D1606347

THE TALENT EDUCATION SCHOOL OF SHINICHI SUZUKI—AN ANALYSIS

THE TALENT EDUCATION SCHOOL OF SHINICHI SUZUKI – AN ANALYSIS

The Application of Its Philosophy and Methods
to All Areas of Instruction

RAY LANDERS

WITH PHOTOGRAPHS BY ARTHUR MONTZKA

Revised and Expanded Third Edition

AN EXPOSITION-BANNER BOOK

Exposition Press   *Smithtown, New York*

Acknowledgment is gratefully extended to the following for permission to reprint from their works:

Specified material abridged from *Revolution in Learning: The Years from Birth to Six* by Maya Pines. Copyright © 1966, 1967 by Maya Pines. By permission of Harper & Row Publishers, Inc.

Excerpts from *The Conditions of Learning* by Robert M. Gagné. Copyright © 1965 by Holt, Rinehart and Winston, Inc. Reprinted by permission of Holt, Rinehart and Winston, CBS College Publishing.

From *A Complete Guide to Therapy: From Psychoanalysis to Behavior Modification* by Joel Kovel, M.D. Copyright © 1976 by Pantheon Books, a Division of Random House, Inc. Reprinted by permission.

From *Word Play: What Happens When People Talk* by Peter Farb. Copyright © 1973 by Alfred A. Knopf, Inc. Reprinted by permission.

From "Why Children Should Draw: The Surprising Link Between Art and Learning," *Saturday Review*, September 3, 1977, by Roger Williams. Copyright © 1977 by Saturday Review Company. Reprinted by permission.

Photographs by Arthur Montzka. Copyright © by A. Montzka. Reprinted by permission.

"Starting Young Pianists with the Suzuki Method," by Constance Starr, *Clavier*, April 1972, pp. 7–13. Copyright © The Instrumentalist Company, 1418 Lake Street, Evanston, Illinois. Used by permission.

Revised 1976 for inclusion in Suzuki Piano School, Volumes 1–2 and 3–4; Summy-Birchard Music Division of Birch Tree Group Ltd., Princeton, N.J. Used by permission.

Introductory remarks by Dr. Suzuki as presented at the beginning of Volume 1 of the Suzuki Piano School. Reprinted by permission of Summy-Birchard Music Division of Birch Tree Group Ltd., Princeton, N.J., Copyright 1978, Zen-On Music Co., Ltd., Tokyo.

From *The Anatomy of Human Destructiveness* by Erich Fromm. Copyright © 1973 by Erich Fromm. By permission of Holt, Rinehart and Winston, Inc.

First Edition published 1980. Second Edition 1981. Third Edition 1984

© 1980, 1984 by Dr. Ray Landers

Library of Congress Catalog Card Number: 83-82386

ISBN 0-682-40154-4 (hardcover)
ISBN 0-682-40155-2 (paperback)
Printed in the United States of America

To Madeline Webster, who taught me to expect much of myself.
To Walter Robert, who taught me that discipline leads to freedom.
To Shinichi Suzuki, who taught me to expect much of all people.
To Suzuki teachers everywhere for their concerns for the growth of children and the happiness of man.

When the artist is alive in any person, whatever his kind of work may be, he becomes an inventive, searching, daring, self-expressive creature. He becomes interesting to other people. He disturbs, upsets, enlightens, and opens ways for a better understanding. Where those who are not artists are trying to close the book, he opens it and shows there are still more pages possible.

—Robert Henri

It is only immoral
  to be dead—alive
    sun—extinct
      and busy putting out the sun
        in other people.

—D. H. Lawrence

We are given as our birthright a Stradivarius and we come to play it like a fiddle. . . . Consider the Stradivarius. Consider the child—the star brighter than any other star man's mind can create a conception of. . . . Talents to last a million years are the mother lode of its molecules. . . . All the future tunings and turnings are already here, latent givens in the once and future child.

—Jean Houston

Our earth is but a small star in the great universe, yet of it we can make, if we choose, a planet unvexed by war, untroubled by hunger or fear, undivided by senseless distinctions of race, color, or theory.

—Stephen Vincent Benét

Contents

Preface

Much has been written about heredity and environment and their effects and impacts on human intelligence and talent. The subject continues to be controversial. One famous educator who strongly believes that the environment is the overwhelming factor is Dr. Shinichi Suzuki of Matsumoto, Japan. Since the mid-1940s, Dr. Suzuki and his colleagues have trained hundreds of thousands of young student musicians throughout Japan. The Suzuki philosophy is applied to the learning of violin, other musical instruments, and other subjects in the Talent Education schools and Early Development Association in Japan.

Suzuki string programs have developed in the United States since the mid-1960s, and other instrumental programs have developed since the early 1970s. For example, through the influence of such educators as Constance Starr, who in 1968 traveled to Matsumoto to investigate the Talent Education method as applied to piano, interest in Suzuki piano instruction is growing. In 1972 and 1973 workshops were held in the United States by Mrs. Starr and other Suzuki piano specialists. The number of workshops has increased immensely since then. By the summer of 1972 Summy-Birchard Company of Evanston, Illinois, published, in the United States, the piano method books and records that have been available in Japan since 1970. The Suzuki flute method was published in America in 1977, the revised cello method in 1978, and the viola method in 1981.

An educational philosophy with the impact in Japan and elsewhere that Talent Education has had should be analyzed in detail to see what possible benefits it might bring to music instruction in the United States and other countries. Conclusions in this analysis are based partly on my own observations at Suzuki schools in Matsumoto, Kyoto, and Tokyo during a trip to Japan in the summer of 1972. While at the Talent Education Summer School in Matsumoto, I observed numerous piano, violin, and cello lessons, attended private and group recitals, and visited lectures and question-answer seminars given by Dr. Suzuki and Mrs. Haruko Kataoka, the head of the piano department and one of the authors of the Suzuki *Piano School* method books. I interviewed Dr. Suzuki and Mrs. Kataoka privately. During July and August I traveled throughout Japan in order to observe aspects of Japanese culture and examine various Suzuki schools. Besides observing Suzuki teachers in Tokyo and Kyoto, I toured a Suzuki violin and cello factory in Nagoya.

In addition to information learned in Japan, much of the material found in this book is based on observations I have made while serving as an observer or clinician at numerous Suzuki workshops, institutes, and conventions since 1969 (see About the Author p. 187) at which I observed classes and workshops by Carole Bigler, Valery Lloyd-Watts, Doris Koppelman, Harlow Mills, Dorothy Mae Charles, Michiko Yurko, Clifford Cook, Shizuko Suzuki, and others. Mrs. Constance Starr was teaching at a Suzuki Institute at Holy Names College, Oakland, California, in 1972, and was able to answer many questions about her observations while in Japan. I viewed videotapes of Mrs. Kataoka's teaching that Mrs. Starr had filmed in Japan. I completed my doctoral thesis on the Suzuki piano method at Indiana University in 1974. I was again able to observe Dr. Suzuki's teaching at the American Suzuki Institute, Steven's Point, Wisconsin, in 1976, Mrs. Kataoka's teaching at Steven's Point in 1978-80, and the teaching of both at the Third International Suzuki Teachers' Conference, San Francisco, California, in 1978 and the Fifth International Suzuki Teachers' Conference, Amherst, Massachusetts, in 1981. In addition, a thorough reading of books and articles about Suzuki as well as general books on education, sociology, and psychology (see the Bibliography) has helped enhance my understanding of the Talent Education philosophy. Through teaching at numerous Suzuki Institutes in the United States, Canada, and Australia and directing the Suzuki Music Academy of Chicago since 1975 and the Summer Chicago Suzuki Institutes and the Chicagoland Suzuki Music Festival since 1981, I have gained firsthand experience of Talent Education's methodology. A visit to the 1982 Chicagoland Festival by Dr. and Mrs. Suzuki helped me to gain more perspective on the success of Talent Education in the United States.

This book is divided into seven chapters through which it is hoped to convey to the reader insights into the Suzuki Method which will help him appreciate the universality and soundness of its ideals.

The First Edition of this book was published in July 1980. The Second Edition of December 1981 contained editorial revisions, the addition of photographs by Arthur Montzka, and the new question-answer section found in Chapter 5. The present Third Edition has been extensively revised to incorporate many new insights. Much new information has been added, including a more thorough bibliography and many pages of new text. Review, games, and other class activities are covered more thoroughly, and the chapter on learning theories has been expanded. These additions are the result of my continued study of the Suzuki™ Method and the experiences I have gained through visiting Talent Education schools throughout the United States and in other countries in recent years. Talent Education is constantly evolving, and publications dealing with it should evolve also.

This book presents a comprehensive survey of the potentialities of Talent

Education. The reader is advised to examine my other book on the Suzuki Method, *Is Suzuki Education Working in America?* (Exposition Press, available in early 1985), for a critical summary of Talent Education's progress in the United States.

I am grateful to Gerard Jarbigian for reading the manuscript and offering valuable suggestions.

The photographs of various Talent Education students, parents, and teachers (including Dr. Suzuki) in this book were taken by Arthur Montzka at various Suzuki Institutes, including the American Suzuki Institute at the University of Wisconsin, Steven's Point, the Fifth International Suzuki Teachers' Conference at the University of Massachusetts, 1981, and the First and Second Annual Chicagoland Music Festival at Orchestra Hall and the Auditorium Theatre, Chicago, 1981-82. They are reprinted with the kind permission of Mr. Montzka.

1
Shinichi Suzuki and Talent Education: Historical Sketch

Shinichi Suzuki, born in Nagoya, Japan, in 1898, grew up as a member of a successful musical family. His father founded the first violin factory in Japan—a large business that in the 1890s employed around eleven hundred workers and manufactured up to one hundred violins daily. The Suzuki family's interest in string instruments dates back to the production of Japanese samisens (three-string, banjolike instruments) by Shinichi's great-grandfather. The Suzuki family still produces string instruments, though not on as large a scale as in the past.

As a child, Shinichi Suzuki worked in his father's factory but showed little serious interest in learning to play the violin. He attended a commercial school in Nagoya and, in his spare time, worked in the factory, thus becoming thoroughly acquainted with the workings of string instruments.

Suzuki says that a passionate interest in playing the violin was awakened in him when he was seventeen years old:

> Unexpectedly we got a gramophone. The first record I brought was Schubert's "Ave Maria" played by Mischa Elman. . . . It made a tremendous impression on me. To think, the violin, which I had considered a toy, could produce such beauty of tone! Elman's "Ave Maria" opened my eyes to music. My profound emotion was the first step in my search for the true meaning of art.[1]

Suzuki then began violin study under a Miss Koda and later, at age twenty-one, went to Tokyo to study violin with Miss Koda's sister, Ko Ando. In Tokyo he also studied acoustics and theory. His progress was rapid, and, at the age of twenty-three, he went to Germany, where he studied with Karl Klingler, the first violinist with the Klingler Quartet. Klingler, whom Suzuki selected after an extensive three-month search, usually did not teach but was sufficiently impressed by Suzuki to accept him as a student. Suzuki said that what he learned from Klingler was "not as much technique as the real essence of music. . . . He would look for the roots underlying a man and his art and lead me to them."[2]

1

In Berlin, Suzuki became more knowledgeable about Western music and ideas. He attended numerous musical events and, through Klingler, met such men as Albert Einstein and Fritz Busch. A major event in Suzuki's life occurred when he attended a concert by Fritz Kreisler. He was so impressed by Kreisler's tone that he has used it since as a model and ideal for his students.

Also while in Berlin, Suzuki met a German singer who became his wife. Mrs. Waltraud Suzuki has been a major force in the administration and development of Talent Education. She translated into English Suzuki's book *Nurtured by Love*. But most important, she has served as a protective force for Dr. Suzuki's well-being.

At the age of thirty-one Suzuki returned to Japan and, with three of his brothers, formed a string quartet that toured extensively and introduced Western chamber music to many Japanese audiences. He taught violin (using "European" traditional methods) in various universities in Tokyo, Yokohama, and elsewhere.

Although it was not until the end of World War II that Suzuki decided to devote his life to the musical education of young children, his interest in childhood education intensified in his seventeenth year. In that year he says, "I was born. . . . I emerged as a human being."[3] Through literature, he became more aware of the importance of growth and education. The discovery of Tolsoy's *Diary* led Suzuki to the words: "To deceive oneself is worse than to deceive others." He investigated the writings of Tolstoy as well as those of many other great Western writers. Suzuki, as he summarizes in *Nurtured by Love*, soon "turned from the 'conscience' of Tolstoy to follow the lead that Mozart provided in his music into the belief that it is the life force itself that is the whole basis of man's being. . . . The image of young growing children, who are the very essence of life's joy, took hold in my imagination then."[4] He began to spend much time with children. He comments:

> The seed was sown of the Talent Education movement that was to be my life work. . . . Most of the beautiful children would eventually become adults filled with suspicion, treachery, dishonesty, injustice, hatred, misery, gloom. Why? Why couldn't they be brought up to maintain the beauty of their souls? There must be something wrong with education. That is when I first began to think along these lines.[5]

Suzuki's first experiment in teaching young children occurred when he was thirty-three years old, but it was not until 1945, at the age of forty-seven, that he settled in Matsumoto and started to develop his Talent Education School.

Two incidents seem to have had a special effect on Suzuki's educational philosophy. The first occurred in his thirty-third year when he taught at the

Imperial Conservatory in Tokyo. A father who had taught his son to play the violin brought the young man of eighteen to audition for Suzuki. Suzuki was surprised at the great resemblances between the father and son in dialect, manner of speaking, greeting habits, laughter, posture, movements, and even the strengths and shortcomings in their violin playing. So impressed was Suzuki with this obvious parental influence on a son that he decided to teach children, stressing cooperation with their parents. Four-year-old Toshiya Eto and three-year-old Koji Toyodo became his first very young pupils under this new approach. Both are now artists of international stature.

A second incident that greatly shaped Suzuki's educational philosophy occurred as a result of World War II. During the war, to avoid the bombings in Tokyo, he lived in the mountains of Kiso-Fukushima with a sister and her small children; he became ill because of malnutrition and during his convalescence had much time for reflection. He observed his sister's babies as they learned to talk. Through his recollections of these two incidents— the similarities he saw between the father and son and his observation of the naturalness of the babies' learning of language—he realized that children could be taught music in ways similar to how they learned to imitate their parents in other skills. Suzuki's initial teaching encounters with Toshiya and Koji were successful enough to encourage him to seek means of further developing his educational ideas.

Suzuki felt pity for the children who suffered during the war; this feeling was instrumental in his decision to devote his life to helping children find happiness through music. Looking for a place to open a school, he was invited to Matsumoto, a city at the base of the Japanese Alps, by Mrs. Tamiki Mori, a singer who had taught with him at the Imperial Conservatory. She asked Suzuki to become a teacher at a school there in 1945. He replied:

> I am not very interested in doing "repair" work on people who can play already. I did enough of that before in Tokyo. What I want to try is infant education. I have worked out a new method I want to teach to small children—not to turn out geniuses but through violin playing to extend the child's ability.[6]

Thus the Talent Education movement began in Matsumoto.

Within a year Suzuki presented some of his students in a concert at the Hibiya Auditorium in Tokyo. There were more than thirty children between four and nine years of age on the program. The audience of about three thousand was astonished to hear children play a beautiful performance of a concerto by Seitz after only one year of lessons. From that day, the Talent Education movement grew rapidly.

Suzuki did much research during the next three decades in developing his violin method books; the first book alone was the result of ten years of experimentation and testing. As his pupils matured, many of them took teacher-training courses at the Talent Education Institute and became instruc̨tors there or at one of the approximately one hundred branch schools that eventually developed in cities throughout Japan. Hundreds of thousands of students have studied in the Suzuki schools. Dr. Suzuki estimates that about 5 percent have carried their studies beyond the completion of all the volumes of study to continue as professional musicians.

Through carefully worked-out instructional programs the Suzuki pupil learns much about playing his instrument. He gains music appreciation through sensitive listening and performance and, as Suzuki emphasizes, seeks to gain happiness through music. So successful has this approach with the violin program been that Talent Education programs have expanded to include instruction in other instruments and other areas outside of music (see later discussion on pp. 42). Courses have also been designed and published for the cello, violin, viola, piano, and flute; in Tokyo, an Early Development Association kindergarten and in Matsumoto, an infant school both apply Talent Education principles to areas such as calligraphy, arithmetic, art, and English. The purpose of the Early Development Association is explained by its president, Masaaki Honda:

> To develop the most scientific, effective educational methods and techniques in line with the truly innovative principles of early childhood development, and thus prove the way for the formation of well balanced personalities in children.
> To invent various new and creative educational methods, put them into experiments and evaluate the results for further studies.[7]

Thus in Japan, with Dr. Suzuki still a very effective teacher and leader, the Talent Education philosophy grows in influence as the numbers of schools, teachers, and students increases.

In the United States interest in Suzuki has increased greatly in recent years. Since Suzuki made his first American tour with ten of his young students in 1964, the number of students who have studied under the Talent Education method in the United States had grown to an estimated one hundred thousand by 1973 and has expanded immensely since then.[8] There are presently Suzuki programs in all fifty states: besides universities or conservatories such as the Eastman School of Music, Oberlin College, the University of Southern Illinois, Holy Names College, and many others, there are numerous public and private schools, as well as individual teachers, with Suzuki-oriented programs. Numerous annual Suzuki teacher-training and family workshops and institutes attract increasing numbers of people; for example, the American Suzuki Institute at the University of Wisconsin in Steven's Point teaches thousands of students, parents, and teachers each summer. According to the *American Suzuki Journal*, more than thirty sanctioned Suzuki institutes hosted in excess of seven thousand families and twelve hundred teachers in America during the spring and the summer of 1980.[9] Forty-five institutes were listed for spring and summer in the *American Suzuki Journal* of February 1983. Many more workshops are held during the year at various schools and universities throughout the country. And, of course, institutes reach only a portion of Suzuki students studying during the year at schools, associations, or with private teachers. The numbers of active teachers listed with the Suzuki Association of the Americas (SAA) in 1983 were 2,228 violinists, 1,828 pianists, 631 cellists, 118 flutists, and 691 violists—a total of 5,496. Many of these are sanctioned by the Suzuki Association of the Americas (SAA) as teacher-trainers; as of 1983, there were 13 cello, 4 flute, 44 piano, 4 viola, and 78 violin teacher-trainers. Many of these Suzuki teachers and teacher-trainers are affiliated with schools, colleges or universities, or associations; many are private teachers that teach in their homes or in facilities such as churches or music stores. People in the United States seem greatly interested in Suzuki and will benefit more and more from his ideas. The founding of the SAA in 1972 has been a major step toward the development of a centrally organized Talent Education Institute in the United States. The SAA publishes the quarterly *American Suzuki Journal* and serves as the official organization for dissemination of Suzuki ideals throughout the Western world. It is in charge of teacher-training programs and sanctioning of teachers, trainers, institutes, and workshops and also provides a central location for listing Suzuki teachers and the training they have received. SAA board members, elected by members of the association, serve for a three-year term and serve on various committees that are continually in the process of providing guidelines for Suzuki education. In 1975, the SAA and other national organizations voted to form the International Suzuki Association to help assure that standards are high in all countries. The International Suzuki Association had its official beginning at the International Suzuki Teachers' Conference held in Japan in July 1983. In announcing the purposes of the association, Dr. Suzuki said:

> We must dismiss all weapons, wars and crime from this world. If every child born on this earth is nurtured in a good environment from the day of his birth, there will be no crime. If a child is not nurtured in love, he will learn to hate others. He will want weapons, and eventually he will create war. Teaching music is one of the ways to guide children to see the beauty of this world. But we must find a way to guide children who are born into unfortunate situations. This is my idea; this is my prayer that every child on this earth be happy. All of you who are here, who understand my wish, I ask that you please work for the happiness of every child in the world.

Many other organizations have also been instrumental in the development of Talent Education. These include the publishers of the excellent *Talent Education Journal* and the Ability Development Company, which publishes the bimonthly *Suzuki World* and numerous Suzuki-related books and recordings. Ability Development has provided a great service through its international catalog distribution of Talent Education supplies and related materials.

Talent Education continues to grow, and its influence has reached many other countries since it first spread to the United States in the mid-1960s. The 1983 SAA membership directory lists Suzuki programs and teachers in all fifty of the United States and in Australia, Belgium, Bermuda, Brazil, Canada, Denmark, England, France, Holland, Indonesia, Israel, Italy, Japan, Mexico, New Zealand, Saudi Arabia, South America, Sweden, Switzerland, and West Germany. Many of these states and countries have organized their own Suzuki associations.

The Suzuki Method, like any new approach, is subject to controversy, as is discussed in more detail in *Is Suzuki Education Working in America?* (available in early 1985) and in Chapter 7 of this text. The method has received much critical acclaim and good publicity, particularly in the United States. Numerous Suzuki students have been featured on national radio and television shows, and Talent Education has been the subject of hundreds of articles in local and national publications. The rate of growth has been phenomenal in both quantity and quality. Many Suzuki groups (Japanese and American) have made national tours, and Suzuki students are receiving increased attention through their performances and their superior abilities, as shown by the number of musical contests they win, the number of scholarships they receive, the number of string students who hold first chairs in their orchestras, but, most of all, the number of "average" Suzuki students who are demonstrating to the world their love for music and their trained abilities that tower over their "average" traditionally trained friends. Another book by the author asks the question, "Is Suzuki education working in America?" and answers with a definite yes, though this yes is qualified with concerns over the need for certain new directions in America's view of Talent Education. The present book's main emphasis is on the great potentials contained within the Suzuki Method.

2
The Talent Education Philosophy

A basic assumption of the Talent Education philosophy, that "every child [can] develop his abilities and talents if suitable and repeated stimulation [can] be given," stems partially from Suzuki's observations of the naturalness of man's language development.[10] When he went to Germany at the age of twenty-three, Suzuki experienced much difficulty in learning to speak German; he recalled by contrast the ease with which he had learned Japanese as a child. This intuitive knowledge of how children learn led him to develop the Talent Education philosophy:

> The fundamental ideology is based on the assumption that originally all humans are born with considerable high potential for developing themselves. . . . This wonderful ability of learning is developed by the environment. What they receive from their parents at the day of their birth is not language itself but the ability to learn and speak language, and provided the babies have no physical defect, all are born with these qualities.[11]

To Suzuki, "talent" is synonymous with "ability." As Honda summarizes: "There is a possibility of cultivating and educating various abilities within any human being to a very high standard."[12] Suzuki does not believe that musical talent is a gift inherited only by certain individuals; he feels, rather, that *all* children can develop musical ability just as they can develop language ability—provided they are trained under proper environmental conditions. Suzuki's "method" is the result of decades of experimentation, research, and teaching that led to the design of an educational system that provides these environmental conditions.

The Talent Education philosophy is concerned with the development of the full human potential; Suzuki believes that music, like language, helps the individual in life. As Honda expresses it:

> Our understanding of the phrase "Talent Education" does not only apply to knowledge or technical skill but also to morality, building character and appreciating beauty. . . . Thus, our movement does not mean to raise so-called prodigies. We must express it in other words as a "total human education" or enriched environment.[13]

7

Suzuki does not give entrance examinations or talent tests to students. His general policy is to encourage any student who desires to study as long as the student and his parents are interested and serious in their intent. The method incorporates many motivational devices on the assumption that all young children, properly motivated, will desire to study. As long as the student wishes to study, lessons continue. Individual differences in growth rate are taken into account; even mentally and physically handicapped children are encouraged to study. The author observed a girl in Matsumoto who had some fingers missing on her left hand and was learning to play the violin in a reverse position. Suzuki discusses an example that demonstrates his attitudes toward instruction of handicapped students:

> The following episode took place at our Nakatsugawa City branch. Among the many students there was a six-year-old girl who had suffered from infantile paralysis. She was not able to control the right side of her body. She had a squint in the right eye. When playing "Twinkle, Twinkle, Little Star," just as she got to the last two notes of the first phrase her right arm and hand would involuntarily give a violent twitch so that the bow flew out of her hand. . . . The teacher patiently went on with the lessons, and every day the mother persistently picked up the bow innumerable times. . . . The great love and persistent endeavor of both mother and teacher won. The time came when the child was finally able to hold the bow throughout the entire piece. . . . Fortunately the little girl kept on practicing, and her right eye, which had been crossed, gradually started moving into the correct position while at the same time she began to gain control of her right side. . . . Gradually she could move normally. . . . All this was achieved through the therapy of her efforts in playing just one piece of music, aided by the endeavors of her mother and her teacher.[14]

The above example illustrates Talent Education's aim to help the development of the "whole" child through music education.

The importance of repetition in achieving development is emphasized by Suzuki:

> Most tone deaf children cannot produce the first four notes of the scale, do, re, mi, fa, without making the semi-tone interval, fa, a little too high. . . . They have already acquired the habit of making fa too high. This "pre-education" cannot be changed. . . . I found that one has to teach them a new fa. If they have learned the wrong fa by hearing it five thousand times, one must make them listen to the right fa six or seven thousand times. . . . At first there are no results, but, eventually, the ability to produce the correct fa begins to take precedence over the ability to produce the wrong fa. . . . A new function has developed.[15]

Suzuki believes that many educators incorrectly blame students' weaknesses on "character" or "nature" and, as a result, are pessimistic about change occurring in certain students through education. Teachers should believe instead that, through good training or "retraining" with much emphasis on repetition, new learning can overcome weaknesses that have developed as a result of poor learning environments.

Having watched Dr. Suzuki teach private lessons and direct performances of small and large groups of children, I am impressed with his genuine love for children. He is an extremely patient teacher and possesses a remarkable ability to help a child instill faith in himself—a faith in his inner good qualities. Suzuki is concerned with maintaining the "precious" attributes of small children:

> They have no thoughts of self-deception. They trust people and do not doubt at all. They know only how to love, and not how to hate. They love justice and scrupulously keep the rules. They seek joy and live cheerfully and are full of life. They know no fear and live in security. . . .[16]
>
> Children in their simplicity seek what is true, what is good, what is beautiful, based on love. That, I believe, is the true nature of man.[17]

Although Dr. Suzuki has a strong belief in the beauty of children, he also expresses sympathy for adults and the need to help them, to be compassionate to those who were not lucky enough to receive the early start he advocates, to realize that we have to help parents to help their children: "When I went to Tokyo [in 1967, says Suzuki], a woman of thirty-five or six said, 'It's said that a child is a gift from heaven. How true. Some are given good children, other terrible children. . . . I, for one, got such a bad child . . . I am truly unfortunate.' 'This won't do,' I thought, [Suzuki continues] so I made a familiar speech on Talent Education, emphasizing that the child reflects how the mother raised him. [She started to cry and said], 'While listening to you, I realized what a terrible parent I have been, I have given my child a hard time.' . . . [Suzuki continued] 'You are a wonderful mother. That very self-criticism makes your child happier. Face your child from tonight with the same heart with which you feel sorry now.' . . . a month later [seeing the mother again], 'what happened?' I asked. . . . 'Since I saw you last, we've stopped fighting,' . . . she said, 'your child will grow up beautifully,' I congratulated her. . . . What is impressive in this story is the heart of the mother who could apologize to the child. This is the heart of a parent who can lead the world from an uncultured age to one of culture."[18]

The Suzuki philosophy, in summary, is based on an ideology that believes in the potential of all (encouraging early education but seeking to help all ages), that encourages the learning of music as a means to a happier life, that advocates growth for each individual at his own rate, that emphasizes high-quality training from the earliest years with emphasis on repetition, and that believes in the basic goodness of man. Suzuki's great appreciation for the naturalness by which man learns a language coupled with his reverence for music eventually led him to develop a method to carry out the goals of his philosophy, a method that is based on learning music just as one learns language—the "mother tongue" approach. As Suzuki states in *Where Love Is Deep*:

> Music is one of the outstanding cultures mankind has created . . . not to know music is a great loss. Born as human beings we are brought up in a society of cultures; how can it not be a loss to live without knowing the world of these great cultures? Among the cultures that mankind has developed, the most universal are "spoken language" and "written language." People all over the world benefit from them. Another world which has developed in parallel with language is music. It is the world of communication between a life and a life. . . . The time will surely come when mankind can cultivate through music a superior sensitivity and beautiful humanity in every child. . . . In order to materialize this hope of mankind, there must be people who work toward this dream, toward the creation of a beautiful human world.[19]

Suzuki's philosophy thus is based on a simple truth: true Talent Education teachers will be people who, through their caring, constantly work to improve the world.

3
The Talent Education Method of Instruction

There are approximately one hundred branches of the Talent Education Institute in Japan. Instructors, who are graduates of the institute, teach, on the average, five to six hours daily. Except for monthly group classes and bimonthly recitals, which are usually held in local school auditoriums, space requirements are small and many of the branch schools consist merely of a small room or rooms. The main school in Matsumoto is housed in a new, modern building, which provides ample studio space for teaching and performance. Situated nearby are the Matsumoto City Auditorium and the Shonan High School; both are sometimes used for the institute's activities, particularly during the summer school.

Lessons are scheduled so that the pupil and parent can be present in the classroom before or after their own lesson times to observe lessons of others. The number and length of lessons each week depend on the concentration span of the student and may vary from several lessons of just a few minutes the first weeks to longer single lessons each week later. Politeness is emphasized; the child, mother, and teacher bow to each other at the beginning and end of lessons. In addition to the private lessons (semiprivate really, because others observe), most students participate in monthly group classes in which they play (the strings sometimes in unison or with harmonized parts), participate in various musical learning games, and play solos for each other. Bimonthly solo recitals are also held.

During the summers, many students and teachers travel to Matsumoto for the annual Talent Education Institute Summer School; concerts featuring large numbers of students giving group and solo performances are held, group and private lessons are given by Dr. Suzuki and other teachers, and seminars are given for pupils, teachers, and visitors. Every other summer, many students and teachers attend the International Teachers' Conference, held in various parts of the world.

Japanese Talent Education has a carefully worked-out graduation system, and mass graduation concert ceremonies are held annually in Tokyo. Dr. Suzuki personally supervises the listening to tapes of all graduating students; he writes personal comments about them and signs all certificates.

A summary of the principles used in the Talent Education method follows. These principles are designed to help the educator, teacher, family members, and student create a natural environment so that learning can occur in a way similar to that in which language development occurs—the "mother tongue" approach.

1. *Emphasis on motivation*, beginning in the earliest years. As Suzuki explains:

> We do not at first have [the student] play the violin. First we teach the mother to play one piece so that she will be a good teacher at home. . . . It is necessary for the parent to have first-hand experience. Until the parent can play one piece, the child does not play at all. . . . The idea is to get him to say, "I want to play too." . . . The mother plays on the small violin more suited to the child.
> The child, after observing the mother's lessons and her practice at home, will naturally before long take the violin from his mother, thinking "I want to play too."[20]

Suzuki parents are instructed in ways to motivate their children. Through listening to recordings (Suzuki Method and otherwise), attending concerts and lessons of Suzuki students, attending cultural events in the community, and observing one of his parents take lessons before he begins, the Suzuki child becomes highly motivated to begin music education. The child is encouraged to begin specialized music listening from birth, following a carefully worked-out series of classical recordings that has been developed in Japan Talent Education schools. These recordings are to be listened to in conjunction with the regular method recordings (violin, piano, cello, or flute). Even though a student's lessons may not begin until age two and a half or three, his development begins from birth. A natural, motivating environment leads to happy and healthy learning (see p. 57 for further discussion of motivation).

2. *Emphasis on listening*. As mentioned above, parents are encouraged to play recordings of music for children as early as infancy.

> A masterpiece by Bach, Mozart or Schubert is . . . played everyday for the baby. . . . At about five months, any baby thus exposed will clearly learn the selection . . . [and] another selection is added.[21]

Sometime between infancy and the age of three, the child is introduced to the music of the first volume of the method through listening to a recording of the volume, attending lessons or concerts of Suzuki students, and observing a parent or sibling perform. The age that the special listening begins varies from family to family, but the general consensus is the earlier the better. Though the entire volume may be listened to daily, at first emphasis is on constant rehearing of the earliest piece or pieces in the volume. Through clapping, marching, or eurythmic games the child can be assigned specific ways to listen. The general approach that I observed in Japan was to have the pupil concentrate mainly on listening to the piece he is currently learning as well as the next few pieces to be learned; sometimes, however, he listens to the other pieces from the volume as well as selections from later volumes. Recordings of performances by Japanese artists are published as part of the methods for the violin, viola, cello, flute, and piano. (There are also American-made recordings of the piano and violin methods as well as the "Children's Listening Library" that Suzuki recommends for the earliest years; see the Bibliography, pp. 158 and 177.) As the child advances, he hears a greater variety of recordings of the same works, but even the beginner is exposed to different interpretations by hearing live performances. Suzuki encourages young beginners to observe the lessons of older students before they begin their lessons at about the age of three. Naturally, the child is encouraged to continue listening to other music in addition to the Suzuki repertoire. The emphasis on listening continues through the advanced levels. (For further discussion on listening, see p. 74.)

3. *Cooperation of the parent in the student's learning process.* The mother (or sometimes the father) attends every lesson, listens attentively, and takes notes so that she may supervise the child's practice at home; and as mentioned in point 1 above, the parent learns to play at least one selection (many learn many more pieces, depending on the child's developing readiness to play) before the child begins to study. A parent may take lessons for as long as six months before the child begins; however, one or two months seems to be the norm. In the early years of instruction, and often in the later years, the child does not practice alone; a parent supervises the home practice. Thus the parent is, in essence, a second teacher and spends more time instructing the child than does the teacher. In later years, when the child becomes more independent, the parent remains very involved but usually supervises less— mainly because of the child's gradual development of note-reading.

4. *Learning through imitation.* The child is encouraged to imitate the teacher and parent; or, rather, the child imitates naturally. He is shown everything exactly—posture, movements, touches, notes, rhythm, and dynamics. There are very few written instructions in the volumes; the teacher or parent demonstrates for the pupil in specific detail; or sometimes the child learns through watching a sibling, parent, or other Suzuki student practice. Verbal instructions are given for clarification. Lessons are times to correct and check all that has been learned the previous week, to teach new material, and to review previously learned repertoire.

5. *Learning without the reading of notes in the first stages of training.* In language development, one speaks the language before he learns to read

or write. Talent Education is similar in its emphasis on the postponement of note-reading. As Constance Starr says:

> [The Suzuki pupil] has not been hampered by learning to read first. He has learned to use the language of music before he learns to read it. He has heard and been made aware of good tone quality, sensitive musical phrasing, and fine rhythmic execution . . . musically.[22]

The Suzuki philosophy emphasizes that the reading of music should begin only when it is most beneficial to the learning of music. The more complex the music, the greater will be the need for a symbolic note system to help the student in his preparation. Until then, reading is unessential and limits the emphasis on musical concentration. For example, reading usually begins in Volume 4 in the violin method and after Volume 1 in the piano method. It is often taught by having the pupil replay all the pieces previously learned while looking at the printed score. He repeats this procedure over a period of time until he begins to make associations between the sounds he is used to creating and hearing and the new symbols he sees on the printed page. He associates the symbols not only with the notes and rhythm but also with the phrasing, dynamics, and tempo markings. Suzuki teachers often use special introductory note-reading books. (For example, *The Method Rose* is sometimes used in Japan for piano. Many American piano teachers use Frances Clark's *Music Tree* series or other books. See my suggestions for learning to read notes on p. 68, Question 3.)

6. *Performance from memory with additional emphasis on special sight-reading material.* Even after pupils begin to read notes they continue to perform from memory at lessons, recitals, and group performances. In home practice the child memorizes as he learns. In the earlier stages (before he begins reading), he follows the guidance of his teacher and parent in checking his memory; later, note-reading is added as a guide and check. Reading is emphasized as a means of helping in performance, not as an end in itself. Thus, just as we do not "read" our everyday conversations, the Suzuki student does not usually read notes at his lessons or performances except for special note-reading assignments. As he advances, he learns reading more and more along with listening and imitation to guide him in preparing for performance, but the eventual end remains the memorization of the selections. The Suzuki string student often practices sight-reading through participation in various ensemble and orchestral groups associated with the Suzuki school or outside the school; in addition, Suzuki students may be given other repertoire books for specific sight-reading assignments. These books are usually at a lower level of difficulty than the corresponding Suzuki repertoire.

The Suzuki Method, like any good approach, emphasizes four kinds of memory: the aural (through listening); the visual (through imitating the teachers' or other models' movements); the kinesthetic or physical (through much repetition of learned movements); and the analytical. (Emphasis on sectional work and learning without the "crutch" of note-reading in the beginning forces the child to be more analytical—to compare sections or phrases, for example. In later years the child becomes more analytical in approaching note-reading, theory, and form.)

7. *Constant review of previously learned repertoire.* The Suzuki instructional system, if taught correctly, ensures the pupil's retention of the repertoire he has learned. At monthly group classes the string student plays, along with other pupils, many of the pieces he has learned, either in unison or in harmonized parts. The classes start with performances of the most advanced literature in the method's repertoire books by pupils who are capable of playing it; as less advanced repertoire is performed, more and more students join in until, finally, the simplest piece is played with all students at the school (except beginners who have not yet mastered it) participating. Even the earliest beginners participate through bowing, playing a few notes, or demonstrating exercises. Similar monthly performances are held by many piano and flute students but with less emphasis on group performance. (These monthly programs are not just recitals but are also lessons; the teacher offers suggestions to the group or individuals and sometimes plays various musical games with the pupils.) Suzuki teachers emphasize review of earlier repertoire at lessons and bimonthly recitals. Many of the earlier pieces serve as technical preparation for later pieces; review is also important for repetition because pieces need to be played and performed many times so they will become a part of the student's musical "vocabulary." To Suzuki, review is one of the more important aspects of the method. As he stated at the 1981 International Teachers' Conference in Amherst, Massachusetts, "If no use were made of words already learned and only new words are learned, wouldn't the speech of all the children in the world become similar to that of a retarded child without ability?" (opening ceremony of the conference, University of Massachusetts, July 27, 1981). The same principle applies to musical selections that were previously learned: they should be reviewed. (For a more detailed discussion of review and for suggestions of review techniques, see Chapter 5, Question 4, p. 72.)

8. *Use of games.* Games are incorporated to motivate, to develop alertness, to help overcome boredom, and to test the pupil's understanding. Dr. Suzuki gives an example:

> When the children have learned how to play "Twinkle, Twinkle, Little Star Variations" easily and freely, I ask them to play them, and I say "Now

let's play a game. I want you to answer my questions while you go on playing. Answer in a loud voice, and don't stop playing." Then, in a loud voice,
I call out, "How many legs have you?" They think this is loads of fun,
and they answer all together at the top of their voices, "Two." If they can
do this while they go on playing correctly, it means that the skill has been
properly inculcated and has become second nature. . . . Another thing is
to play the first part of a piece in mime only—with empty hands. I play
it only once. Then I say "Get set—go." Having carefully watched my
movements, they play the piece with one accord.[23]

Other games request that the pupils march, stand, or stoop in different
ways while playing; or they stand quietly while another group performs and
then join in the performance at a certain signal such as a hand clap. In
another example, two students play the same violin—one bowing and the
other fingering.

As Dr. Honda points out, these games also serve to motivate the
occasional bored student:

There is a time when a child and mother get tired and weary of their
lessons, a kind of slump that comes to us in our daily life. This occurs when
the child makes little progress or none. . . . In this case playing with other
children is very useful. It not only encourages them, but enables them to
find the pep to solve the distressed mood. . . . In this case, games help
a lot.[24]

The use of games is highly individualized, the types and approach varying from teacher to teacher. Many teachers are creative in their structure
of games. Games are usually used at monthly group classes but are sometimes
incorporated into the regular lessons. (See Chapter 4, Question 8, p. 76 for
a list of additional possible games.)

9. *Perfection of one piece before starting a new one.* Suzuki believes that
discipline is hindered and certain concepts essential for future Talent Education
study are not developed if a piece is not thoroughly mastered. The repertoire is
presented in a carefully organized order; often concepts learned in one selection
are preparatory for pieces that follow, therefore it is essential that each composition be learned with correct notes, rhythm, and technique. The amount of emphasis placed on various musical aspects (dynamics, phrasing, interpretation)
varies from child to child in the beginning stages of instruction, but after each
selection is accurately learned it is reviewed with more and more emphasis in
developing interpretive ideas. As new pieces are learned, the older ones are reviewed, often with new techniques that have been developed through the newer
repertoire. For example, in piano one may review the "Twinkle Variations" with
new emphasis on larger tone after having learned a larger wrist movement in
"Cuckoo."

Much attention is given to the importance of every note. Each detail is carefully prepared; a spirit of respect is taught for each and every phrase. Through learning to bow to his teacher and parent, a pupil is taught the importance of mutual respect; this respect is carried over to the music. In Japan, young students often spend several months at lessons learning how to bow correctly, to sit or stand with good posture, and to make the movements appropriate for the first note. This slow, careful emphasis develops good attitudes for study through the advanced levels.

10. *Learning the repertoire in the order presented in the method without any omissions.* This is essential because of the organized presentation of concepts and techniques. An easier selection often follows a difficult one as a reward, something to look forward to. In addition to gaining a thorough technique and large repertoire, the student is motivated through this practice; if he particularly likes a selection that is ahead of his present "position" in the method, he will be challenged to learn what comes before so eventually he can learn the favorite to which he aspires, thus expanding his repertoire and musical ability.

There is a certain flexibility on this point from teacher to teacher. Some occasionally change the order slightly if to do so will motivate the student, but such changing is not generally encouraged. Students enjoy the security of having goals. Learning the repertoire in order gives them something for which to work.

11. *Learning an excellent repertoire.* The repertoire in the Suzuki volumes includes familiar folk melodies and classical music of the baroque, classical, and romantic periods. No modern repertoire is used; after mastering all the volumes of the method, however, the student and teacher choose further repertoire for study, and many select contemporary music. Music of varying periods, including some contemporary, is often inserted between some of the pieces of the method. For example, a student may express a special appreciation for a Bach selection found in a volume of the method, and the teacher will assign additional Bach selections. The repertoire is conceived as a foundation from which the student learns basic tools of performance. He is then free to learn a much broader repertoire. (See later discussion on p. 68, point 2.)

12. *Learning technique through the repertoire.* Suzuki emphasizes that technique essential for good performance can be learned through carefully structured repertoire and teaching. Pedagogical devices that are used are modern and up to date. (See later discussion by John Kendall on p. 131.) He suggests that special exercises, scale and chord studies, and other technical approaches be introduced as needed by each student; this is an individual matter. As in note-reading, the child is introduced to general rules for scales,

chords, and theory at the times most beneficial to him—when they will help with his music-making rather than being ends in themselves. Learned pieces also serve as "etudes" at times because they are often reviewed in various technical ways—often with the emphasis on improving technical points of the current new repertoire through practicing similar points in previous repertoire.

13. *Individuality*. Dr. Honda suggests that individuality is encouraged rather than hindered by the Suzuki method:

> In the past twenty years, more than ten thousand children graduated from our school, but not one played absolutely the same. Though the foundation was the same, the buildings constructed on this base are all different. The influence of the teaching is indeed strong, but there are many other factors that combine to make the character. The children speak through their violins, and, though they speak in the same language, the feeling and the expression are all different. The children are encouraged to hear the records of famous artists. They must absorb the feeling, expression and the musical sensitivity of these artists. But it is difficult to acquire all these and each child receives different feelings and develops his own sensitivity. We cannot lose our individuality even if we are taught from the same books, the same religion, the same living.[25]

The Talent Education philosophy encourages the idea that "discipline leads to freedom." If students can play a piece correctly one way, such as that heard on a recording, they are much freer to play other approaches. At lessons, group classes, and recitals teachers often ask students to play various ways in order to test their flexibility and true knowledge of the repertoire; for example, tempo and dynamic changes and different interpretations are sometimes requested. Thus the child actually learns many ways to perform; he learns a flexibility that helps him find his own "creative flow" and style. As he matures, the student is encouraged to listen more and more to various repertoire and interpretations. At the completion of all the volumes of the Suzuki repertoire (this often happens at age eight or nine for Japanese students), the student has a thorough "alphabet" on which to build his individuality. He is then encouraged to learn future repertoire to suite his interests, thus further encouraging his individuality.

14. *Learning at each student's own rate of development with emphasis on patience, praise, and constructive, positive corrections with much repetition*. This Talent Education philosophy is explained by Dr. Honda:

> If a hundred-meter race is carried out by several children, there are some who are faster than others. But even those who are slow will reach the goal if they continue to run. . . . This is also true in violin. When several children

the same age begin a violin lesson, there are some who learn much quicker than others. We say that these children inherit the sensitivity of grasping the music quicker than others.[26]

Students are not pushed beyond their present levels of development, and emphasis is on thorough learning and much repetition. Some children can learn several ideas at one lesson; others may be able to cover only one idea. Generally, Suzuki suggests that teacher and student concentrate on one new idea or problem at a time.

In Japanese Talent Education schools, ridicule of slow learners is not accepted; there is little emphasis on competition as to which students can learn the fastest. Emphasis is on the learning of music, and all pupils are complimented for each proper step in this direction. The use of monthly group classes, in which students of varying levels observe each other, helps create a less competitive situation. The six-year-old learning "Twinkle," for example, feels less threatened by the three-year-old playing the same selection when he also observes an older student performing it. In a sense, each child is being taught to compete with the potential within himself. Suzuki teachers are expected to be extremely patient in allowing even the slowest of students to develop at his natural pace. According to Constance Starr:

> Mr. Suzuki has said that the word "patience" should never be applied to the learning experience by either teacher or parent. Patience has the connotation of controlled frustration, yet the parent . . . should enjoy the learning process. He must be helped to understand that the learning process of a small child is often very slow, that every effort, every step, no matter how small, should be a pleasure to watch. . . . In place of criticism, praise should be plentiful. . . . No matter how bad a performance may be, there is always some aspect of it that can be praised. . . . A sincere "good" may be the response to even this small effort building confidence, and . . . stimulating the positive desire to do better.[27]

Thus the Suzuki teacher, to allow each student's best rate of development, is patient and emphasizes his good qualities; at the same time, he encourages the student to continue to improve and grow. Through much praise and positive reinforcement along with carefully structured constructive criticism, the child is motivated to learn.

15. *Emphasis on slow practice and final performance in correct tempo.* According to Mrs. Starr, "Mr. Suzuki says that teachers must change their idea that young children cannot play fast. . . . They can do what most adults can do."[28]

Yet to achieve this goal of fast playing, or, more correctly, of playing a piece in the tempo indicated, slow, careful practice to master one point at a time is emphasized by Dr. Suzuki: "If one hurries and collapses or tumbles down, nothing is achieved. . . . Without stopping, without haste, carefully taking a step at a time . . . will surely get you there."[29]

Talent Education makes much use of a "stop and prepare" approach. While learning to hear entire pieces and units through listening to the recordings, the child is taught to practice slowly and carefully. To become more aware of the appropriate movements necessary for each sound, the child often practices sections up to speed with long "stop and prepare" analytical pauses between them. During these pauses, the student learns mentally to prepare all the needed movements before he plays. For example, in the first Twinkle Variation of the *Piano School*, the child, after playing ♬♫ on C, will be instructed to "stop and prepare" before playing ♬♫ on G. During this stop, he thinks of the appropriate movements needed to continue—slide or stretch to the fourth finger, play G, use ♬♫ rhythm, keep the finger curved, and so on. Eventually, this pause becomes shorter and shorter as the analytical process becomes more ingrained. As the student advances to later repertoire, often the amount of material analyzed in these pauses becomes longer, depending on factors such as the number of problems involved and the student's level of concentration.

16. *Emphasis on constant performance.* Through the use of monthly group lessons and bimonthly solo recitals and other special concerts, and through the emphasis on attendance of other children and parents at his private lesson, the Suzuki student is, in a sense, always "performing"; he is usually playing in front of others with larger audiences in attendance at the concert programs or group classes; smaller "audiences" (other students and parents) attend his lessons. Even in practice, particularly during his beginning years, he often plays in front of a parent who helps in his supervision. There he usually is corrected with others present. The student develops an attitude that others in his environment want to help him learn. A mistake can be corrected through the contributions of others; a loving, caring atmosphere prevails. He becomes a "natural" performer and develops a more relaxed attitude about playing in front of others. When he performs in concert he is much less nervous than the average "traditional" student because he realizes that even the concert is a learning situation, that the audience is "pulling" for him and believes in his potential—they are there to enjoy him, learn from him, and help him. (See Question 9 on p. 78.)

17. *Use of an organized instructional system that incorporates semiprivate lessons, group classes, parent meetings, and recitals.* Weekly private lessons (varying in length according to the concentration span of the child but usually one-half hour) are given. In Japan the child is asked to observe the lesson of the student (or students) preceding or following him—thus the lessons are really semiprivate. In America many schools and teachers schedule students together in groups of two to four for lessons varying from one to one and

one-half hours (or even two in the case of older students). This system seems to work better than asking students to observe earlier or later lessons. The student still receives private attention but also learns the importance of learning from his peers. Sometimes two or more students and perhaps the parents also participate in group games or listening or reading activities. The pace of these weekly lessons can be better geared for each child's concentration level with this "master class" approach. Students may alternate with each other, for example, in five- to fifteen-minute segments, depending on their levels of attention on that particular day.

A monthly group lesson (size varies, but approximately six to twelve students is a recommended number) allows for ensemble playing, games, and repertoire (solo and group) performances. Many Suzuki schools also have parent meetings (often monthly)—a time in which parents and teachers can analyze problems and offer suggestions for each other. Sometimes a specific topic or lecture is presented. Bimonthly recitals are held in Japan. For example, all the students who study on Mondays meet together on a Monday every other month for a concert of solo performances; those who study on Tuesday meet together on a Tuesday, and so on. These recitals sometimes replace regular lessons during the weeks they are held. In America many schools schedule concerts for their students at times varying from monthly to annually. It is suggested that they be held (for *all* students) at least once every two to four months. Even the beginning students should participate through bowing, showing correct posture or something else learned at the lesson, or playing the few notes they know. Even some of the parents and teachers should be encouraged to perform. (In addition, separate faculty concerts should be held periodically.)

18. *Use of instruments of varying size.* Violins that are as small as one-sixteenth and cellos one-fourth the regular size are used for the smallest students. As the student grows, he is given larger instruments. These instruments, many produced in Suzuki family factories, range in quality, but adequate ones are available at reasonable prices because they are produced on a mass scale. Piano and flute students use regular size instruments. This does not interfere with the early start for pianists because playing the larger instrument requires the student to use the larger wrist and arm movements that the piano method advocates; in flute, however, because of embrochure problems, a regular size instrument is used, and instruction begins later— around five or six years of age, although in America some teachers encourage beginning recorder at an earlier age as preparation for flute study. (A recent development is the production by the Sankyo Company of an "elephant trunk" flute, an instrument with a curved head joint. Because this flute is shorter in length, a smaller child, as young as four, might use it.)

19. *Use of qualified instructors.* The teachers of the Talent Education schools in Japan are required to take extensive teacher-training courses at the institute in Matsumoto. They are expected to master performance of the repertoire and the teaching techniques of the method. Many of the teachers

are former Talent Education students who have completed the method; thus they have become thoroughly familiar with its philosophy and methods through firsthand experience. To ensure that the teachers maintain high standards, annual review seminars are supervised by Dr. Suzuki in Matsumoto and other cities in Japan. Also, many attend the teachers' conference mentioned below. (For further discussion of this topic, particularly in relation to America, see Chapter 5.)

20. *Attendance at an annual summer institute.* Many students and teachers from the schools throughout Japan attend the annual Talent Education Summer School at the main institute in Matsumoto. Solo and group recitals, master classes on repertoire, seminars for teachers and visitors, lectures by Dr. Suzuki and other members of the faculty, and a final mass concert that features hundreds of performers are held during the nine-day event. In America there are numerous annual institutes that follow this plan. A biannual International Teachers' Conference is also held in Japan, America, or Europe with many teachers, students, and families in attendance.

21. *Graduation System.* Concerning the Talent Education philosophy about graduation, Dr. Honda says: "Though there is no end in the world of arts or education, we thought it important to encourage the parents and children. Setting up a high aim and trying to gain this peak would make it easier for people to attempt it."[30]

A system has been developed for each of the methods (piano, violin, viola, cello, flute) whereby students receive certificates at different levels of achievement. For example, in Japan the violin student, after completing Volume 3, will record on tape the last piece in the volume, a Louré by Bach, and mail the tape to the main institute. Dr. Suzuki or another teacher will listen to the tape and send the student an elementary graduation certificate. There are eight certificates for the *violin* method: Level 1—At the completion of Gavotte by Gossec (Volume 1); Level 2—Bourée by Bach (Volume 3); Level 3—Concerto in A Minor, 1st movement, by Vivaldi (Volume 4); Level 4—Concerto in G Minor, 1st movement, by Vivaldi (Volume 5); Level 5— La Folia by Corelli (Volume 6); Level 6—Concerto in A Minor by Bach (Volume 7); Level 7—Concerto in D Major by Mozart (Volume 10); Level 8—Rondo by Mozart and Sicilienne by Paradies (beyond Volume 10) (See Chapter 4, part 4, p. 39, for a listing of the Japanese requirements for the *piano* certificates). The *cello* graduation system has five certificates: Level 1—Minuet 2 by Bach (Volume 1); Level 2—Minuet in G by Beethoven (Volume 3); Level 3—Sonata No. 5, 1st and 2nd Movements, by Vivaldi (Volume 5); Level 4—Sonata, 1st and 2nd Movement, by Eccles (Volume 7); Level 5—Concerto in C Minor, Allegro molto maestoso, by J. C. Bach (Volume 8). The *flute* has five certificates: Level 1—Minuet 5 by Bach (Volume 2); Level 2—Intermezzo by Bizet (Volume 2); Level 3—Minuet from

L'Arlésienne Suite (Volume 3); Level 4—Sonata by Blavet (Volume 4); Level 5—Carnival of Venice by Genin (Volume 5). For *viola* the requirements have not, as of early 1984, been formulated for levels above Volume 1: Level 1—Gavotte by Gossec (Volume 1). In America, some schools and teachers follow the levels of graduation suggested by the Japanese, but many others give students certificates at the end of each volume instead.

As Lorraine Fink explains, "It is actually the teacher who decides the student will be permitted to graduate . . . when the teacher and student agree that the best possible job has been done the tape is sent off—with great anticipation—to be heard and to receive comment . . . no student who submits a tape can fail to graduate . . . thus, following the Suzuki philosophy, the child will not fail to be passed, not because the standards are low, but because the parent and teacher will set the stage for the child to succeed."[31]

Students receive their certificates at annual graduation concerts held in each school. An annual Graduation National Concert is also held in Tokyo. Ragner Smedsland, then the Finnish minister, attended one of these concerts during a trip to Japan in 1955. His comments convey the general excitement of such an event:

> The scene is Tokyo's new sports hall—a Sunday in March. The galleries are full of 10,000 spectators who, spellbound, are following the spectacle on the arena where 1,200 violin playing children of the age of four to fifteen are playing Vivaldi's Concerto in A Minor. In the middle of the arena there is a platform with a grand piano and on the four sides thereof the children are lined up. The program was commenced by the first movement of Mozart's Violin concerto in A Major played by the eighty most advanced violinists. Thereupon 120 of the next lower class joined them for playing the first movement of Bach's Violin Concerto in A Minor. And for each new item on the program a new group marched in until the total reached 1,200.[32]

Thus the National Graduation Concert is similar to the monthly concerts held at each branch school, the main difference being the large number of performers and audience. As of 1980, as many as thirty-five hundred children perform at these concerts.

Though no national graduation concerts of this scale are held in America, numerous regional group concerts have been presented by schools or institutes. For example, the Chicagoland Suzuki Music Festival, of which I am director, attracts students annually from numerous states. The 1982 Festival, held in the Auditorium Theatre, featured about 950 violinists (including 150 teachers), 125 cellists (25 teachers), and 275 pianists (75 teachers). The string students participated in a playing concert similar in design to the one mentioned above. Dr. Suzuki was in attendance and also visited similar festivals in Philadelphia, Pennsylvania, Monroe, Louisiana, Tucson, Arizona, and Honolulu, Hawaii. The combined festivals attracted more than 4,000 students and teachers from all fifty states. Many American Talent Education schools have their own special concerts or ceremonies for the awarding of certificates.

Of course, for the Talent Education method to be most successful, it is not enough merely to follow the twenty-one principles outlined above. A Suzuki teacher should have a basic humanitarian approach, a belief in the great potentiality of man, and a reverence for the child. In general, he must be in agreement with the Talent Education philosophy outlined in the previous chapter. (See Chapter 5, Question 9, p. 78, for a discussion of the special respect for the child's basic goodness that is required.) Also, the Suzuki teacher must be aware of modern pedagogical approaches. Talent Education makes use of up-to-date pedagogy and techniques. (See discussion of pedagogy on pages 13–15, 17–18, 19–20, 32–33, 35–36, 41, 46, 50, 67, 108, 123, 131, 135–39, and 148.)

4

The Suzuki Method Applied to All Areas of Instruction of Various Instruments and Other Subjects: Analysis of Suzuki Piano Instruction

It was only natural that Shinichi Suzuki, having grown up around his father's violin factory, would apply his educational ideas originally to violin instruction. Suzuki believes, however, that principles of Talent Education can and should also be applied to other musical instruments and areas of human growth. The Early Development Association was created in Tokyo with this idea in mind. Calligraphy, art, arithmetic, English, gymnastics, and musical instruction in various instruments are offered at the association and in Matsumoto, all using the Suzuki approach. Inherent in the Talent Education philosophy is the ideal of using music and general education as a means to happiness. Suzuki believes the "mother-tongue" learning method to be best and most natural; Talent Education can and should be applied to all areas of instruction.

The Suzuki Method is currently published for violin, viola, cello, flute, and piano. In addition, various schools in America have adapted Suzuki techniques for instruction in other instruments. Numerous papers have been written on the wide range of application of the method. (See the Bibliography.)

SUZUKI PIANO INSTRUCTION

To demonstrate the possible use of the Talent Education philosophy and method for instruments beside violin, the following discussion of Suzuki piano instruction is included. The reader is encouraged to study how the Talent Education philosophy has been applied to piano instruction and to analyze its possible uses for other areas of musical and general study.

The Talent Education philosophy was not applied to piano instruction on a large scale until recently. Although from the formative years of the

25

institute piano has been taught by Suzuki teachers in Japan, only in 1970 were the repertoire-method piano volumes printed in Japan by the Zen-On Company. They were first printed in the United States by the Summy--Birchard Company in 1972. Mrs. Haruko Kataoka of Matsumoto and Mrs. Shizuko Suzuki of Tokyo (the sister-in-law of Dr. Suzuki) developed the piano method under the guidance of Suzuki. Both are presently teaching in Japan; Mrs. Kataoka is in charge of the piano teacher-training program there and also gives teacher-training seminars in other countries, including the United States.

Many Americans, including the author, have traveled to Japan to observe Suzuki piano instruction. For example, Constance Starr spent thirteen months in Matsumoto in 1968–69. Her articles, videotapes, and teacher training at various institutes have been instrumental in introducing Suzuki piano to the West. Of special importance are Carole Bigler and Valery Lloyd-Watts, whose book *Studying Suzuki Piano: More Than Music* (see Bibliography) has become a best-seller and a leading force in the diffusion of Talent Education. Ms. Lloyd-Watts's recordings of the Suzuki repertoire have also been a welcome addition to American Suzuki study. Ms. Lloyd-Watts, Ms. Bigler, Mrs. Kataoka, and numerous other Suzuki piano teachers have taught piano teacher-training courses through North America since 1972. (The 1983 SAA *Directory* lists 44 sanctioned piano teacher trainers as well as 78 violin, 4 viola, 13 cello,—and 4 flute.) Rapid growth in attendance at these workshops and in membership in the Suzuki Association of the Americas attest to the growing popularity of Suzuki piano. Since I attended one of the first American workshops offered in Suzuki piano, at Holy Names College, Oakland, California, in 1972, I have observed a tremendous yearly growth in the number of students and quality of performances.

BASIC PRINCIPLES OF THE PIANO METHOD

The Suzuki *Piano School* method consists of six volumes (seven in Japan) of repertoire-instructional books and a series of corresponding recordings. Volumes 1 through 4, available through Summy-Birchard in America, are recorded by Meiko Miyazawa, a Japanese artist. The recordings for Volumes 5 and 6 have not yet been produced in the United States, but Volumes 5 and 6 are available in the Valery Lloyd-Watts series (Ability Development Co., Athens, Ohio). The recordings used in Japan are not the same as those sold in America. The Japanese (Fontec Label) recordings are by Klaus Hellwig, Walter Gieseking, and Dinu Lupatti; they are excellent, musical performances. Though not available for purchase in America, they may be ordered from Japan through the Talent Education Institute. (see Bibliography p. 166 for address.)

Basically, the piano method is to be taught using the principles mentioned in the preceding chapter; however, because of the nature of the piano, there are some differences:

1. The *Piano School* method does not use instruments of different sizes. The reason is not merely the unavailability of smaller instruments, but, because as Mrs. Kataoka suggests, the regular size instrument is actually preferred. In playing it, the beginning child is required to use the larger motions that the Suzuki piano method emphasizes—arm and wrist action along with finger action.[33] And as Mrs. Starr summarizes: "The use of arm action to achieve a tone when beginning at the keyboard answers the needs of the child as well as the demands of tone quality. The fingers (alone) of a four year old are too small and too weak to produce a tone of volume and quality."[34]

2. To make sitting at the piano more comfortable for the smaller students and to ensure proper posture, adjustable chairs or cushions and footstools of various heights are used. Special devices are used to fit over the piano pedals and connect them to higher pedals, thus making them accessible for the smaller child. (Pedal boxes are available from Rantapaa Enterprises, 1398 Grantham, St. Paul, Minnesota 55108, and from Electro Enterprises, 323 S. Franklin St., Suite 804-E30, Chicago, Illinois 60606.)

3. Because of the general lack of studios with large numbers of pianos and the complexity of two-hand playing, the piano method places less emphasis on performance in groups than does the violin method. Many teachers, however, hold monthly group classes at which students participate in eurhythmics, games, and other group activities. Sometimes two students and/or the teacher will perform together. Mrs. Kataoka was uncertain as to whether group performances would be planned if facilities for such programs were available. She does not seem to encourage monthly group classes as much as Dr. Suzuki and some others do. In the United States, several programs that have access to piano labs have tried group performances with varying degrees of success.[35] Because of the more complex nature of piano performance, a result of one's often playing more than just melody, group playing is more difficult for pianists. For it to be effective, all pianists involved must know their repertoire and be highly flexible.

The author highly recommends the incorporation of monthly group classes, in addition to the weekly semiprivate lessons, into a Suzuki piano program. (See Chapter 5, question 8, p. 76 for suggestions on structuring group activities.)

4. Reading is emphasized earlier in the piano method than with violin; it is usually started after the completion of the first volume. Because the pianist learns in the early repertoire to think and play contrapuntally and harmonically, it is necessary for him to start reading earlier than the violinist,

who initially thinks linearly. Many teachers use texts such as the Frances Clark's *Music Tree* series or Michiko Yurko's *No H in Snake* games from the initial stages of instruction to introduce reading concepts. Some Japanese teachers use the *Method Rose.* (See discussion in Chapter 5, question 3, p. 68.)

The piano method requires other subtle differences in approach which will be emphasized in the following summary of its instructional materials. The method also varies in certain aspects from teacher to teacher. For example, many teachers incorporate the music theory approach of Michiko Yurko.[36]

PIANO REPERTOIRE: THE SIX VOLUMES

The six volumes of the *Suzuki Piano School* published in the United States are, except for minor differences in cover design, similar to those published in Japan.[37] There is, however, a revised edition of Volume 1 (*New Suzuki Piano School*, Zen-Oh Music, 1979) available only in Japan that features, in addition to all the original material, arrangements of all the pieces with melodies placed in the left hand and accompaniments in the right hand; also, the Twinkle Variations are presented as in the earlier edition and in new versions that feature melody in one hand, accompaniment in the other. Both the original American and Japanese editions have English and Japanese titles and instruction. The newest Summy-Birchard edition (1978) is printed in English, Japanese, French, German, and Spanish. The following list is the repertoire found in the *Piano School* (sources, when from a collection or series, are added in parenthesis by the author):

VOLUME 1

Twinkle, Twinkle, Little Star Variations	S. Suzuki
Lightly Row	folk song
The Honey Bee	folk song
Cuckoo	folk song
French Children's Song	folk song
London Bridge	folk song
Mary Had a Little Lamb	folk song
Go Tell Aunt Rhody	folk song
Clair de Lune	J. B. Lully
Long, Long Ago	Bayly
Little Playmates	F. X. Chwatal
Chant Arabe	anonymous
Allegretto	C. Czerny
Adieu (Goodbye to Winter)	folk song
Allegretto	C. Czerny
Christmas Day Secrets	Dutton
Allegro	S. Suzuki
Musette	anonymous

VOLUME 2

Ecossaise...J. N. Hummel
A Short Story......................................H. Lichner
The Happy Farmer (Album for the Young)..........R. Schumann
Minuet in G (Notebook for Anna Magdalena Bach)......J. S. Bach
Minuet in G (Notebook for Anna Magdalena Bach)......J. S. Bach
Minuet in G (Notebook for Anna Magdalena Bach)......J. S. Bach
Minuet in G Minor (Suite, BWV 822).................J. S. Bach
Cradle Song..................................C. M. von Weber
Minuet in F (Serie 22, No. 2).....................W. A. Mozart
Arietta..W. A. Mozart
Melody (Album for the Young).....................R. Schumann
Sonatina in G (Serie 16, No. 160)...............L. van Beethoven
Moderato and Allegretto
Musette (English Suite No. 3).........................J. S. Bach
Minuet in G Minor (Notebook for Anna Magdalena Bach)...J. S. Bach

VOLUME 3

Sonatina in C, Op. 36, No. 1......................M. Clementi
Allegro, Andante, and Vivace
Sonatina in C, Op. 55, No. 1........................F. Kuhlau
Allegro and Vivace
Theme (arranged from Symphony No. 3).........L. van Beethoven
The Little Rough Rider (Album for the Young)..........R. Schumann
Ecossaise in G (Serie 25, No. 306)...............L. van Beethoven
Sonatina in C, Op. 36, No. 3.....................M. Clementi
Spiritoso
Sonatina in G....................................W. A. Mozart
Allegretto

VOLUME 4

Rondo in C (arranged from Divertimento No. 17).......W. A. Mozart
Minuet in C (Eight Minuets with Trio)..............W. A. Mozart
Minuet in D (Eight Minuets with Trio)..............W. A. Mozart
Minuet in G (Eight Minuets with Trio)..............W. A. Mozart
Musette (Notebook for Anna Magdalena Bach).........J. S. Bach
Sonata in G, Op. 49, No. 2....................L. van Beethoven
Allegro, ma non troppo and Minuetto
Gavotte in G Minor (Suite, BWV 822)................J. S. Bach
Minuet in B Flat (Partita No. 1)......................J. S. Bach
Minuet II in B Flat (Partita No. 1)...................J. S. Bach
Gigue in B Flat (Partita No. 1)......................J. S. Bach

VOLUME 5

Fur Elise (Serie 25, No. 298)....................L. van Beethoven
Arabesque (Twenty-Five Progressive Studies).........F. Burgmuller
By the Limpid Stream
(Twenty-Five Progressive Studies)...................F. Burgmuller
Sonatina in F (Serie 16, No. 161)...............L. van Beethoven
Allegro assai and Allegro
Old French Song (Album for the Young)...........P. Tchaikovsky
Prelude in C (Well Tempered Clavier, Vol. 1)...........J. S. Bach
Two-Part Invention in C.............................J. S. Bach
Sonata No. 48 in C (Hob. XVI: 35)...................J. Haydn
Allegro con brio, Adagio, and Allegro
Siciliano (Album for the Young)....................R. Schumann
First Loss (Album for the Young)...................R. Schumann
The Cuckoo.......................................L. C. Daquin
Little Prelude in C Minor
(Twelve Little Preludes).............................J. S. Bach
Sonata in C, K 545..............................W. A. Mozart
Allegro, Andante, and Allegretto

VOLUME 6

Sonata in C, K 330..............................W. A. Mozart
Allegro moderato, Andante cantabile, and Allegretto
Sonata "Pastorale" in D Minor.....................D. Scarlatti
Sonata in A, K 331..............................W. A. Mozart
Andante grazioso, Minuet with Trio, and Allegretto
Prelude in G (Amriti Sammbung No. 8).............G. F. Handel
The Harmonious Blacksmith (Air and Variations—Suite 5).G. F. Handel
Minuet in G, Op. 14, No. 1....................I. J. Paderewski

As mentioned on page 26, the Japanese Suzuki recordings of the above repertoire are not the same as those published in America by Summy-Birchard. The Japanese recordings, available through the Talent Education Institute in Matsumoto (see address on page 166) contain seven volumes. Volume 1 contains the selections found in Vols. 1 and 2 of the Summy-Birchard version; Volume 2 contains selections from Vols. 3 and 4; Volume 3 has certain selections from Vols. 5 and 6. In addition, there are three other Japanese volumes: Volume 4 includes the Sonata in A Major, K. 331 by Mozart; the Italian Concerto BWV. 971 by Bach; and the Sonata No. 23 in F minor, Op. 57 ("Appassionata") by Beethoven. Volume 5 contains the Sonata in C Major, K. 330 by Mozart; the Sonata in C Major, K. 545 by Mozart; the Sonata No. 17 in D Minor, Op. 31, No. 2 ("Tempest") by Beethoven; and the "Fantasia" in D Minor, K. 397 by Mozart. Volume 6 contains the Partita in B Flat Major by Bach; the Sonata in D Minor, L. 413 ("Pastorale") by Scarlatti; the Sonata in E Major, L. 23 by Scarlatti, "Jesu, Joy of Man's Desiring" by Bach; Siciliana by Bach; Impromptu in G Flat Major, Op. 90, No. 3 by Schubert; Impromptu in E Flat Major, Op. 90,

No. 2 by Schubert. Volume 7 contains the Concerto No. 26 in D Major, K. 537 ("Coronation") by Mozart; and the Concerto in D Major by Haydn.

AFTER VOLUME 6

After completion of Volume 6, Mrs. Kataoka recommends the study of repertoire such as Inventions of Bach, Sonatas of Scarlatti, the Italian Concerto of Bach, the Op. 57 Sonata of Beethoven, the "Ah! vous dirai-je, maman" Variations of Mozart, The D Major Concerto of Haydn, and the "Coronation" Concerto of Mozart. She suggests that the teacher follow the interest of the pupil in selecting further repertoire.

The only instruction given in volumes of the *Suzuki Piano School* is the introductory preface found in the beginning of Volume 1. Otherwise, only a few directions about phrasing, legato and staccato playing, and a few preparatory exercises are given in the first two volumes; except for one legato exercise in the third volume, the last four volumes consist entirely of repertoire.

The preface is written by Dr. Suzuki and summarizes some, though not all, of the concepts of the Talent Education philosophy. For the reader to grasp the extent of the Suzuki philosophy discussed, I have included this preface (as well as an explanatory section that is not included in the new 1978 edition) in Appendix 2 (see p. 146). The reader is advised to check the *Piano School* (Volume 1, pp. 10–11, 15, 17, 18, 19, 20, 22, 30; Volume 2, pp. 4, 6, 8, 10, 14, 19; Volume 3, p. 7) for examples of the preparatory exercises. (Page numbers refer to the 1978 edition.)

The qualified Suzuki teacher is, of course, dependent on more information about the method than is printed in the volumes of repertoire. Talent Education in Japan emphasizes learning through imitation more than through reading; it is only natural that the books contain few instructions. Teachers are encouraged to learn from other teachers and students. The Western as well as the Japanese teacher must go beyond the context of the repertoire books through private music studies (perhaps in colleges), thorough readings of Suzuki-related and other educational material, and through attendance at SAA-sanctioned institutes and workshops. This issue will be discussed in more detail at the conclusion of this chapter and in Chapter 5.

PIANO—VOLUME 1

This section contains a summary of the *Suzuki Piano School*. The reader is encouraged to familiarize himself with the music and recordings of all the volumes. Volume 1 may be summarized as follows:

1. The key of C is predominant with sixteen of the pieces in C, one in A minor (Chant Arabe), two in G (Goodbye to Winter and Allegro), and one in D minor

(Musette). The authors suggest transposing some of the earlier pieces; for example (on page 16)[38], "All of the previous pieces should be played in the key of G Major." Many North American teachers are teaching the transposing of Volume 1 pieces to other keys—ranging from just a few to all major and minor keys. I suggest a review system that eventually makes use of transposition of Volume 1 pieces to all keys—not necessarily learning each selection in each key but learning to play in all keys through a carefully structured review system that incorporates a combination of learning new keys by ear and by guidance from the teacher. While a student is learning Volumes 2 and 3, he could be reviewing Volume 1 pieces in a few new keys—perhaps one to three—weekly (along with other review techniques suggested in Chapter 5, question 4, p. 72).

2. The first piece, Twinkle, Twinkle, Little Star Variations, provides a technical introduction that emphasizes the use of the arm and wrist motions. (Please read comments in Chapter 5, Question 1, p. 67, and note that the following summary should be analyzed in broad terms. The movements suggested do not necessarily apply to all students at the places suggested.) As Mrs. Starr summarizes (in an article originally published in *Clavier*):

> The small child delights in big motions. He likes to feel rhythms with his body. . . . With this in mind, the use of arm action to achieve a tone when beginning at the keyboard answers the needs of the child as well as the demands of tone quality. The fingers of a four year old are too small and too weak to produce a tone of adequate volume and quality. . . .

Mrs. Starr discusses various pedagogical approaches to the variations. Concerning the first variation, she says:

> The teacher should play this variation at this brisk tempo [the tempo on the recording] when presenting it and the student should be expected to play at this tempo when performing it himself. From the beginning he must be encouraged to develop quick, fast movements. . . . The hand should be relaxed and the thumb positioned so that it will touch the key on the spot at the side of the thumb next to the fingernail. It is important that the teacher keep the wrist straight, using the forearm and hand as a unit so that the tone is produced by the weight of the arm. . . .
>
> Even though the curved position of the hand is ideal, some children will at first play with stiff and straight fingers. The teacher helps the child assume a better position by shaping the hand and placing it on the keyboard in a relaxed position in preparation for playing each individual note of "Twinkle." . . .
>
> Some children may be able to imitate the teacher's arm action, tone, rhythm, and tempo after observing the teacher demonstrate a few times.

If the child needs further help, the teacher may take the child's right hand in her right hand, holding his thumb between her thumb and middle finger and guiding his forearm with her left hand. In this way she may guide his hand and arm as he plays. . . . This procedure may have to be repeated again and again. . . .

This same instruction should be given each time a new finger is introduced, second finger on D, third finger on E, etc.

As soon as the child can do this with some ease, he may practice the interval at the beginning of the "Twinkle" melody. He plays the ♫♫ ♩♩ with the thumb on C. Then the teacher moves the child's hand so that the fourth finger is poised above G, and he plays the same pattern on G. He may then try this by himself, but always with the stop and preparation between the notes. If necessary the teacher may point to the G key from beneath the child's hand until he is able to find this easily by himself. Following this he may be instructed to play the entire first phrase, taking time before playing each note to prepare and poise the hand properly. With a very young child this may take many lessons. The student may practice the five-finger exercise and the first phrase of "Twinkle" for some time before advancing. He may then play the entire first variation, with a stop before each change of note. Only after this preparation does he play the first variation continuously as it is written.[39]

Mrs. Starr discusses the rest of the piece (the entire article is printed in the appendix, see p. 133) and mentions other concepts that are introduced in the following variations and theme: legato touch through the use of a good hand position (theme), flexible up-down wrist motions (second variation), and forearm action (third variation).

3. The first piece also provides an introduction to other Suzuki principles: slow practice, "stop and prepare" technique, learning through listening and imitation (the student, of course, rarely looks at his copy of the music until after learning all the pieces in the book), and perfecting a section before starting a new section.

4. Some of the pieces are preceded by preparatory exercises (see p. 31 for a list of the examples). According to Mrs. Kataoka, these exercises are not necessarily meant to be taken literally; they serve as examples of exercises the teacher might devise for special technical or musical problems. (Later volumes present even fewer such exercises; see the discussion on p. 35 of this chapter.)

5. No biographical or historical information about the music and composers is included. This subject is left to the discretion of each teacher. No dynamic and tempo marking are given until the thirteenth piece (Little Playmates), and phrasing marks are found in only some of the pieces (pp. 17, 18, 23, 25, 26, 28, 29, and 33). The only tempo markings defined are

"allegro" and "allegretto." Obviously there is no need for a thorough written explanation in this volume because most such information is relayed orally by the teacher, parent, or recording. The markings or explanations that are given serve merely as examples for the teacher to follow. Each teacher or parent should use his intuition in explaining terms, phrasing, dynamics, composer, and so on.

6. Basic pentachord positions are used through the thirteenth piece; there are, however, occasional slight shifts of positions (see London Bridge, p. 21, the first measure compared with the last two measures of the right hand part, for example). The last seven pieces introduce other concepts of positioning: moving to new positions within a piece (Christmas Day Secrets, pp. 30–31), expanding the fingers within one position (Chant Arabe, p. 26, the left hand part, or Christmas Day Secrets, p. 31, top line, the right hand part), turning the thumb under to reach a new position (Christmas Day Secrets, the eleventh and twelfth measure of the left hand), crossing a finger over the thumb (Musette, p. 33, the sixth measure of the right hand part, or Allegro, p. 32, the third measure of the right hand part).

7. The harmonic structure of the repertoire is based mainly on I, $IV^{6/4}$, V^6, or $V^{6/5}$ chords. During lessons, the earliest pieces, the first four of which are written as melody (played by the student with one hand or with two hands two octaves apart) with no accompaniment, are often accompanied by chords or chordal patterns played by the teacher at a second piano or at the upper keyboard of the student's piano. (There is no mention of this in the volume; this conclusion comes from my observation of Mrs. Katako and other Suzuki teachers.)

8. There is a wide range of tempi in the recordings of the repertoire of the first volume. The Chant Arabe is slow and the Christmas Day Secrets very fast, for example. The Japanese, the Summy-Birchard, and the Lloyd-Watts recordings often offer contrasting ideas on tempo.

9. Much of the repertoire is based on familiar folk tunes. (See the list on pp. 28–31 of this text.)

10. Some other concepts introduced in the first book are: lifting the wrist slightly at the end of phrases (see p. 17); using larger wrist motions for repeated staccato notes (pp. 11 and 29); training the hands to use slightly different motions at the same time to achieve correct musical effects (p. 28, measures 1, 3, 9, and 11 or p. 33, measure 5); learning the technique of legato playing through "tonalization" (beautiful tone) exercises (pp. 15, 20, 22, 36); and learning the ability to change tempo and dynamics within a piece (pp. 25, 27, 31–32).

11. Although not precisely stated in Volume 1, good posture and mental preparation are emphasized from the very first lesson:

> The child's posture must allow for maximum freedom and relaxation in his playing. He must not have unnecessary strain in any part of the body. For this reason he should sit with back straight and far enough away from the keyboard to allow him to lean slightly forward with arms hanging comfortably at his sides. . . . Not one note is played during beginning instruction without careful preparation of posture and hand position.[40]

Often several weeks or even months are spent at beginning lessons working only on posture, bowing, hand positions, or movements required for the first note.

Thus the first volume of the *Suzuki Piano School* introduces the beginning student to many important concepts and approaches. The following five volumes basically are books of repertoire that develop and expand these concepts; through the gradually increasing complexity of the music, the student reinforces the concepts already learned while learning new ones.

SUMMARY OF PIANO REPERTOIRE VOLUMES

In addition to the above comments about Volume 1, *a general summary of all the volumes follows*:

1. Even fewer preparatory exercises are found after Volume 1. Volumes 2 and 3 have a few "tonalization" exercises (Vol. 2, pp. 8, 19, and Vol. 3, p. 7), a couple of technical "preparatory" exercises (Vol. 2, p. 4—a grace note study, and, p. 6—a chord study), and four scale exercises (Vol. 2, p. 4—C major, p. 8—F major, p. 10—G major, and p. 14—G minor), which are based on traditional fingerings. Otherwise, no exercises or instructions are given. Mrs. Kataoka says that technical studies are to be introduced by the teacher at times when the student will benefit the most; readiness varies with individual students. The preparatory exercises and scales given merely serve as examples and are not necessarily meant to be taught in the sequence in which they are inserted in the books. Mrs. Kataoka suggests that for especially difficult passages, preparatory exercises could be devised well ahead of the actual study of the composition. Technique is introduced, not as an entity in itself but as a means of achieving the goal of making music.

2. All the volumes are fingered extensively. The fingerings merely serve as a model and are not always meant to be followed literally; the teacher should seek the best fingering for each student. The printed fingerings emphasize the following points: use of different fingers on repeated notes to help in the development of a loose wrist and a more relaxed hand position (see Bach Minuet 1, Volume 2, 1st measure, right hand, for example); use

of a finger at the end of a phrase that will prepare the hand position for the next phrase (see Short Story, Volume 2, measures 6–7, right hand); no emphasis on using similar fingerings for sequential passages (see Minuet by Mozart, Volume 2, measures 9–16); and frequent use of a fingering that requires a more spread hand position (see Allegro from Sonatina, Op. 36, No. 1 by Clementi, Volume 3, measure 1, right hand, fingering 3-5-3-1-1 would make for a more relaxed hand position). In general, the fingerings emphasize traditional scale and chord fingerings. I suggest that the student learn the fingerings as presented for the Volume 1 selections. These pieces are basically in simple pentachord position, and the fingerings serve to present basic concepts. More and more after Volume 1, however, the teacher needs to look at each individual's hand shape and size in determining the best fingerings. Naturally, the teacher needs a good basic knowledge of fingering approaches, the depth of knowledge learned through years of performing and in teaching college pedagogy courses.

3. Some music is extensively edited with phrase, dynamic, touch, and tempo markings. The markings of the editors are not differentiated from those of the composer or the original publications. Some pieces are edited thoroughly, but others have no added markings. For example, in Volume 4, the Mozart Rondo (pp. 4–5) is edited but the three Mozart Minuets (pp. 6–8) are not. The baroque repertoire presented in Volume 2 has dynamic and tempo markings, but, except for some "tonalization" markings to indicate legato, phrasing is not indicated; the baroque repertoire in the third through sixth volumes is thoroughly edited and includes extensive phrase markings.

No ornamentation charts are given; as presented on the recordings, the stylistic correctness of the performance of the ornaments might be questioned by some scholars, but one should remember that the recording is not presented as the definitive interpretation. The Suzuki teacher can present a more thorough approach to ornamentation through re-recording some of the baroque repertoire with more elaborate ornamentation or through presenting additional repertoire. (See Chapter 5, p. 75, question 7.)

Editing is not presented in any unified way throughout the books. In a sense, the recordings and teacher serve as the "editors" through their suggested tempi, dynamics, and so on. The Suzuki teacher should compare other editions of the repertoire selections to help the child realize there are other interpretations.

4. The performance on the corresponding recordings sometimes differs from the editorial indications in the music. For example, in the Summy-Birchard recordings, the Mozart Rondo (Volume 4, pp. 4–5) is marked with much dynamic contrast but is performed by Meiko Miyazawa at a similar dynamic level throughout; the Clementi Sonatina, Op. 36, No. 1 (Volume

3, pp. 4-9), is performed in a way that differs in some aspects from the printed score—repeats are not played in the first movement, dynamic markings are not always followed, and all three movements are played at practically the same tempo although the markings are "allegro," "andante," and "vivace"; the Bach Minuet (Volume 2, p. 25), though marked "allegretto," is played extremely slowly.

In general, the repertoire is performed well by Miyazawa in the Summy-Birchard version. The performances are accurate as far as notes and rhythm are concerned, and the playing is often very musical. The Suzuki student should remember that the record is only a "stepping-off point" for further learning and listening; it is because of the subjectivity of one's interpretation while performing and while listening that the Suzuki Method emphasizes listening to other performances as well (Valery Lloyd-Watts has recorded all six volumes in musical performances, and the Japanese recordings present yet another version; see Bibliography); the student is asked to be flexible and to be able to play in many ways in order to find his own interpretation.

5. The titles only rarely indicate the source of the repertoire. For example, a Bach Minuet is listed merely as "Minuet 1" (Volume 2) and the Beethoven Sonatina is listed without any source (Volume 2). (I have added the sources, when available, of those pieces from collections in the list of repertoire on pp. 28-31.) The teacher is responsible for being familiar with this information in order to share it with the student.

6. Because there is no special emphasis on the use of the printed books as the fundamental learning tool, they contain no art work or special materials that would distract the student's attention from the music. The books are supplementary to the educational process and are for guidance in learning the music; however, they are attractively organized and designed.

7. No pedaling marks are given until the last two pieces of the fourth volume. Though presented in certain selections in the last two volumes, the marks are not uniformly organized. For example, the Haydn Sonata found in Volume 5 contains only thirteen measures (out of 270) that have pedal indications. About the teaching of pedal, Mrs. Starr wrote:

> The editors of the method feel that if the child has learned to play with a sensitive legato from the start, pedaling is unnecessary until the end of the fourth volume. Most of that previous repertoire does not require pedal to give a good musical performance. Pedal may be, and sometimes is, introduced in the Bach Minuets and Gigue (Volume 4). Often when this is done by the younger children it is necessary to use the pedaling box so that the child *can* use the pedal.[41]

The only mention of pedal in the text is found in the "explanatory note" section toward the front of the earlier editions of the first four volumes:

> When should pedal be introduced? Not until Vol. 6. All pieces in the earlier books sound well without pedal. By not using pedal, the child learns to play cleanly and to produce legato with his hands rather than with the pedal.[42]

Thus there is a contradiction; though Mrs. Starr says the end of Volume 4, the text says that Volume 6 is the proper place to begin pedaling. This difference is perhaps an example of the flexibility that Talent Education emphasizes; teachers often vary in their presentations of certain concepts, and one teacher may vary from child to child depending on the age, height, maturity, motivation, and goals of each student.

8.   The emphasis on repertoire in the key of C continues through all the volumes. There are thirty-six pieces or movements in C, two in D, one in E, nine in F, seventeen in G, one in A, three in B flat, one in C minor, and seven in A minor. Not represented are the keys of B, D flat, E flat, G flat, and A flat majors and F, B, C sharp, E flat, G flat, or F sharp, A flat or G sharp, and B flat minors; of course, some of these keys are presented in sections of the repertoire.

No attempt is made to present the keys in a structured way. The method does not place as much emphasis on early coverage of all keys as found in some other modern approaches. A student naturally continues to learn new keys as he continues to study; repertoire selected for study after completion of the six volumes eventually can cover other major and minor keys as well as other modes and tonalities used in contemporary music. Also, if the teacher desires, repertoire that introduces wider ranges of tonality may be included between the pieces found in the method, and, as mentioned earlier, transposition of the pieces in Volume I to other keys is encouraged even in the beginning stages of instruction.

9.   The volumes do not present biographical or historical information, nor is there a glossary of terms. At a lecture-seminar in Matsumoto in August 1972, Dr. Suzuki explained that the student best learns the meaning of terms through experience. He hears performances and learns the music and eventually begins making associations with all the symbols on the printed page. The student is taught the importance of checking the accuracy of his concepts through the use of other sources such as a good musical encyclopedia or through consulting his teacher.

The terms and symbols presented are not meant to be comprehensive, but they are important in developing the concept of symbolic terminology and its use in learning music.

10. The six volumes do not present a thorough survey of forms but rather serve to introduce the student to the most common classical and baroque forms. The early examples of form are simple; as the volumes progress, the forms presented become longer and more complex in key structure and organization. Volume 1 emphasizes short pieces with two- or three-part sections and simple variations; Volume 2 introduces sonatina form; Volume 3, rondo and larger sonatina forms; Volume 4, minuet-with-trio and sonata forms; Volume 5, free prelude and invention forms; Volume 6, large theme-and-variation and romantic free forms.

11. The pieces are presented in such an organized order that earlier repertoire often serves as preparation for later selections. For example, all the left-hand patterns of the sixth through the ninth pieces of Volume 1 prepare for the tenth and many other pieces that follow; the rhythmic pattern of Allegretto 2 (Volume 1, p. 29) prepares for the rhythm of Christmas Day Secrets (Volume 1, p. 30). The two-, three-, and four-note articulations found in the right hand of Ecossaise (Volume 2, p. 5) prepare for similar articulations in a Short Story (Volume 2, p. 6) and some other pieces that follow.

12. Although not stated within the text of the volumes, there is, in Japan, an organized graduation system for Suzuki piano. The following graduation pieces are used in Japan: *Level 1*—Minuet 2 by Bach (Volume 2); *Level 2*—Sonatina, Op. 36, No. 1, by Clementi (Volume 3); *Level 3*—Partita in B flat, Minuets and Gigue, by Bach (Volume 4); *Level 4*—Sonata in A, K. 331, by Mozart (Volume 6); *Level 5*—"Italian" Concerto by Bach (beyond Volume 6); *Level 6*—Concerto in D ("Coronation") by Mozart; *Level 7*—Partita in B flat by Bach; and *Level 8*—Sonata No. 33 ("Appassionata") by Beethoven. Mrs. Starr suggests that the American teacher adopt this graduation idea as a motivational aid if he wishes.[43] (As mentioned in point 21, p. 52, many American schools present certificates at the conclusion of each volume.)

OFTEN MENTIONED CRITICISMS AND STRENGTHS OF THE PIANO METHOD

The volumes of the *Suzuki Piano School*, judged alone and not in relation to other aspects of the Suzuki teaching philosophy, have been unfairly criticized by some music educators for the lack of detailed instruction and explanations, the lack of technical exercises and theory work, the lack of biographical and historical information, the lack of a glossary, the lack of drawings and art work, the use of extensive fingerings (some which certain critics disagree with), the unevenness in the presentation of pedal markings, the lack of modern or much romantic repertoire, the lack of any organized presentation of note-reading, and the occasional discrepancies between the performances on the corresponding records and the indications in the printed score. As explained in the sections of this chapter that discuss the above points, however, there is often a purpose for these various omissions or discrepancies; they are not true weaknesses when judged in context of the entire Suzuki philosophy. For example, the repertoire encompasses very little romantic and no contemporary music. If judged as a comprehensive introduction to piano literature, the method would be inadequate; but the method was not designed as a totally representative repertoire but more as a basic "alphabet" from which a student will gain a sound technique and musicality; from this viewpoint it is excellent. The music presented is of high quality, and other repertoire can be incorporated. (See Beverly Graham's *Suzuki Pianists' List for Supplementary Materials* for an extensive, graded listing of compositions that might be taught in addition to the basic Suzuki repertoire.)

The reader should also remember that, according to some writers, the Japanese are not as literal-minded as the Americans (see Chapter 7, Question 13, p. 129, and comments under Question 1, Chapter 5, p. 67). They do not place as much emphasis on detailed written instructions and explanations; they believe information is best transmitted from teacher and/or parent to student; therefore, the method should be judged by its comprehensive pedagogical presentation rather than its printed volumes.

There are, however, two criticisms some would consider valid: the lack of any differentiation between the interpretive markings of the composer and the editors and the lack of adequate instructional manuals or thorough training programs for the teacher.

The lack of adequate instructional manuals and thorough training programs has been a frequent criticism of the piano method as it is presented in the United States. According to Mrs. Starr, Dr. Suzuki encouraged the publication of the *Suzuki Piano School* in the United States in 1972 although there were no training centers or teacher manuals there then. He did not insist on implementing the same requirements for teachers then found in Japan because he believed these would develop naturally over the years. His prophecy is coming true; now teacher-training programs are being held at various Suzuki institutes, and the Suzuki Association of the Americas initiated sanctioned teacher-training programs in 1979. Since then, guidelines and requirements have become clearer and standards have risen. Memphis State University (Tennessee), in 1979, began the first Master of Music degree course in Suzuki piano pedagogy, and other institutions, including Ithaca College (New York), have added Suzuki teacher-training piano courses and degrees to their curriculums. The publication in 1979 of the text, *Studying Suzuki Piano: More Than Music* by Carole Bigler and Valery Lloyd-Watts, has, to some extent, satisfied the need for a teacher manual. Numerous books and articles on Suzuki piano, including *Introducing Suzuki Piano* by Doris Koppelman and *How to Teach Suzuki Piano* by Shinichi Suzuki, have been published since then (see Bibliography.) The Japanese Suzuki piano teacher is expected to attend training courses under a sanctioned teacher such as Mrs. Katoaka in Japan and fulfill certain requirements in order to become a certified Suzuki teacher. The American teacher, however, can purchase the books and records at a local music store and claim to be a Suzuki teacher without comprehending the Talent Education philosophy. Even if one has attended some Suzuki workshops and has read books and articles on the Suzuki philosophy, he may lack a thorough pedagogical background. The introduction and explanatory remarks presented in the earlier volumes are not comprehensive enough for the inexperienced teacher; it is hoped that the sanctioning program of the Suzuki Association and the publication of texts such as those of Bigler and Lloyd-Watts and others will help to rectify this problem. A partial solution will come gradually through a natural evolution as students and parents are attracted to the more qualified, caring instructors. By seeing the results (at workshops, institutes, concerts, and so on) of good teaching and good learning, teachers and students alike will seek to emulate the roles presented. The teacher with an extensive background and with SAA teacher training will naturally attract families that want the best education. (This matter is discussed further in the next chapter.)

In conclusion, there are many strengths of the *Piano School* even when the books are judged without considering the Talent Education teaching philosophy. The volumes are excellent in their presentation of fine literature and well-performed corresponding recordings, their coverage of a wide range of concepts, their organized order of repertoire that emphasizes preparation for later pieces through the learning of concepts found in earlier pieces, their gradual expansion from simple pentachord positions in the first volume to more complex hand positions later, their thorough presentation of basic musical concepts (particularly in the first volume), their use of the arm and wrist as well as the fingers from the initial lessons, and their lack of detailed instructions that could, as in some other methods, take the focus away from the music.

No matter what instrument, piano or otherwise, the Suzuki instructor teaches, he should incorporate good, sound pedagogy in his methodology. The *Piano School*, like the methods of the violin, cello, viola, and flute, has been designed with the most up-to-date pedagogy. Hopefully, any future Suzuki Method courses designed for other instruments or subjects will be as conscientiously constructed. Any educator interested in using the Talent Education approach in a curriculum he designs should be thoroughly introduced to the Suzuki philosophy through study of at least one of its instrumental methods, a study that would include a complete analysis of the repertoire and pedagogical techniques. From reading books and articles, he should be aware how the Suzuki Method differs from the traditional approach. (Especially recommended is an article by Nancy Greenwood Brooks, "Toward a Deeper Understanding of Suzuki Pedagogy," which discusses the "essence" of Suzuki's approach, the core innovations.[44])

TALENT EDUCATION FOR ALL SUBJECTS

The Talent Education method is best judged by its overall philosophy rather than simply by its repertoire books. Suzuki is concerned above all with nurturing children from birth through use of a Talent Education approach for all subjects:

> Once about 20 years ago I shed tears in the middle of the night thinking of all the babies born on the earth who were in a miserable state because they were being educated in the wrong way. They were left without anything being done for them. I thought of all the human beings in the world as well. I got the idea that we should establish a national system for nurturing children beginning at zero years old from the tears I shed that night. The system that I envisioned is like this: A country should develop specialists for nurturing children. These leaders should go to all cities, towns, and villages in the country. When the government received a birth report, the specialist would go to the newborn baby's house. First, he would congratulate the family, then he would give advice to the parents on how to educate the baby at home. He would give them knowledge on how to raise the baby, how to keep the baby in good health, how to develop his ability, and how to make this baby become a fine human being with a beautiful heart. All of these things would be taught through education at home, starting at zero years of age.
>
> The specialist would have a geographical area of responsibility. Within this area he would visit every child until the age of 5 or 6. He would see how the child was being raised and help the baby by the authority of the government. Then no one in the country would be improperly raised.
>
> If a certain family was too poor to take proper care of the baby, or spend money on the health of the baby, then the government (either federal, state or local) should give financial help to the family.
>
> We should have this kind of system so that every child would grow into a fine and virtuous person from being watched with a warm heart and educated in the right way.[45]

Suzuki describes his own preschool in Matsumoto:

> Next I would like to report on the experimental pre-school (that is, pre-primary school) methods we conduct at Talent Education Institute for the purpose of applying educational methods that develop children's individual abilities so that the ability becomes an integral part of the child. Twenty-five years ago I founded in Matsumoto the Talent Education Institute for pre-school children, called in Japanese "Yoji Gakuen," and invited Mrs. Yano, an educator in this part of the country, to start the project in this method of learning so that every child might develop his ability to the point where it becomes a part of him. The children were, and are, accepted without any tests. This school has been continuing for twenty-five years. There are

sixty children in the class, comprising in age those of three, four and five years. We do not separate them according to age, which normally is done in regular schools, because we know very well that the three year olds grow up steadily under the stimulating environment afforded by the older children. In one year, they usually acquire the ability to memorize one hundred and seventy to one hundred and eighty haiku, and they are able to repeat any one of them clearly upon demand. A haiku is a short Japanese poem of five, seven and five syllables in three lines. Of course, we train them to develop many other abilities, such as physical education and the development of quick reflexes, writing numbers correctly, and reading kanji. Drawing and calligraphy are taught as is English conversation. They are also taught to speak their mother tongue, Japanese, clearly and correctly. To do this we use the same training methods as are used to train TV announcers. To observe the enthusiasm and happiness of these tiny children is the deepest source of satisfaction for those who work with them. During the last seven years we have tested the I.Q. (Tanka-Binet system) for the five year olds who graduate from pre-school to primary first grade. The average I.Q. has been near 160. In 1973 the average was 158.[46]

Dr. Suzuki discussed the Talent Education approach to teaching arithmetic:

> Why do we not teach arithmetic by the same method that we teach our mother tongue? A child will learn four or five words and use them many times every day and therefore will be able to use them quite freely. Ability to use the words comes only from using them. A few words can be increased gradually and naturally. Then ten words will become the basis for the next increase. This is the method by which the mother tongue is learned by the child.
>
> I have tried out my new method of teaching arithmetic at some primary schools. We taught about 40 pupils by what I call "The full-mark method." We teach until every pupil in the class gets full-marks (100%) and education begins from this stage. We teach how easy it is to get full-marks and the method we use is the same as teaching the mother tongue. According to our tests of teaching arithmetic for five years, we found that all pupils were able to get full marks, every time without exception.[47]

A thorough discussion of Talent Education principles applied to various subjects may be found in Masaru Ibuka's *Kindergarten Is Too Late.* Mr. Ibuka is a former president of the Sony Foundation which has been instrumental in sponsoring the Early Development Association in Tokyo. Also recommended is an article about a Suzuki-oriented art curriculum for children—"The Young Masters Art Program" by John Gordon. (*Suzuki World*, September-October 1983, p. 12.)

In conclusion, the Suzuki educator should emphasize the Talent Education objective of cultivating an artistic appreciation and discipline in people to help them achieve happier, more successful lives. Whether the curriculum is math, music, English, science, or another subject, Talent Education does not necessarily strive to create professionals in these specific areas but rather desires to create "professionals" in the area of life—in living. Learning a subject well will help one learn to live well.

5
Teaching the Suzuki Method

What is required of a good Suzuki teacher? This chapter presents a summary of the author's own ideas. The Suzuki Association of the Americas (SAA) has developed suggestions for teacher sanctioning, which are also discussed in this chapter.

SUZUKI ASSOCIATION OF THE AMERICAS GUIDELINES

The SAA is the official organization for the development of Suzuki teacher training. Through its board of directors and committee members, it provides guidelines for sanctioned teacher-training courses which are held at various colleges, schools, and institutes. Records of teachers who have taken the various training courses are maintained in the SAA offices in Muscatine, Iowa. To be sanctioned, the SAA courses must be taught by a teacher trainer approved by the Association. The following courses are offered: Foundation Course 1–*A*—a basic introduction to the history, philosophy, and methodology, which is an overall view of the Suzuki Method presented with special emphasis on the beginnings of instruction, the "pre-Twinkle" stage; and the earliest pieces in Volume 1; Foundation Course 1–B—a review of all the pieces in Volume 1; *Numbered Courses* (each corresponding to the volume and instrument studied) present study of the repertoire including pedagogical and technical approaches. Each course (representing study of one volume of the repertoire) presents a minimum of twenty-three hours of study (taught over a minimum of five days) including lectures, repertoire study, observations of Suzuki students and teachers, and performances by the trainees. (A minimum of fifteen class hours is required for each course; in addition, eight hours of supervised observation is mandatory.) Discussions are held on pedagogical points, subjects such as listening, review, technique, incorporating extra repertoire, note-reading, and whatever is appropriate for the volume being studied. In order to gain admission to one of these courses, one must submit an audition tape to the institute director where the course is being taught—for courses 1-A, 1-B and 2, two major pieces from Volume 3 should be submitted; for courses 3 and up, two major pieces or movements from the next volume should be submitted. One may audit or take these courses for SAA credit and/or college credit. To receive credit, the trainee must be able to perform the corresponding repertoire musically and accurately from memory and meet attendance and reading assignment requirements. For college credit, a term paper is required. To receive SAA credit, the trainee is also required to become an Active Member of the SAA, which includes the benefits of a subscription to the *American Suzuki Journal*, institute listings and other mailings, a membership directory, and special rates on health insurance programs. (For further information, guidelines for teacher-trainer application, and a list of sanctioned training centers, write the SAA (Batterson Buildings 319 E. Second Street, Suite 302, Muscatine, Iowa 52761). The units described above are usually offered as week-long courses at a sanctioned institute; although some are offered as more expanded courses. The SAA recommends that one study with a teacher-trainer over a longer period of time, preferably for two years. Such a course would be taught at a college, university, music school, or Suzuki program. Just as with the shorter courses, the student would have the option of registering the completion (upon approval of the teacher) of each volume of study with the SAA. This longer course, while basically following the format of the week long courses, would be more comprehensive and would incorporate supervised practice teaching, extensive private lessons, and a more thorough study of various pedagogical approaches and repertoire.

The SAA record-keeping procedure is not a certification process. It is designed as a service to Suzuki teachers to provide them with a central location to record their progress.

Like any fine teacher, the Suzuki teacher should have an extensive pedagogical background. The author recommends that a Suzuki teacher have a minimum of a Bachelor of Music (or its equivalent degree or experience); a Master's degree is preferred. The teacher should have had repertoire and pedagogy courses that thoroughly cover literature for his instrument and various approaches to teaching. He should be able to perform accurately and musically, preferably from memory, the Suzuki repertoire that he teaches and, finally, he should have developed the attitude and taken the Talent Education–sanctioned courses needed for good Suzuki instruction. These points will be expanded upon below.

TEACHER ATTITUDES AND QUALITIES

Standards very somewhat throughout America with regard to the specific requirements for Suzuki teachers. What follows are the expectations for the faculty of the Suzuki Music Academy of Chicago, of which the author is the director.

First, the Suzuki teacher should have certain philosophical beliefs that are conducive to good Talent Education. The following guidelines by the Suzuki Association of the Americas are distributed to all faculty members of the Academy. The author's additions are in brackets.

PHILOSOPHY AND ATTUTUDES OF
TALENT EDUCATION TEACHERS[48]

The Suzuki teacher should have:

(1) Genuine interest in and affection for children as developing human beings, as well as musicians.

(2) Capacity to work well with children of different ages and with parents and colleagues in a pleasantly cooperative atmosphere.

(3) Recognition of the importance of continuing study and self-improvement for the teacher-performer, at the highest level possible.

(4) Belief in the importances of:

a) Beginning early

b) Postponing reading until readiness is established by teacher and parent

c) Listening to recordings

d) Following the Suzuki repertory sequence [and not omitting any Suzuki repertoire]

e) Private lessons plus group classes

[In addition to their own lessons, students should observe the lessons of other Suzuki students or take their lessons in small semiprivate groups of two to four students plus their parents.]

f) Training parents to be auxiliary teachers at home

g) Cooperation, not competition.

Since a minimal amount of traditional etude and drill materials are included in the Suzuki books, the teacher must use creative and imaginative approaches to the repertory and build exercises and studies relating to specific problems and new techniques in each piece.

Merely teaching the student to play the pieces is not enough. Making productive use of constant review, reinforcement, and performance are intrinsic to this way of teaching.

In order to teach effectively, the teacher must memorize the repertory and know it inside and out, both from the playing and pedagogical standpoints. Keeping "one step ahead of the student" will not succeed in this method.

PERSONAL QUALITIES OF A SUZUKI TEACHER

1. Love of Children
2. Love of Music
3. Enthusiasm
4. Personal Warmth
5. Self-Discipline
6. Sensitivity to Varied Personalities

7. Ability to Praise
8. Ability to Organize
9. Good Personal Practice Habits

[The Suzuki teacher believes, with all his heart, that *all* children can be educated; *all* children have music talent that can be brought out through proper environmental stimulation. Though children move at different paces, they will all reach their goals if caring, high-quality instruction is given along with environmental motivation.]

REQUIREMENTS FOR TEACHERS

It is suggested that each Suzuki school or association devise its own requirements for teachers according to its needs. The following are the requirements of the Suzuki Music Academy of Chicago.

REQUIREMENTS AND STANDARDS FOR TEACHERS

1. Potential Suzuki teachers should read the "Philosophy and Attitudes of Talent Education Teachers" (printed above) and honestly ask themselves if they are "Suzuki-oriented." Good attitudes are essential.

2. The following books on Talent Education, educational psychology, childrearing, and education and pedagogy are recommended. (The first seven are to be read and discussed with the director and other teachers before beginning the first teaching assignments; other books should be read for further growth and stimulation.)

Ability Development from Age 0 by Shinichi Suzuki.

Kindergarten Is Too Late by Masara Ibuku.

Nurtured by Love by Shinichi Suzuki.

In the Suzuki Style, Elizabeth Mills, Editor.

The Suzuki Concept, Elizabeth Mills, Editor.

The Secret of Childhood by Maria Montessori.

The Talent Education School of Shinichi Suzuki—an Analysis by Ray Landers.

Where Love Is Deep by Shinichi Suzuki.

See Bibliography for other books and articles.

Other Suggested Books:

P.E.T. in Action by Thomas Gordon, (Parent Effectiveness Training).

T.E.T. by Thomas Gordon, (Teacher Effectiveness Training).

Children: The Challenge by Rudolf Dreikurs, M.D.

Escape from Childhood by John Holt.

Improving Your Child's Behavior Chemistry by Lendon Smith.

Death at an Early Age by Jonathan Kozol.

Revolution in Learning (The Years from Birth to Six) by Maya Pines.

What Is Zen? by D. T. Suzuki.

Zen and the Art of Motorcycle Maintenance by Robert Pirsig.

Growing Up Absurd by Paul Goodman.

Summerhill by A. S. Neill.

How Children Learn by John Holt.

How Children Fail by John Holt.

Body, Mind, Behavior by Maggie Scarf.

The Third Force by Frank Goble (Maslow's Self-Actualization Theories).

The Conditions of Learning by Robert Gagné.

Piaget's Development Psychology by Ruth Beard.

Selected materials on Zoltán Kodaly, Carl Orff, Emil-Jaques Dalcroze, and Maria Montessori and their educational philosophies.
(See additional suggestions in Bibliography.)

REFERENCE BOOKS

Piano

How to Teach Piano Successfully by James Bastien.

The Art of Piano Playing—A Scientific Approach by George Kochevitsky.

Suzuki Piano: More Than Music by Carole Bigler and Valery Lloyd-Watts.

Violin and Cello

Playing the String Game by Phyllis Young.

Violin

The Suzuki Violinist: A Guide for Teachers and Parents by William Starr.

Cello

Teaching Suzuki Cello: A Manual for Teachers and Parents by Charlene Wilson.

A teacher should own these reference books and other books on pedagogy so they are available when help is needed.

3. Intensive training period with Dr. Landers or another approved SAA teacher-trainer (on philosophy and repertoire study) and attendance at a two-week Suzuki Institute before beginning teaching. Every year the teacher should take a course of Suzuki pedagogy at a week-long Suzuki Institute and study with an SAA-sanctioned teacher-trainer (either at an institute or privately) until completion of all levels of teacher-training courses. After this, he should attend a week-long national Suzuki Institute annually. It is recommended that a new instructor have a minimum of Units A, 1, and 2 before beginning teaching.

4. Active teacher membership in the Suzuki Association of the Americas.

5. Minimum degree requirement: Bachelor of Music (or its equivalent). In exceptional cases, an outstanding teacher who does not have the B.M. may be hired—if he agrees to pursue the degree while teaching and complete it within a time period prescribed by the board members or the director.

6. Completion of the Master of Music degree (or its equivalent) or study toward the degree while teaching or continued private study (weekly lessons with a reputable teacher) until all volumes of the Suzuki repertoire are mastered.

7. Completion of pedagogy and repertoire courses at the Bachelor's or Master's level (usually part of B.M. or M.M. degree requirements). In certain cases, weekly lessons with the director may substitute for this requirement. Thorough knowledge of sound pedagogical techniques and repertoire is required.

8. Eventual memorization and perfection of all the repertoire found in the Suzuki volumes; continued private study until this is accomplished. Adherence to the pedagogical approaches used by Talent Education. All selections should be taught from memory.

9. Attendance at special faculty meetings that might be required. Active participation and involvement in Academy activities such as concerts and special programs.

10. Cooperation with the director, other faculty members, the board, and the association's students and parents. Agreement to follow the policies, attitudes, and instructional techniques prescribed by the faculty, board, and director.

11. A caring attitude: "Higher, higher, we must always improve!" (Shinichi Suzuki)[49]

CONTRACTS: EVALUATION FORMS FOR PARENTS AND TEACHERS

Suzuki teachers should sign contracts with their employers in which all requirements are specifically stated.

A Suzuki organization should undertake an evaluation, probably annually. Teachers should appreciate the opportunity to grow from the suggestions of their students, students' parents, colleagues, board members, and administrators. The Suzuki Music Academy of Chicago gives its Suzuki parents two evaluation forms to complete each year. The first is a self-evaluation for the parents; the second is an evaluation of teachers for the parents to fill out and return to the director. The director meets with each teacher at least once yearly to discuss the evaluation forms and his own observations. The academy's parent and teacher evaluation forms are reproduced below:

THE SUZUKI MUSIC ACADEMY OF CHICAGO
SELF-EVALUATION FOR SUZUKI PARENTS*

*(Form by Diane Kleidon)

1. Number of lessons missed this term ———
2. Number of late arrivals this term ———
3. Number of early departures this term (remember that learning from other childrens' lessons is a part of your child's lesson) ———
4. Number of parent meetings attended this term ———
5. Number of recitals or activities missed (remember that leaving after your child's performance is not really attending a recital) ———
6. Do I assist my child at home as often as I would like? ———
7. Do I assist my child at home as often as he/she would like? ———
8. Do I make sure that there is time for uninterrupted practice? ———
9. Do I make sure that my child practices? ———
10. Do I make sure that the Suzuki record/tapes (and other recordings) are played often? ———
11. Have I arranged for my child to perform for the family or friends? ——— (Remember that it is important for the child to get recognition at home for his/her musical ability.)
12. Have I discussed problems or areas of concern with the teacher or others who might help? ———
13. Do I convey a positive attitude about the Suzuki program to my child? ———
14. Am I doing my best to ensure that my child enjoys learning about music? ——— (This includes encouragement, patience, understanding, and, of course, loving care.)

This evaluation form is for your own use to assess how you are doing as a Suzuki parent. Complete the form at the end of every term and keep it where you can see it frequently.

THE SUZUKI MUSIC ACADEMY OF CHICAGO
TEACHER EVALUATION FORM

Teacher's Name:_____Term:_____

Your name: _____

I. *KNOWLEDGE OF MATERIAL*: Does the teacher seem competent in his teaching abilities? Does he* know the Suzuki repertoire thoroughly? Does he possess a broad range of problem-solving abilities as a teacher? Does he understand the Suzuki philosophy? (*or she; he refers to both he or she throughout this form)

(Check one below)

Rating: —— excellent   COMMENTS:

—— good

—— needs improvement

II. *COMMUNICATION ABILITIES*: Does the teacher communicate well with the children and parents? Does he know how to handle difficult situations? Does he know how and when to use discipline? Does he talk with parents about certain problems? Do you and the children feel comfortable with him? Does he ever put the children down? Does he speak in terms and language understandable to the children and parents?

Rating: —— excellent   COMMENTS:

—— good

—— needs improvement

III. *FAIRNESS AND PROMPTNESS*: Does the teacher treat all parents and children equally? Does he avoid favoritism toward certain children? Is he generally on schedule? Does he give sufficient notice if he has to miss classes? Does each child get adequate time and attention?

Rating: —— excellent   COMMENTS:

—— good

—— needs improvement

IV. *APPEARANCE*: Does the teacher dress in a manner appropriate to the situation? Is he neat in appearance?

Rating: —— excellent   COMMENTS:

—— good

—— needs improvement

V. *ATTITUDE*: Does the teacher seem genuinely concerned about teaching? Does he show the special caring attitude required of a Suzuki teacher? Does he have a cooperative spirit toward his students, students' parents, and colleagues?

Rating: —— excellent   COMMENTS:

—— good

—— needs improvement

VI. SUGGESTIONS OR COMMENTS CONCERNING THE
OVERALL PROGRAM: _____

_____

_____

_____

_____

It is recommended that a Suzuki school also have evaluation forms concerning the school and its administrators.

FACULTY-PARENT MEETINGS

Talent Education colleagues should have continual contact with each other. Meetings once a month or more often with three or four teachers at a time would be beneficial to all. Repertoire could be played and analyzed; problems could be discussed; pedagogical suggestions could be offered; and, most important, a spirit of growth and mutual cooperation could be maintained by all members of the school or association.

Meetings with parents are essential. Parents need suggestions from other parents, their teacher, other teachers, and the program administrators. Meetings also give teachers a chance to learn more about the needs of their students. Such meetings should be held at least once every two or three months (monthly if possible) and include open discussions as well as specific lectures or panel discussions on various topics related to Suzuki.

PURPOSES OF SUZUKI ORGANIZATION

Any Suzuki organization, to function at its best, must have a clear definition of its purposes. For example, the purposes (as stated in the Articles of Incorporation as a Not-for-Profit Corporation) of the *Suzuki Music Academy of Chicago* are as listed below:

(1) To provide a music education program in the following areas: applied cello, flute, guitar, piano, recorder, and violin (and eventually more instruments); music history; music appreciation; music fundamentals and theory; and eurythmics. The program is for children (ages 3 to 16) and features the method and philosophy of Shinichi Suzuki, which incorporates the involvement and teaching of parents of the students.

(2) To offer a high quality music instruction program at the most reasonable cost so that children of all levels of society might enroll.

(3) To, through special fundraising activities, provide a special scholarship fund for those needy children who otherwise might not be able to enroll.

(4) To provide special educational programs, symphony programs, operas, concerts, ballets, seminars, lectures, etc. for the children enrolled.

(5) To adhere to the specific aspect of Suzuki's philosophy that requires the involvement of the parent and the individual attention to each child so that all the children may strive for an appreciation of music that they might not gain elsewhere. To adhere to all elements essential to Talent Education.

(6) To make accessible a program that motivates children and parents to appreciate the discipline and joy of music—a discipline and joy that can be transferred to other educational endeavors.

(7) To provide the best facilities, instruments, and equipment so that the above goals might be met.

(8) To provide the best administration and teachers in order to maintain the high standards that the Suzuki Method requires.

(9) To provide opportunities for its students, as well as students from other Suzuki schools, to perform at various Chicago area locations; to sponsor regional and national tours for area Suzuki students.

(10) To educate the general public about Talent Education through publicity, brochures, television and radio programs, and concerts.

(11) To help bring Talent Education students together through sponsorship of festivals, workshops, and institutes.

(12) To be an institutional member of The Suzuki Association of the Americas and to adhere to the policies of that organization.[50]

Although this chapter has dealt mainly with the Suzuki teacher who is involved with a school or association, the private teacher can incorporate many of the ideas presented into here into his methodology. Many cities have Suzuki organizations which private teachers can join; the teachers thus maintain their independence and at the same time cooperate in activities such as concerts, master classes, seminars, lectures, and special events that an association might sponsor.

ORIENTATION MEETINGS

It is important that potential students have a clear understanding of Talent Education before they begin instruction. A teacher, association, or school should have periodical orientation meetings that include performances by Suzuki students, a lecture, films on the basic philosophy, interviews with Suzuki parents and students, and a question-answer period. Brochures and any relevant information about Talent Education and the organization should be handed out. Potential Suzuki parents should be asked to read books on Talent Education (including *Nurtured by Love*) and to attend Suzuki lessons and concerts before their child begins lessons. Special classes for parents of infants could be offered to teach them how to listen, to discuss the method thoroughly, and to offer beginning instruction for the parent.

Many Suzuki organizations have their students' parents sign annual contracts or statements agreeing to adhere to certain Talent Education principles—listening, group classes, daily practice, recital attendance, parental involvement and so forth.

The following is a statement given to Suzuki Music Academy of Chicago families at the beginning of each term: Parents are asked to pursue these expectations each term.

What's expected of a Suzuki Music Academy family? In order for each student and family member to benefit fully from the program and for each teacher to be able to work at his fullest capacity, the Academy requests the following:

(1) Keep your instruments in excellent shape. Pianos should be tuned often—at least two or three times yearly (call the office for names of reputable tuners.) Be sure your instrument is of good quality (Don't use electronic instruments for Suzuki practice.)

(2) The parent who attends the lesson should be the one doing the home teaching and supervision. Remember—the amount of energy you expect from the child should be equalled by your energy. You should supervise carefully all practice and listening. Work carefully with your teacher weekly to be sure you understand your assignments.

(3) A cassette (battery powered) tape recorder is required at all lessons and master classes. Record each lesson to be sure all assignments are understood. Also bring a notebook to write down assignments.

(4) Be sure that you receive and follow through specific daily listening and practice assignments from your teacher.

(5) You are expected to devote a certain amount of time *daily* to your Suzuki study. This will be determined by you and your teacher, but in general 3 to 4 year olds should spend 5 to 10 minutes daily in practice and 10 to 15 minutes daily in specific listening *at a minimum*; 5 to 8 year olds—10 to 20 minutes practice and 15 to 30 minutes specific listening minimum; 9 to 10 years—20 to 40 minutes practice and 30 to 50 minutes specific listening minimum; 11 to 13 years—40 to 60 minutes practicing and 50 to 70 minutes specific listening minimum; 13 and above—60 to 90 minutes of practicing and 70 to 100 minutes specific listening minimum. *Please note that*

the times listed are minimum times—it is hoped that each child will want to do much more. Also, the times for listening are for specific assignments; you should, in addition, do much general listening (contact the office for an Ability Development catalog which lists many pages of recommended albums and collections.) Remember—much less television and more listening and practicing. Practice and listening assignments should be spread throughout the day with each child's concentration span considered for the length of each session.*

(6)   Review is an essential aspect of the Suzuki philosophy. Each lesson will be devoted in part to review selections. Earlier learned pieces are used as "etudes"—pieces to learn new techniques. You are expected to cooperate with your teacher on special review assignments.

(7)   Attendance at lesson—for full benefit of the Suzuki philosophy, you are expected to attend lessons with one or more other children. Under no circumstances should a child attend a lesson without his supervising parent.

(8)   Siblings are encouraged to attend lessons, but only if they do not distract the progress of the class. A teacher may on occasion, ask a parent to temporarily take a sibling from the studio.

(9)   Recital Performance and Master Classes—Plan on playing a composition that is securely learned—preferably one that has been thoroughly mastered (memory, technique, musicality) for at least two weeks. Practice in different sections (pianists hands separately)—play the memory "scramble game—divide the piece into different numbered sections—scramble the numbers up—draw different numbers to practice. Violinists are required to rehearse with an Academy accompanist at least twice in order to perform on a recital.

(10) You are expected to remain until the end of the concerts you attend. Hearing other children perform, is in many ways, more important to your child than his performance. It is motivational and helps create a healthy spirit of cooperation.

*The author encourages that practice be aimed more toward quality rather than quantity; for example, an assignment might be, "Play the right hand of 'Cuckoo' twenty times daily with correct notes and rhythm," rather than an assignment such as, "Practice for 30 minutes." However, the times listed under point 5 are suggested because the academy has found this gives a sense of structure and expectation for many parents; a common question heard at Suzuki institutes is: "How long should my child practice?" A teacher should answer that it depends upon the individual child, that quality is more important, but yet he should feel free to recommend a time span. After all, Dr. Suzuki has often stated that children should practice two hours a day and, at other times, has stated that only a few minutes a day are suitable for some children.

(11) Attendance at all master classes is required.
Attendance at lessons and at the end of the term recital is required.

(12) You are expected to attend several concerts or recitals held in the Chicago area. This will help motivate you and your children and provide a natural musical environment. Recommended: at least one concert per month. Call the office for a special brochure about Orchestra Hall programs.

(13) You are expected to be responsible to your teacher about notifying him or her about any lessons you must miss. Even if you don't expect a make-up for a missed lesson, please call the teacher if you must miss. . . . He/she may be making a special trip to give you your lesson.

(14) Your teacher has the right to ask you to try another Academy teacher if he feels you aren't adhering to the expectations listed above. If the second teacher believes that you are not giving the involvement that the method requires, he will encourage you to seek instruction in a more traditional approach.

* * *

PARENTS—PLEASE REREAD THE ABOVE 14 POINTS CAREFULLY. Remember that your teacher and the Academy are willing to offer full involvement for you. We agree to give our full energy and hope to receive the same from you.

* * *

MOTIVATION

In conclusion, a Suzuki teacher needs to realize the importance of motivation in Talent Education. His students and their parents should be made aware of the value of attending concerts; they should be given many opportunities to perform; they should be provided with lists of recordings in addition to the Suzuki records or tapes and reading lists; and motivational games should be used at lessons and group classes—for example, a "name that tune" or "guess that rhythm" game using Suzuki repertoire could be played with a group of students to test how well they have been listening and to motivate them to listen better. In other words, a Talent Education teacher deals with much more than just the lesson—he is involved in a total environmental approach. Through an approach that uses the following devices, a strongly motivational learning situation can develop: (1) *creative listening* (through recordings, concerts, observing lessons); (2) *creative teaching* (demonstration of a high-quality musical level, teaching from memory, using interesting games and stories, performing at lessons and recitals, making specific assignments, seeking the best pedagogical devices); (3) *parental involvement* (a parent learning beginning pieces, being as involved as the child in practice, and showing genuine interest); (4) *total Suzuki approach in instruction* (semiprivate lessons, group monthly classes, bimonthly recitals, and other chances to perform); (5) *natural musical environment* from birth (child surrounded by music—Suzuki repertoire and other music, attendance at many concerts and other Suzuki lessons, observation of parents and siblings studying and practicing); (6) *constant review* of all repertoire (practicing in various keys, tempi, moods, touches, and styles, performing many pieces in different situations such as in home recitals and recitals at the completion of each book; (7) *contests* that motivate (games, play-a-thons, listen-a-thons, or practice-a-thons). For example, in a practice-a-thon, the student is asked to keep a record of how much he practiced during a designated period. For fund-raising purposes, he could be asked to seek a list of sponsors who agree to pay from one to ten cents for each minute he practiced during that time. A special concert for all participants (to which their sponsors are invited) could be held with prizes for (a) those who practiced most, (b) those with the most sponsors, and (c) those who raised the most funds. (8) *Careful, structured organization of home practice and listening time* (the teacher should give specific assignments at each lesson); (9) *creative note-reading assignments* (sight-reading pieces should be at an easier level than the corresponding Suzuki repertoire); (10) *discussion with the child* about his needs and feelings—*truly caring* for him; and (11) most important, *highest expectations* for the students, parents, and teachers—the greatest motivational device of all.

STRUCTURING THE SCHOOL YEAR

To give the reader an idea of how a Suzuki organization might structure its academic year, a Suzuki Music Academy of Chicago registration form, term schedule and various activity forms for the fall 1983 term are reproduced below. Because of variance in fee schedules from term to term, fees are not listed here. The academy operates on a three-term schedule: fall (September through December), winter (January through April) and spring-summer (May through July). Because of its not-for-profit, tax-exempt status, it is able to incorporate several fund-raising projects into its program. (Any Suzuki organization would benefit from seeking not-for-profit and tax-exempt status; contact a lawyer about the processes involved.) The forms, especially the schedules printed here, are representative of only one term; different special activities are offered each term.

THE SUZUKI MUSIC ACADEMY OF CHICAGO

The Fine Arts Building • Suite 401 • 410 S. Michigan Avenue • Chicago, IL 60605 • (312) 663-0038

REGISTRATION FORM - FALL TERM 1983
September 6 - December 18

☐ Beginning Parent's Group: 11 - one hour long sessions for parents (6 parents per group) of children 1 or 2 years old: Instruction on beginning the instrument will be given each parent; Methods of listening and motivating students will be demonstrated; Lectures and discussions will be presented to clarify the Suzuki philosophy. Each parent enrolled will receive a pass to observe any of the Academy's group classes, lessons and recitals.
Tuition = $ _____ + $ _____ for 3 books and record. (Includes *Nurtured by Love* and *Where Love is Deep* by Suzuki, and one music book and recording.)

☐ Beginning Children's Group: (2½ to 4 year old beginners) 11 - hour long or 22 half-hour long semiprivate lessons (4 children per group) plus 3 hour long or 6 half hour long master classes (12 children per group) plus 1 formal recital = 15 hours or 30 half hours of instruction Designed for the 2½ to 4 year old just beginning; emphasis will be on listening and teaching a parent ahead of or along with the student.
Tuition = $ _____ + $ _____ for 3 books and record.

☐ Beginning Children's Group: (4½ to 5 year old beginners) Same outline as above except there will be 3 children per group for the lessons and 9 children per group for the master classes.
Tuition = $ _____ + $ _____ for 3 books and record.

☐ Beginning Children's Group: (6 years old and above) Same as above but with 2 children per group for lessons and 6 children per group for the master classes.
Tuition = $ _____ + $ _____ for 3 books and record.

CONTINUING STUDENTS

☐ 3 to 5 year Olds: 11 one hour lessons (groups of 3) + 3 hour master classes (groups of 9) + one formal recital = 15 hours of instruction.
Tuition = $ _____ .

☐ 6 Years Old and Above: 11 hour lessons (groups of 2) + 3 hour master classes (groups of 6) + one formal recital = 15 hours of instruction.
Tuition = $ _____ .

OR ***

For Those 6 Years and Above Who Choose Longer Lessons: (for purposes of introducing a more comprehensive repertoire review, note-reading, and theory program.)

☐ 11 - 1½ hour lessons (groups of 2)+ 3 one hour master classes (groups of 6) + one formal recital = 20 hours of instruction.
Tuition = $ _____ .

or

☐ 11 - 2 hour lessons (groups of 2) + 3 one hour master classes (groups of 6) + one formal recital = 26 hours of instruction.
Tuition = $ _____ .

**Check above which schedule you are registering for.

59

THE SUZUKI MUSIC ACADEMY OF CHICAGO

The Fine Arts Building • Suite 401 • 410 S. Michigan Avenue • Chicago, IL 60605 • (312) 663-0038

REGISTRATION APPLICATION - Fall 1983
Continuing Students:
COMPLETE THE FOLLOWING AND RETURN TO YOUR TEACHER.
(New students - Mail form and check to above address)

Your Name:_____

Address: _____ City: _____ Zip: _____

Phone (day): _____ (night): _____

____I'm registering for Adult Class.
____I'm registering a child (if so, complete below).

Child's Name: _____ Age: _____ New: _____ Continuing: _____

Instrument:_____   Teacher Preference:_____
                                       (if any)
Time Preference:_____   Location Preference:_____

Child's Name: _____ Age: _____ New: _____ Continuing: _____

Instrument:_____   Teacher Preference:_____
                                       (if any)
Time Preference:_____   Location Preference:_____

****

Minimum deposit of $40.00 due immediately (by July 15) for continuing students. Give to your teacher during the week of July 11th.) Final payment due (postmarked by or in our office) by August 15th. After this there will be a $10.00 late charge per student.

Full payment now due for all new students. Mail immediately.

****

During July new students will be sent information about an orientation meeting. The meeting will feature a concert by Suzuki students, a lecture by Dr. Landers and a parent representative, a film of Dr. Suzuki teaching. Books, records, and brochures will be available as well as scheduling for lessons. New students and their parents will be also required to observe several academy concerts, classes, and lessons before beginning their own lessons.

Amount Due For Tuition: $_____
                For Books - Record: $_____
                Total Due: $_____

☐ Continuing students only:
I enclose a deposit of $_____ ($40 minimum) per registrant and will mail the final payment by August 15. (Those wishing to pay in two installments may do so by making special arrangements with the office. You will be required to complete a special agreement form.)

☐ Continuing and New:
I enclose the full payment now.
(Checks payable to Suzuki Music Academy of Chicago.)
[All fees, minus a $15.00 registration charge, are refundable through Sept. 1.]

THE SUZUKI MUSIC ACADEMY OF CHICAGO

The Fine Arts Building • Suite 401 • 410 S. Michigan Avenue • Chicago, IL 60605 • (312) 663-0038

FALL TERM SCHEDULE, 1983
September 5 through December 18

****

SEMIPRIVATE LESSONS (groups of 2, 3,
or 4) Adult classes (groups of 5)
Weeks of Sept. 5, 12, 19, 26
　　　　　　Oct. 10, 17, 24
　　　　　　Nov. 7, 14
　　　　　　Dec. 5, 12
(NOTE: No lessons or classes will be given
November 21 through 27, the week of the
Thanksgiving holiday.)

FORMAL RECITALS (each registered student will perform or bow - each string student will play in the play-in concert plus perform a solo on another program.)
*For downtown and north side students:
Sherwood Music School, Recital Hall 2nd
floor, 1014 S. Michigan—Saturday, December
17th - 9:30 a.m., 11 a.m., and 12:30 p.m.
*For Beverly, Homewood, & Kankakee
students: Beverly Arts Center, 2153 W.
111th—Sunday, December 18th - 9:30 a.m.,
11 a.m., 12:30 p.m., 2 p.m. (violin play-in),
3:30 p.m., and 5 p.m.

SPECIAL ACTIVITIES:
*Listening-a-thon: October 24-30,
Information will be mailed in late September.
*Daley Center Concert: Daley Plaza—East
Wing, Randolph at Clark, Thursday, Oct. 27,
11:30 to 1:30 (students selected by teachers.)
*Pot Luck Dinner-Faculty Concert: Sunday,
December 4, 5 to 8 p.m.,
Morgan Park Methodist Church.
Information will be mailed in late September.
*Other concerts at schools, churches, retire-
ment homes-teacher will notify various
students of dates.
*Coming Events: 3rd Chicagoland Suzuki
Music Festival (Feb. 24-26); Summer Institute
at Lake Forest College (July 8-13).
*Neediest Children's Fund Special Concerts
at the Chicago Hyatt Regency - December 21.
Information to be mailed.

MASTER CLASSES FOR CHILDREN (attendance required)

*Piano and Cello: (all students) Weeks of Oct.
3, Oct. 31, & Nov. 28 - arranged by each
teacher and held at your lesson location-
groups of 6 - 12 students per hour class.

*Week of December 12-18. Those book 2 and
above piano students who wish may attend 2
special *Orff Classes* taught by Dr. Landers.
(This is at no extra charge. Call office by Dec.
1 to reserve space. These classes are held at
our downtown location.)

Dec. 6 & 13 at 4:00, 5:30, or 7:00
Dec. 7 & 14 at 4:00, 5:30, or 7:00
Dec. 8 & 15 at 4:00, 5:30, or 7:00

Select one set of dates & a time - call early
for best selection. (Note - Orff classes feature
our newly purchased xylophones,
metalophones, and percussion instruments
performed in conjunction with piano solos.
Violin students will have a chance to work
with the instruments next semester.)

*Violin: Mondays, Oct. 3, Oct. 31, Nov. 28,
Dec. 12: Held at Morgan Park Church, 110th
& Longwood. *All students* from all locations
should attend.

6:00-6:45 p.m. Room 203-Pre-Twinkle &
　　　　　　　　Twinkle students
　　　　　　　　Room 205-Lightly Row
　　　　　　　　through May Song (Bk. 2)

7:00-7:30 p.m. All students in Parlor for
　　　　　　　　play-in.

7:45-8:30 p.m. Room 203-Long, Long
　　　　　　　　Ago through Gavotte
　　　　　　　　(Bk. 1)
　　　　　　　　Room 205-Books 2, 3, 4

THE SUZUKI MUSIC ACADEMY OF CHICAGO

The Fine Arts Building • Suite 401 • 410 S. Michigan Avenue • Chicago, IL 60605 • (312) 663-0038

FALL TERM SCHEDULE, 1983
page 2

Sundays, Oct. 9, Nov. 6, Dec. 4: Held downtown—410 S. Michigan, Suite 401.
Volume 2, 3, 4 students only. Note-reading, chamber orchestra, master classes with Roland and Almita Vamos.

1:00-2:00 p.m. Book 2 - Witches Dance through Minuet (Boccherini) - Mrs. Vamos
                Book 2 - Chorus (Handel) through Two Grenadiers - Dr. Vamos

2:00-3:00 p.m. Book 3-4—Gavotte (Martini) through Gavotte (Becker)—Mrs. Vamos
                Book 3-4 - Gavotte (Bach) through end of volume—Dr. Vamos

3:00-4:00 p.m. Faculty session with Mrs. Vamos.
                Chamber orchestra—note-reading session with Dr. Vamos. (book 3-4 students)

(Repertoire to be studied at Monday sessions include the following:
Book 4 - Rondo (Seitz); Book 3 - Humoresque (Dvorak), Minuet (Bach); Book 2 -Chorus (Handel), Witches Dance (Paganini), Waltz (Brahms), Gavotte (Mignon); Book 1- Gavotte (Gossec), Minuet 2 (Bach), Andantino (Suzuki), Perpetual Motion (Suzuki), Allegro (Suzuki), Long, Long Ago, May Song, O Come Little Children, Go Tell Aunt Rhody, Song of the Wind, Lightly Row, Twinkle Variations.
NOTE: All violin students should review all the previous selections they have learned with special emphasis on the above selections. In addition, Book 3 and 4 students should learn the duet parts to the following selections: Twinkle Variations, Perpetual Motion, Minuet 2, and Chorus from Judas Maccabaeus.

MAKE-UP POLICY: Your teacher is not required to give more than 1 make-up lesson for any lessons that you miss. Except in the case of emergencies, make-up lessons will not be given unless the teacher is given 24 hours of notice. The Academy gives no refunds after the first day of the new term. No make-ups are given for missed master classes. List your teacher's phone number in case you need to reach him/her:

Post this schedule.

62

THE SUZUKI MUSIC ACADEMY OF CHICAGO

The Fine Arts Building • Suite 401 • 410 S. Michigan Avenue • Chicago, IL 60605 • (312) 663-0038

LISTENING-A-THON   FALL 1983   November 7 - 13

In order to motivate our students to listen more efficiently and pleasurably and to educate their parents about the value of listening, a Listening-a-Thon contest will be held during this term. Funds raised from this contest will benefit the Academy through helping in our instrument purchases and in our rental expenses.

During the master class week of October 31st through November 5th, your teacher will discuss at your classes special listening techniques to follow during the Listening-a-Thon week. These will include clapping, marching, moving in the direction of the melody with the hand or body, dancing, singing, or just listening quietly. During this week, keep track of how much you listen and mail this information along with your parent's signature and a list of sponsors to our office by November 30th. It is up to you to ask your friends and relatives to be sponsors—to offer to pay the Academy ½ to 10 cents for each minute that you listen during the Listening-a-Thon week. You will send us their names, addresses, amount of pledge. . . and our office will be responsible for collecting the contributions from all sponsors.

Each participating student will be asked to play in our special Listening-a-Thon Concerts at Sherwood Music School on December 17th or The Beverly Arts Center on December 18th. Each student will receive a certificate that indicates the amount of time listened, the number of sponsors, and the amount of funds raised for the Academy. In addition, SPECIAL PRIZES WILL BE AWARDED TO THE
*10 STUDENTS WHO LISTENED THE MOST
*10 STUDENTS WITH THE MOST SPONSORS
*10 STUDENTS WHO RAISED THE MOST FUNDS

The top prize in each category will be a choice of a complete 21 album record collection of classical, folk, semi-classical, and pop selections by Arthur Fiedler and the Boston Pops Orchestra, or a $40 gift certificate for record purchases through Ability Development Co. Second prizes in each category will be two cassette recordings and program booklets - Child's Listening Library - a collection of a wide variety of music that Dr. Suzuki recommends. The other eight prizes in each category will be special musical books or records.

IN ORDER TO RECEIVE YOUR PRIZE IT IS ESSENTIAL THAT ALL FUNDS BE RECEIVED BY THE TIME OF THE DECEMBER AWARD CONCERTS.
SPECIAL NOTE: YOU SHOULD *NOT* PRACTICE YOUR INSTRUMENT DURING THE LISTENING-A-THON; YOU SHOULD DEVOTE YOUR ENTIRE PRACTICE TIME TO LISTENING. ALL ACADEMY STUDENTS ARE EXPECTED TO PARTICIPATE-EVEN IF YOU HAVE ONLY ONE SPONSOR.
Please complete the following and mail it to the above address by Nov. 30th.

STUDENT'S NAME_____TEACHER_____
Address_____Phone_____
I listened the following amount of time each day:
Monday_____minutes;   Tuesday_____minutes;   Wednesday_____minutes;
Thursday_____minutes;   Friday_____minutes;   Saturday_____minutes;
Sunday_____minutes.
GRAND TOTAL = _____Minutes. Mom or Dad's signature: I have supervised my child's practice and confirm that the time listed is correct.

PLEASE LIST ALL SPONSORS ON THE BACK OF THIS SHEET OR ON ANOTHER SHEET.
Include (1)Name, (2)Address, City, Zip. (3)Phone and (4)Amount pledged per minute (½, to 10 cents). (In early December we will contact all your sponsors and notify them of your amount of time listened and bill them. . .you will not have to collect the funds.)

THE SUZUKI MUSIC ACADEMY OF CHICAGO

The Fine Arts Building • Suite 401 • 410 S. Michigan Avenue • Chicago, IL 60605 • (312) 663-0038

POPS CONCERT
and
POT LUCK DINNER
featuring
ACADEMY FACULTY

A BENEFIT PROGRAM

SUNDAY, DECEMBER 4, 1983
5 to 8 P.M.
MORGAN PARK UNITED METHODIST
AUDITORIUM-SOCIAL HALL
110th and Longwood, Beverly
(Get off of I 57 at 111th St.;
Drive west on 111th (Montery)
to Longwood, turn right 1 block)

Featuring:

Virginia Burkhart, piano	Etude in A^b Major by Chopin Arabesque by Burgmuller
Joan Engelstad and George Watkins, violin	Suite Antique for Two Violins by Stoessel
Pat Heineman and John Reglin, piano	Two Piano Music of Schubert
Jill Kaeding, cello	Sicilian by Fauré
Ryna Krysiak and Sally Sloane, piano	Sabre Dance from "Gayne Ballet" by Khachaturian
Ray Landers, piano	Selections from Pictures at an Exhibition by Mussorgsky
Linda Poquette, piano	Rhapsody in B Minor, Op.79, No.1 by Brahms
John Reglin, piano	Maple Leaf Rag by Joplin
Lisa Richter, piano	Sonatina in C, 1st mvt. by Kabalevsky
Sally Sloane, voice	Summertime by Gershwin
Julie Thies, piano	Consolation No. 3 by Liszt
George Watkins, violin	Perpetual Motion by Novacek
Randy Wilkinson, piano	Cuckoo Variations by Wilkinson
Linda Poquette and Ray Landers	Christmas Duets

Tickets are available by mailing a check with self-addressed, stamped envelope and attached order form to the office. Tickets may also be purchased from your teacher. Ticket price: Adults-$10 and Children (age 12 and under)-$5 (Children under 3 who sit in parent's lap - no charge.) . . . or IF YOU CHOOSE TO BRING A DISH (enough to feed 4 to 6 people) TICKET PRICES ARE LESS . . . $6 and $3 for those who bring a meat dish and $8 and $4 for those who bring a vegetable, casserole, salad, dessert, or coffee-punch-cola.

THIS WILL BE A BENEFIT PROGRAM TO HELP RAISE FUNDS TO ASSIST THE ACADEMY IN RENTAL PAYMENTS, AND IN INSURANCE PLAN PAYMENTS FOR OUR FACULTY.

In order to provide you with three convenient locations, the Academy pays much more rent per term than can be possibly covered through your tuition payments. Also, we have recently instituted a Blue Cross-Blue Shield Health-Insurance program for our faculty. Through attending this special event, you can financially help the Academy in these expenses and, at the same time provide your family with a fun, relaxing, and motivating evening of popular and light classical music.

The Parent Club will be in charge of organizing the pot-luck dinner. If you have any questions regarding the dinner, call the Academy office.

THE SUZUKI MUSIC ACADEMY OF CHICAGO

The Fine Arts Building • Suite 401 • 410 S. Michigan Avenue • Chicago, IL 60605 • (312) 663-0038

Order Form for December 4th Faculty Concert - Pot Luck Dinner.

Your Name _____

Your Child's Teacher_____

☐ I will be attending the program but am unable to bring food.
    Send me _____ adult tickets at $10.00.
              _____ child (age 12 and under) tickets at $5.00.

☐ I will be attending the concert and will be bringing the following vegetable, casserole,
    salad, dessert, bread, or coffee-punch-cola. (Enough to serve four
    to six)_____
    Send me _____ adult tickets at $8.00
              _____ child tickets at $4.00.

☐ I will be attending the concert and will be bringing the following meat dish. (Enough to
    serve four to six.) _____
    Send me _____ adult tickets at $6.00.
              _____ child tickets at $3.00.

☐ I will not be able to attend, but would like to contribute the following
    amount. $_____.

I include a check for $_____, payable to The Suzuki Music Academy of Chicago, and
a self-addressed, stamped envelope for return of tickets.

Deadline for ticket purchase:

December 1

65

THE SUZUKI MUSIC ACADEMY OF CHICAGO

The Fine Arts Building • Suite 401 • 410 S. Michigan Avenue • Chicago, IL 60605 • (312) 663-0038

. . . . . . a special invitation from Ray Landers and The Suzuki Music Academy of Chicago.

SPECIAL CONCERTS AT THE CHICAGO HYATT REGENCY BALLROOM, CONCERT STAGE, and ATRIUM MALL

WEDNESDAY, DECEMBER 21 GALA VIOLIN PLAY-IN CONCERT - 5:30 to 6:45 P.M. A Benefit Program for WGN's NEEDIEST CHILDREN'S FUND, narrated by Wally Phillips

DECEMBER 1 and 2 at Noon and DECEMBER 21 at 4:30 and 7 P.M. - CONCERTS for selected soloists

The Academy is very honored to be invited to present a series of concerts at the Hyatt Regency Hotel, Wacker Drive between Michigan and Columbus Drive. All area Suzuki students are invited to play in the Dec. 21 5:30 Play-in Concert. Several students will be selected by their teachers to play in the solo concerts.

There will be a gala play-in concert for violinists on December 21st at 5:30 to 6:45 P.M. in the Ballroom. All Academy violinists as well as guest violinists from other area Suzuki programs are invited to participate. The following repertoire will be played: Book 1 - Twinkle Variations, Lightly Row, Song of the Wind, Go Tell Aunt Rhody, O Come Little Children, May Song, Long Long Ago, Allegro, Perpetual Motion, Andantino, Minuet 2, Gavotte; Book 2 - Chorus from 'Judas Maccabaeus,' Brahm's Waltz, Witches' Dance, Gavotte from Mignon; Book 3 - Book 3 - Minuet, Humoresque; Book 4 - Seitz Concerto #2, Vivaldi Concerto 1st mvt. . . . . If you can play (accurately, musically, memorized) any of the above selections, you are invited to participate. THIS WILL BE A VERY SPECIAL EVENT WITH SEVERAL THOUSAND in attendance! We hope many area students will participate; by doing so you will help a worthy cause and at the same time help spread the spirit of Talent Education through performing in a spectacular setting. In addition to the thousands of people in attendance who will be contributing to the Neediest Children's Fund, Wally Phillips and 100 other movie, sports, and arts celebrities will be participating. In order to participate, please mail the enclosed coupon to our office by December 16 (or you may call the office by then) and plan on meeting (in order to be tuned and to receive your entrance badges and food coupons) on Dec. 21st at 5 P.M. in the Belmont Room (West Hyatt Regency Tower-151 E. Wacker-Concourse Level). ALL STUDENT PARTICIPANTS WILL RECEIVE COMPLIMENTARY ENTRANCE TICKETS AND COMPLIMENTARY FOOD AND BEVERAGE. Parents and siblings of the performers would be asked to contribute a toy or $2 to the Neediest Children's Fund in order to be admitted.

MAIL THIS COUPON TO OUR OFFICE BY DECEMBER 16 (or call the office) (or by November 21st for Dec. 1 and 2 concerts)

_____I wish to play in the December 21st 5:30 P.M. violin Play-in concert at the
Chicago Hyatt-Regency. Name_____ Phone_____
Most advanced piece from above list_____ Teacher_____
School (if applicable)_____ Age_____
_____I would like to be considered for one of the solo concerts and would be willing to participate in the following concert: _____Dec. 1, noon at the Atrium Mall; Dec. 2, noon, Atrium; _____Dec. 21, 4:30 P.M., Concert Stage; _____Dec. 21, 7 P.M.; _____I'd be available for any of the times.
NOTE: IN ORDER TO BE CHOSEN FOR ONE OF THESE CONCERTS IT IS ESSENTIAL FOR YOUR TEACHER TO RECOMMEND YOU THROUGH SIGNING BELOW OR CALLING THE OFFICE.
Name_____ Instrument_____ Performance piece_____
length_____minutes, Teacher_____Suzuki School_____
Phone_____ _____name of accompanist (for violin or cello):_____
Recommending teacher's signature _____ (Note: Students performing for these programs will receive meals or refreshments)

QUESTIONS TEACHERS OFTEN ASK

1. *Question*: I am confused because I have attended several Suzuki method teacher-training seminars and find conflicting pedagogical approaches among teachers; often even one teacher changes basic ideas from year to year.

Answer: First and foremost, a good Suzuki teacher should be able to perform (preferably from memory) the repertoire he is teaching and be thoroughly trained in pedagogy and literature; he thus clearly understands the teaching problems. Pedagogical suggestions he receives from workshops should be viewed in the context of each situation. A teacher with a good musical and teaching background knows that he should not always take another teacher's ideas literally but should use them in appropriate situations. Too often a workshop teacher makes suggestions that are applicable for the present moment (for example—in piano, an exaggerated movement to loosen a very stiff wrist or use of flat fingers to correct an excessively curved position), and some teacher trainees mistakenly think that the specific suggestion applies to all children when they learn that specific piece or section. A good Suzuki teacher understands pedagogical techniques and the basic tenets of the Talent Education method; he knows, for example, what physical movements and musical aspects to teach and that beyond these, flexibility is desirable. Americans studying with Japanese teachers either in Japan or the United States should be aware of the problems of communication caused by Japanese-English translations. As Edwin Reischauer writes in *The Japanese*:

> Even assuming a perfect knowledge of both languages on the part of the interpreter, which is rarely the case, English and Japanese both suffer a radical transformation in being converted into the other. Word order is in large part reversed; clear statements become obscure; polite phrases become insulting; and a remark, even though accurately translated in a literal sense, may take on an entirely different thrust. Simultaneous interpreters, for all their wizardry, often can cover only about two thirds of the original statement. And simple errors of translation are all too common. . . . However unsatisfactory the translation process from foreign languages into Japanese, the reverse flow is much weaker. Foreign audiences for the most part have . . . no tolerance to literal translations from Japanese or even for more skillful translations of materials written for Japanese audiences. . . . Certainly the Japanese, with their suspicion of verbal skills, their confidence in nonverbal understanding, their desire for consensus decisions, and their eagerness to avoid personal confrontation, do a great deal more beating around the verbal bush than we do and usually try to avoid the "frankly speaking" approach so dear to Americans. . . . They prefer . . . suggestion or illustration rather than sharp, clear statements.[51]

The Talent Education teacher trainee must be aware of this communication difficulty and judge each situation he observes with Japanese teachers in a broader context.

2. *Question*: How does one incorporate additional repertoire into the method?

Answer: There is no one approach for all children. Some children may complete all the volumes before adding new repertoire whereas others may add constantly from the beginning. Extra repertoire may be used for motivation (teaching popular songs, for example), for expanding the child's knowledge of literature (such as incorporating additional Scarlatti sonatas when the student completes the one in Volume 6 of the *Piano School* or incorporating music of other eras or composers), for special work on note-reading, or for allowing the child's natural interests to be followed. A child who is encouraged to perform special music he appreciates will be more open to learning repertoire that a teacher or parent suggests. For example, at the Suzuki Music Academy of Chicago, piano teachers often record (on cassette) several selections from the Frances Clark *Supplementary Solo Series* (Summy-Birchard Company) for their students; the parents and children listen to this special recording along with the Suzuki records. One of these songs is taught when it can be most beneficial for motivation, often after every five to seven Suzuki songs. The academy has had excellent results with this approach and finds that it helps children to become more interested in the Suzuki pieces as well. The teacher should use his own judgment in dealing with each student. Even if little extra repertoire is incorporated into a given student's lessons early, the teacher should remember to plan a balanced study of music from various eras and composers at the completion of the volumes. In Japan many students complete all the volumes by the ages of eight to ten and thus are ready, at about the age many American students are beginning music instruction, to learn more advanced repertoire. (See "After Volume 6," p. 31 and Supplementary Repertoire—Bibliography, p. 178.)

3. *Question*: I believe in Suzuki's idea of postponement of note-reading in the beginning stages but am at a loss concerning how to teach reading. Also, how does one introduce theory and sight-reading?

Answer: Books such as Michiko Yurko's *No H in Snake: Music Theory for Children* and the *Music Tree* series (Summy-Birchard) are excellent for introducing note-reading. These texts, if taught in a creative way, might be used separately for music appreciation and note-reading classes, in the monthly group lessons, or even in the weekly lessons. The teacher is cautioned, however, that the introduction to note-reading should be taught mainly as a preparatory phase that helps the child to become aware of certain concepts (such as up-down, long-short, or loud-soft) so that reading, when incorporated, will be easier (see p. 122). In the beginning stages, introductory reading materials should require very little time at the lesson or at home (perhaps one-tenth of the lesson or practice time daily). The Suzuki approach emphasizes the review of all the learned repertoire when one begins reading: through looking at music already learned, the child begins to make associations and learns to read in large units as well as single notes. I recommend the following approach: When the child is ready to begin reading (about the end of Volume I for piano or the end of Volume III for violin), the teacher should ask him to review the earlier book(s) in the following way. The child is asked to put slips of paper containing the names of the pieces he performs in a box. Every day he draws out a slip and plays the song named (if he has been reviewing his previously learned selections correctly, he will remember it). He follows the following procedure:

First weeks (number of days depends on the number of songs): One song per day is played, or, perhaps, part of a song or, in the case of piano, the right or left hand of a song. It is probably more important to set aside a certain amount of time, perhaps one-fifth to one-tenth of the practice time, for note-reading review rather than being very specific with how much material to cover. In other words, concentrate on quality rather than quantity; be sure that the time spent on the reading process remains a small part of the practice time. The procedure will vary from child to child because it is important to give attention to each level of development. First the melody (usually the right hand in piano) is played while the parent points (with his hand or a pencil) to the music score. The child is instructed to keep his eyes on the music because at this stage he should know his pieces well and all the pedagogical movements will be ingrained. The parent should occasionally change tempo or stop on a certain note while pointing to ensure that the child is visually following the score. For piano this procedure is repeated with the left hand and then again with both hands. For other instruments with one melodic line, the procedure need only be done once correctly. Very little time is required—only that needed to play the piece or section one to three times. After working on one selection or section daily and completing all the pieces the child knows, the teacher should assign the second step.

Second period of study: Again one song or section per day is played. In the case of piano, first one hand is played, then the other, then both together. Then the parent points to the notes as in the previous week's review. This time the emphasis is on melodic direction: the parent and/or child sings "up," "down," or "same" (to match the direction of intervals) while the child plays the melody—or perhaps sings alone first and then sings and plays. Obviously in piano, only one hand at a time should be played while this exercise is being done.

Third period: The same procedure is followed, but this time emphasis is on saying "long" or "short" for note lengths. Since this is relatively easy perhaps more than one composition can be played daily, enabling the child to progress through this period of study faster.

Fourth period: Emphasis is now on saying "start," "skip," or "step" or "same" (in reference to each note's relation to the previous note) while the teacher or parents point to the notes. For those students who have had no introduction to note-reading concepts, it may be necessary to explain the concept of lines and spaces in relation to skip, step, or same.

Fifth period: Emphasis is now on saying specific intervals (second, third, fourth, and so on). This step is more complex, and more weeks of study will probably be needed. Perhaps smaller sections daily should be reviewed during this step.

Sixth period: Emphasis is on specific rhythmic values (playing or clapping and saying "two counts," "one count," "four counts," "one-half count," "three count rest," and so on.

Seventh period: The seventh period of study involves playing, as in all the other steps, and saying the actual names of the notes (letters). By this time the children should be very aware of concepts (up-down, intervals, melodic line, and so on), and the use of the names of the notes will flow naturally. Many students will have already learned the actual names through separate studies (*Music Tree, No H in Snake*) or classes and will find this easy.

Eighth period: This step follows the same procedure as step seven, except that emphasis is now on the actual names of the rhythmic values (quarter notes, half notes, eighth notes, whole rests, and so on). This is a good time to explain the basics of time and key signatures; more comprehensive explanations should be presented later, however, as the student learns more complex music. It is important to follow the earlier steps even if the student knows the names of the notes and rhythmic figures in order to help him think conceptually and in larger lines to help him read in larger sections and phrases.

The Suzuki teacher or parent is free to follow this suggested plan (which follows Suzuki's idea of learning reading through making associations with already learned music) or to devise his own. The teacher should bear in mind that there is little emphasis on specific ways to teach reading in Suzuki's books because most Japanese students learn music reading in the public schools and therefore need less training from their Suzuki teachers. The American student, however, often has little music reading training in school and needs help from his Suzuki teacher. Whatever plan one follows, he should make certain that the notes are learned as an aid in the learning of music, not as ends in themselves. Also, in any approach to note-reading, one should sometimes use "mental preparation" exercises—clapping, singing, marching, shaping melodic direction with the hand, and eurhythmics (using the entire body in various rhythms); these are all good devices to help the student become more aware of the composition he is about to read.

While the Suzuki student is becoming more and more proficient in his reading, he continues to learn new repertoire through the usual approach—listening, imitating, and so on; as the music becomes more complicated, he will naturally need the score more to help in his learning. Thus, as outlined in the my approach, the reading will become more and more clear and defined according to the student's needs. The approach described above is incorporated into the Suzuki Music Academy of Chicago program as follows:

A. Pre-Twinkle through Volume I (piano) or through Volume 2 (other instruments). At regular weekly semiprivate lessons, teachers use creative listening games and eurhythmics to help introduce concepts of long-short, loud-soft, up-down, and so on. Monthly repertoire classes use the same techniques plus note-reading games, particularly the Michiko Yurko *No H in Snake* approach. In addition, some students are assigned books such as *Time to Begin* from Frances Clark's *Music Tree Series*. The main emphasis remains listening and repertoire study. Only a few minutes, perhaps five out of sixty, are devoted to this introductory approach.

B. Volume 2 (piano) or Volume 3 (others). The note-reading system outlined above is started at the beginning of study of these volumes. The students have been reviewing all their selections and have presented a recital of them and are already used to daily review of a part of a selection, an entire selection, or several selections. Through the games and eurhythmics mentioned above, they are already familiar with many reading concepts and are ready to make associations with the printed page. Usually by the completion of Volume 2 to mid-Volume 3 (piano) or Volume 3 to mid-Volume 4 (others), all eight steps outlined have been completed. About one-fifth to one-tenth of the lesson time is devoted to checking out the assignments made by the teacher. In the meantime, the student continues to learn new repertoire and review old repertoire. As new repertoire is learned, the music is placed in front of the student more and more often and is used for reference. By the completion of his current volume of study, he should be able to read accurately and use the music as a learning tool to memorize from and to check out the teacher's instructions. The academy's approach, however, is not to use the Suzuki repertoire books as sight-reading material but as guides to help the student in learning what he hears and what the teacher demonstrates. To develop sight-reading, supplementary materials are introduced beginning at this point. The student rarely "reads" the new Suzuki repertoire from beginning to end but memorizes it in sections as he learns. He is assigned other, much simpler, repertoire for sight-reading purposes.

C. Volume 3 (piano) or Volume 4 (others) and above. Emphasis is now on introducing supplementary sight-reading materials, always assigning levels of repertoire that are about two volumes easier than the volume currently being studied. In addition, simple introductory note-reading theory books (e.g., in piano, Alfred *Basic Piano Library* series by Willard Palmer, Morton Manus, and Amanda Lethco) are introduced so that students begin to learn to write what they have already discovered. Lessons are necessarily longer (usually one and one-half hours for two students) than previously in order to incorporate this aspect. About one and one-quarter hour is spent learning new Suzuki repertoire and reviewing old repertoire and about fifteen minutes for sight-reading and review of written note-reading theory assignments. The academy has a structured system in which by the time the student finishes the most advanced Suzuki volumes, he has had enough preparatory theory training to understand the chordal structure of the repertoire presented in them. Care is taken, however, to organize the classes and lessons so that the emphasis is on the Suzuki repertoire and incorporated repertoire. The theory study is incorporated as a means to an end and is carefully introduced later and in smaller steps than would be done in a "traditional" approach. Our main emphasis is on giving names to what the student already knows so as to be sure he knows material in a constructive way—to help in the learning of other repertoire. One positive way of developing this attitude is to associate theory study, as with note-reading, with previously learned Suzuki repertoire. The student, while learning Volume 4, for example, can be learning the names of the chords of the selections in the earlier volumes, following a system similar to that used in the teaching of note-reading.

4. *Question*: Dr. Suzuki stresses the importance of review of earier repertoire. In violin, viola, cello, and flute, it is easier to achieve a thorough review because of the ease with which these instruments can perform together. Review for piano students seems more difficult. Even some string and flute students do not review as thoroughly as Suzuki suggests. How does one develop good review habits?

Answer: At the introductory session of the 1981 Fifth International Suzuki Teachers' Conference (University of Massachusetts, Amherst, July 27, 1981), Dr. Suzuki said that review was the "most important point of the Suzuki Method," and he suggested the use of a musical lottery game to help the children in their review. At practice, lessons, and group lessons the child should draw out of a box containing names of all the songs he has learned a selection which he would then perform. A child would thus be motivated to review all his selections because he might be called upon to play any of them for the teacher. Review *is* extremely important for many reasons: many techniques, patterns, and concepts of earlier pieces are found in later pieces, and remembering them makes the learning of later repertoire less time-consuming. The similarity to language review is obvious. As Suzuki said in his speech at the conference, "If no use were made of words already learned and only new words are learned, wouldn't the speech of all the children in the world become similar to the speech of a retarded child?" As in language, the more music (or words) available to the child, the freer he is—the more choice he has, for the child who is able to play many compositions has more freedom in performing or playing in a large variety of situations; psychologically the more one knows, the more easily one learns new materials, or as Jean Piaget put it, "The more new things a child has seen and heard, the more he wants to see and hear . . . the greater variety of things a child has coped with, the greater his capacity for coping. Thus, both curiosity and rate of intellectual development are tied to the variety of situations that have forced the child to modify previous patterns of thought" (see p. 86 and footnote 82). In order to "modify previous patterns of thought" most effectively, the Suzuki student should review the pieces that he knows while learning new repertoire; and the child able to perform a large repertoire should be able to transfer this organizational ability to real life to situations at home and employment, to appreciation of the arts, creativity, and so forth.

Talent Education teachers disagree about how much of the old repertoire should be reviewed. Suzuki seems to encourage review of all the literature, whereas Haruko Kataoka, co-developer of the *Piano School*, suggests that certain selections may be omitted. I believe that all pieces can and should be reviewed. This does not necessarily mean that all selections must be played every day; rather, one should develop a system whereby pieces are learned thoroughly to begin with, are repeated enough initially to become "ingrained" in one's system, and then are reviewed periodically. Simply being in an environment where other Suzuki students are performing helps a pupil retain his learned repertoire; the constant rehearing of already learned pieces helps a student maintain those pieces. (This is one of the reasons why recitals and monthly group classes should contain a mixture of students at varying levels of advancement.)

Many students, teachers, and parents believe review to be too time-consuming and are unaware of how it can occur naturally. Perhaps the following suggestions will help. (1) The teacher should spend time at every lesson working on review. Some Japanese teachers, at some lessons, spend more time on review than on "new" literature. Constant emphasis on reworking technical or musical points of pieces will enhance the student's respect for the pieces' importance. (2) Specific assignments should be made for home practice—for example—"practice ten minutes daily on review—practice five songs this week." Dr. Suzuki's the lottery game idea, quoted above, is excellent for this purpose. (3) Review in numerous ways (for piano, for example—cross hands, different keys or modes, different touches or phrasings, various tempi and interpretations, different fingerings); these methods of review for each composition will help the student understand even more its "essential" meaning. (4) Provide motivational situations such as formal and informal recitals for the student at the completion of each volume. (For example, the child completing Volume 2 could perform all the pieces of Volumes 1 and 2 at a recital; the child finishing Volume 6 could perhaps play a recital of all Volume 6 pieces and certain selections from the other volumes; the audience members could draw other selections by lottery.) The student should have numerous other opportunities to perform (such as churches, schools, club programs, neighborhood concerts, and group classes). (5) As mentioned above, be certain that programs and group classes in which students perform contain all levels of Suzuki repertoire; hearing previously learned selections performed by others will encourage mental review by more advanced pupils.

5. *Question*: What is the best approach for listening?

Answer: As in review and note-reading, it is important for the teacher to help the parent and student by giving specific assignments for home practice. Again, through use of a lottery game, a child might be instructed to listen to one or two compositions daily (in addition to general listening, which might include other Suzuki repertoire as well as additional music) with specific instructions such as "clap the rhythm, dance to the rhythm, shape the melody with your hand," or "sing words." The listening approach varies among Suzuki teachers; in general, however, it is best to aim for a combination of "general listening" with less emphasis on intense concentration expected and specific listening with daily assignments given—often the piece being learned plus one or two of the following selections. It is especially important that parents be taught ways to listen. From their earliest instruction, parents should be educated about the importance of a natural listening environment through concert attendance and general and structured listening in the home. Dr. Suzuki suggests that newborn infants should listen to excellent classical recordings—the Suzuki repertoire as well as a general listening library. (See Bibliography for his recommended "Children's Listening Library" as well as numerous collections recommended by the author in supplementary listening recordings, p. 177.)

Students at the Suzuki Music Academy of Chicago are advised to maintain a home library that includes all volumes of the Suzuki method recordings (Summy-Birchard and Ability Development versions as well as individual recordings of various selections), the "Children's Listening Library," and numerous other collections and individual albums. Teachers instruct parents and students on how to listen. Specific instruction is given at lessons on what to listen to during the week. Occasionally, students are asked to concentrate entirely on listening (with no practicing) to help them become more aware of its importance. (See the Listen-a-Thon information on p. 63). Even though the specific listening emphasis is on the volume being learned, the academy encourages periodical listening to the later volumes. For example, a student may be instructed to listen to the pieces in his current volume from Monday through Friday and to listen to other volumes during weekends. It is important to use listening as a motivational tool. To avoid boredom, occasional changes of format are encouraged. Listening to new repertoire motivates a student toward the future and makes return to the listening of earlier repertoire more rewarding and enjoyable.

6. *Question*: There is disagreement among piano teachers concerning hand separate and sectional practice and memorization. What are your thoughts?

Answer: I am a strong advocate of hand separate practice and memorization for all piano literature. The Talent Education approach assumes an almost Zenlike reverence for every single note and rest; hand separate practice will increase the child's awareness of the importance of each part. Also, recent brain studies have shown that different parts of the brain control the different hands (see the summary of Roger Williams's article on p. 116) and are, therefore, "developed" more by hands alone practice. The right hemisphere of the brain is thought to be nonverbal, synthetic (seeing things as a whole), concrete (relating to the present moment), analogic, nontemporal, nonrational, spatial (seeing where things are in relation to other things), intuitive, and holistic (perceiving overall patterns and structures). The left hemisphere is verbal, analytic, symbolic, abstract, temporal, rational, logical, digital (using numbers in counting), logical, and linear (thinking in terms of linked ideas).[52] The right hemisphere, which controls the left hand, develops the more artistic aspects of our personality, whereas the left hemisphere, which controls the right hand, is more analytical. Not only will hands separate practice help one become more aware of musical concepts, but it will also help in developing awareness in general—it will help one become more well-rounded.[53]

Of the four types of memory (visual, kinesthetic, aural, and analytic) the analytic probably has the strongest long-term retention; hands alone and sectional practice (dividing a piece into numerous sections and practicing starting at any point with either hand) is excellent in developing this analytic process. The question of how large a section to learn or review at one time depends on factors such as age, level of concentration, and difficulty of the music. The teacher should assist the student in dividing pieces into sections. A good practice device is to put the numbers of sections into a box (for example, for piano, left hand—section 2, or both hands—section 3) and draw numbers out daily for special practices.

At the Fifth International Teachers' Conference in Amherst, Massachusetts, in July 1982, Mrs. Kataoka was asked if she has her students practice hands separately or in small sections. Her answer was, "Do they perform it that way?" leaving some teachers with the wrong conclusion that Mrs. Kataoka does not believe that method to be important. Any observer of Mrs. Kataoka's students will note, however, that they are capable of playing left or right hand at any spot in the music they are performing. The Japanese culture has developed a more holistic use of both hemispheres of the brain; there is a more natural consciousness of the playing of both hands, thus less need to draw as much attention to it as the more right-handed Western culture would require.

7. *Question*: What about adding ornaments to the baroque repertoire found in the Suzuki method?

Answer: I recommend that after thoroughly learning a selection such as a Bach minuet, the student might add ornaments. Children enjoy this and, if taught carefully, find the learning or ornaments both rewarding and challenging. For advanced students and teachers, *The Baroque Era* edited by Willard Palmer and Margery Halford (in the Alfred piano series) is highly recommended. Even though the repertoire is keyboard music (of composers such as Rosa, D. and A. Scarlatti, Pasquini, Blow, Clark, L. and F. Couperin, Chambonnieres, Rameau, Pachelbel, Telemann, Böhm, Handel, and J. S. Bach), the introductory remarks cover a wide area that would apply to all Suzuki instruments. Besides ornamentation (with thorough explanations that are understandable even by laymen), other topics discussed include good taste in baroque music, the theory of affects, pedaling, various keyboard instruments, and baroque musical styles of various countries. Numerous keyboard selections are presented with suggested ornamentation and other editorial markings in light print. (Caution—any ornaments for string or flute students should not be played in group performances unless specifically requested; they are mainly for practice and solo performances.) Also recommended is *The Pianists' Bach: Baroque Performance Practice* by Laurette Goldberg, Musical Director, a cassette recording that contains many pieces from the Suzuki piano literature with suggested ornaments and styles.

8. *Question*: Would you recommend some games to incorporate into monthly group classes?

Answer: Listed below are some of the games that Suzuki Music Academy of Chicago students participate in (originally printed in *Suzuki World*, July/August 1982 and revised for inclusion here). Most of these games can be used by students on various instruments:

1   NAME THAT TUNE
The first note or chord from a Suzuki piece is played. The first student to guess that tune correctly has the choice of performing a piece or perhaps, for fun, having his mother or father dance. As the children develop in their abilities or recognize the first note or chord of a tune, other parts of Suzuki pieces can be played, such as the last note or a middle note.

2   GUESS THAT RHYTHM
In a variation of "Name that Tune," a rhythm is clapped by the teacher, and the children guess the selection. The winner can either play a tune or clap his own Suzuki rhythm for the group to guess.

3   PLAY THE THE FIRST NOTE (second note, last note, and so on) OF THE TUNE
The children line up behind the piano or another instrument, and the teacher calls out the name of a Suzuki song that they have all played at one time. If a child is able to play the notes or chords requested (for example, in piano, the first notes of French Children's Song, using both hands, with correct fingering), he remains in the game. The game continues until only one child remains; he is the winner, but, of course, all the others have also won because their listening ability and motivation have been heightened.

4   COMPOSING

Students should be encouraged to play their own compositions (many like to create titles and/or accompanying poems). Special assignments can be made that incorporate certain concepts found in Suzuki tunes. (For example, ask pianists to compose a song that uses the patterns found in the left hand of Cuckoo.)

5⁻   STORYTELLING

Teachers can make up interesting stories that help in the interpretation of selections. For example, Allegro could be described as the story of a race car driver whose car runs out of gas in the middle of the song. The teacher should be thoroughly knowledgeable about composers and music history and be imaginative in sharing this information.

6   INTRODUCTORY NOTE-READING and THEORY GAMES

Michiko Yurko's *No H in Snake* provides many interesting music concepts. The creative teacher knows how to make learning fun and comprehensive through the use of Ms. Yurko's system or one of his own.

7   IMPROVISING DUETS and ACCOMPANIMENTS

Children love having accompaniments added while they are performing. The group class is a perfect time for the teacher to improvise to play along with a student (but only if the student knows the selection thoroughly). Students enjoy improvising or composing new accompaniments for their pieces—for example, a pianist playing Twinkle with an Alberti-type bass. Often, it is fun to ask the parents and students to sing, tap, or clap accompaniment patterns while a child performs.

8   SINGING SPECIAL WORDS to SUZUKI TUNES

It is fun to make up words to help in understanding certain aspects of the repertoire. For example, to help clarify the concept of the three-count note that appears in French Children's Song, one might sing:

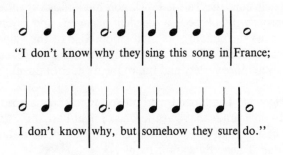

"I don't know| why they| sing this song in| France;

I don't know| why, but| somehow they sure| do."

The use of the word "why" for the long note can be emphasized by having the children and parents stand up when they sing it. The teacher should find words appropriate to each situation.

9 REVIEWING THE PIECES IN VARIOUS WAYS

Have a student play selections with different tempi, touches, keys, modes, phrasings, interpretations, or in various ways such as (for pianists) with hands crossed, or with addition of ornamentation. These variations can add greatly to his knowledge. At the same time, these exercises expand his thinking, test his conceptual and musical understanding, and add variety and enjoyment to the learning situation.

10 RHYTHM GAMES

Marching, clapping, dancing, or making small or large movements with the hands, feet, or entire body, all in conjunction with familiar Suzuki tunes, can help relax and calm students, and, at the same time, teach them certain basic concepts.

For example, in the Bach Minuet 3 for pianists, the children can sing and shape (up and down) the right-hand part while marching to the rhythm of the left hand. In another instance, one child could play Allegro by Suzuki (Book 1) while the other children clap their hands on the quarter notes, snap their fingers on the eighth notes, touch their faces on the half notes, and stomp their feet on the whole notes.

The possibilities are endless, and the creative teacher will use his imagination to make each group class a novel experience. Books or articles on Dalcroze eurhythmics are good sources for other ideas. The articles on Dalcroze eurhythmics (listed in the General Bibliography) by Leslie Pastor and Donald Roach are excellent sources.

11 LOTTERY GAME for REVIEW

Review of earlier repertoire is an essential part of the Suzuki method. Making use of a lottery game motivates children in both listening and playing. Names of individual selections from a volume should be put on cards (perhaps using some creative design such as fish) and placed in a large bowl. One or more children draw one card and perform the selection for the group. If they have not learned how to play the selection, they either clap the rhythm or sing the melody. (See also Question 4, p. 72)

In conclusion, the Talent Education method is organized and thorough in its approach. It is based on excellent pedagogy and psychology. Most important to its methodology is motivation. Use of the games outlined here, and others like them, will help create motivation, encourage learning and review, and add even more variety and fun to the wonder of Suzuki education.

9. *Question*: The Suzuki method seems to show a special reverence for the child—an attitude that some teachers might have difficulty grasping. How can one best explain or understand this attitude so as to be the truly caring teacher that Talent Education requires?

Answer: Edwin Reischauer, in his chapter titled "Relativism" in *The Japanese*, discusses a basic difference in attitude between East and West:

In modern times in Japan there has been growing emphasis on the individual and his rights and an increasing tendency to see things in universalistic terms, as in the West. Still, there undoubtedly remains a deep underlying difference with the West in the greater emphasis on particularistic relations and relativistic judgements . . . the whole social organization of feudal times leaned heavily in that direction up into the nineteenth century . . . both the East Asians and Westerners saw the world in terms of a basic duality, but there was a significant difference. In the West the division was between good and evil, always in mortal combat with each other. In East Asia the division of Yang and Yin was between day and night, male and female, lightness and darkness, that is, between complementary forces which alternate and balance each other. There was no strict good-bad dichotomy but rather a sense of harmony and balance of forces. Much of the flavor of these . . . attitudes . . . lingers on in contemporary *Japan*.[54]

Thinking in terms of the Eastern attitude, the Suzuki teacher should strive more for a "natural" balance of forces in each student. When things are not going well in the student's learning situation (for example, poor practice habits, concentration, or attitudes), the teacher's approach should be to correct the environment surrounding the student—to help him find balance—rather than emphasizing that things are going wrong because the student "has no talent" or is a "bad" child). This approach naturally requires much responsibility for the teacher and parent. Good Suzuki teachers and parents work hard to help each child; if things are not right they search deeply for solutions. It is easy to find simple answers such as "Johnny simply doesn't have talent" or "Johnny has a stubborn personality and will never play the piano," but a good educator takes on a great challenge to search much deeper through continued self-growth, questioning, and caring.

10. *Question*: There is great emphasis in Talent Education on patience. Many teachers seem to think that patience implies never getting angry or making demands—can this approach really work at all times?

Answer: In a lecture on March 20, 1954, "Those Who Do Not See What Is before Their Eyes," Dr. Suzuki tells of a student he once taught who, over a period of two years, did not follow his instructions and did not improve. Finally, as Dr. Suzuki summarizes,

> Losing in the game of patience, one day in the second year I gave the student an ultimatum: "I have showed you and explained to you at every lesson how to use the bow in order to create a sound. I wonder if you are making any effort to understand what I say, I have already been doing the same thing with you for two years. Regretfully I no longer find it meaningful to give you lessons. This may be our last. I must decline to continue with you if, when you play here a week from today, there is no indication that you have followed what I will show you today." The following week when he returned to play for me, for the first time I recognized a trace of practice according to my instructions. . . . I poignantly realized that, no

matter how obviously I might hang a message before someone's nose, it does not enter his eyes if his heart is not ready.[55]

Yes, patience is important, but love is the overriding factor. The caring teacher knows how to make the pupil aware of his expectations; sometimes a harsh demand or change in attitude may be required but if the student senses the request comes out of genuine caring, he will respect it. With this attitude patience need never be the "controlled frustration" that Suzuki dislikes. It is, rather, controlled sensitivity to what to expect and how to achieve it without losing the caring between teacher and student.

CONCLUSIONS

This chapter has presented numerous ideas on the teaching of the Suzuki method. Particular emphasis has been given to a broad approach—an approach that goes way beyond the Talent Education pedagogy—that offers special suggestions for the Western Suzuki teacher. Simply learning certain aspects of the Suzuki approach to the instrument is not enough. One teacher was quoted in an *American Suzuki Journal*: "If you understand the Twinkles, the techniques involved, and how they apply to other pieces in Book One, you will be able to teach all volumes of the Suzuki repertoire."[56] My answer to this statement is that the Suzuki method is a comprehensive educational system. To teach the method requires much more than merely understanding the Twinkles, or Volume 1, or all the volumes. It requires this plus much more. It also requires understanding of the social aspects of the method, such as how much of the method is a natural part of the society out of which it grew and how much of it is contrary to that society and how much we can learn from studying aspects of the Japanese or American educational systems in general. These points are discussed in greater detail in the final chapter. Especially recommended is the entire August 1, 1983, issue of *Time* magazine, titled "Japan—A Nation in Search of Itself." The sections on education, culture, art, design, music, and people (including an article about Dr. Suzuki) are of special interest to Talent Education teachers. Successfully teaching the method requires an intuitive understanding of the importance of motivation, of flexibility toward the individual child and society, and of the basic principles outlined in Chapter 3. Yes, a thorough grasp of the pedagogy is essential, but it alone will lead one only to what is often found in the traditional approach: fine teaching to a select few. Talent Education strives to reach *all* children. Doing so requires the utmost intelligence, growth, flexibility, knowledge, and intuition, in sum—caring—of the Suzuki teacher.

6
Talent Education and
Modern Learning Theories

This chapter compares the philosophies and methods of Shinichi Suzuki with those of various other educators, learning theorists, and authors of the present century to help the reader gain further insights into the universality and soundness of Suzuki's "mother tongue" approach. Throughout the chapter, similarities between the ideas of the authors being discussed and those of Suzuki will be summarized.[57]

JOHN GARDNER ON EXCELLENCE FOR EVERYONE

John Gardner expresses many ideals similar to those of Suzuki in his book, *Excellence: Can We Be Equal and Excellent Too?* He says, "I once asked a highly regarded music teacher what was the secret of his extraordinary success with students. He said, 'First I teach them it is better to do it well than to do it badly.' Many have never been taught the pleasure and pride in setting standards and then living up to them,"[58] Gardner, like Suzuki, believes that all men can achieve excellence:

> Standards! That is a word for every American to write on his bulletin board. We must face the fact that there are a good many things in our character and in our national life which are inimical to standards—laziness, complacency, the desire for a fast buck, the American fondness for short cuts, reluctance to criticize slackness, to name only a few. . . . The transformations of technology and the intricacies of modern social organizations have given us a society more complex and baffling than ever before. And before us is the prospect of having to guide it through changes more ominous than any we have known. This will require the wisest possible leadership. But it will also require competence on the part of individuals at every level of our society. . . . Keeping a free society free—and vital and strong—is no job for the half-educated and the slovenly. Free men must be competent men. . . . But excellence implies more than competence. It implies a striving for the highest standards in every phase of life. We need individual

excellence in all its forms—in every kind of creative endeavor, in political life, in education, in industry—in short, universally.[59]

Gardner offers many ideas concerning an individual's achievement of excellence. For example, he discusses the importance of high morale and hopeful attitudes and the motivational aspects of having high expectations and a constant emphasis on excellence.[60] In discussing motivation, Gardner relates its degree of intensity in any individual directly to the degree of what is expected (or asked) of him: "More and more we are coming to see that high performance, particularly where children are concerned, takes place in a framework of expectation. . . . If there are no expectations, there will be little high performance."[61] Gardner's belief that all members of society, whether cabinet members or first grade teachers, should be excellent in their fields is similar to Suzuki's philosophy that all people can develop superior abilities and that all students, whether at the beginning or most advanced levels, can and should aim for perfection.

Like Suzuki, Gardner believes that the purpose of education is to help people become happier. He says that "learning for learning's sake isn't enough."[62] He discusses how happiness involves striving toward meaningful goals:

> The dedicated person has not achieved all of his goals. His life is the endless pursuit of goals. . . . We want meaning in our lives. When we raise our sights, strive for excellence, dedicate ourselves to the highest goals of our society, we are enrolling in an ancient and meaningful cause—the age-long struggle of man to realize the best that is in him. . . . In short, Americans cannot and will not find happiness in apathy, aimlessness or the pursuit of momentary pleasures. They can—and I believe will—find both meaning and happiness in dedication to the highest goals of their society.[63]

E. F. SCHUMACHER—FREEDOM VS. DISCIPLINE

In *A Guide for the Perplexed* E. F. Schumacher analyzes the discipline versus freedom controversy in relation to education. He discusses one group of educators who believe that learning calls for the "establishment of authority for the teacher and discipline and obedience on the part of the pupil."[64] Another group believes in the establishment of the greatest possible freedom: "Education is nothing more nor less than the provision of a facility. The educator is like a good gardener, whose function is to make available healthy, fertile soil in which a young plant can grow strong roots; through these it will extract the nutrients it requires. The young . . . will develop best when it has the greatest possible freedom to choose exactly the nutrients it needs."[65] Schumacher suggests that the best education is one that combines the two aspects of liberty and discipline with a third factor—brotherliness: "Brotherliness is a human quality beyond the reach of institutions. . . . It

The photographs on the next fifteen pages were taken by Arthur Montzka (unless otherwise noted). They feature Talent Education students, teachers, and parents at various locations, including the American Suzuki Institute (Steven's Point, Wisconsin, held every summer), the First and Second Annual Chicagoland Suzuki Music Festivals (Chicago, Illinois, 1981 and 1982), the Fifth International Suzuki Teachers' Conference (University of Massachusetts, Amherst, 1981), and the Suzuki Music Academy of Chicago (year-round classes, Chicago, Illinois).

The pictures present a broad perspective of the Suzuki approach. They show students in solo and group performances, in semiprivate and group lessons, in formal and informal situations. Also, the photographs show the involvement of parents and teachers in the Suzuki learning environment and the combinations of seriousness and fun, discipline and games, and joyous respect of learning that is found in Talent Education.

Though the photographs speak for themselves, a few words of clarification follow: first and second pages—Dr. Suzuki with students in Steven's Point and Chicago and with Bette Dyer, Ray Landers, and Mrs. Suzuki at the Chicagoland Suzuki Festival, 1982 (*second page, top*); fourth page—Kay Slone (*middle left*) and Linda Wear (*lower left*), with students and parents at the American Suzuki Institute; fifth page— Gail Lange (*bottom*) with a Suzuki student and parent; seventh page—Dorothy Jones (*top left*), Margery Aber (*top right*), and Haruko Kataoka (*middle left*) with students; eighth page— Ray Landers (*top, photo courtesy of Chicago State University*) and Yvonne Tait (*bottom*) with students; tenth page—Margery Aber (*middle*) with students; twelfth page—Wendy Fain, a special child who, through her adjustment to her cerebral palsy, has gained the kind of openness to education and growth that Suzuki advocates (*top left, photo by Harold Day*); fourteenth page—Suzuki students in play-in concerts at the Chicagoland Suzuki Music Festival (*top and bottom*) and the American Suzuki Institute (*middle*); fifteenth page—Ray Landers in performance (*photo courtesy of Chicago State University*).

can be achieved only by individual persons mobilizing their own higher forces and faculties, in short, becoming better people."[66] Brotherliness suggests a caring, growing, and sharing. Schumacher's suggested combination of discipline, freedom, and brotherliness is certainly in agreement with Suzuki's philosophy. The Talent Education teacher provides a most disciplined educational system but presents it in such a stimulating, motivating environment that the gaining of knowledge is much freer. Suzuki emphasizes the need to move in steps appropriate for each child; no child should study against his wishes, yet any child, when properly motivated, will want to study. The role models of the knowledgeable and caring teacher, parents, and other music students help the Suzuki student see the freedom that comes with experience, discipline, and learning. Suzuki education strives for the balance of forces that Schumacher recommends.

MAYA PINES—REVOLUTION IN LEARNING

A highly recommended book is Maya Pines's *Revolution in Learning (The Years from Birth to Six)*, a comprehensive summary of many recent innovative schools, modern educational programs, and learning theories concerning young children. The theories of such psychologists as Piaget, Bruner, and Hunt are analyzed; revolutionary educators such as Montessori are given historic perspective; special programs such as Head Start, numerous day-care centers, and certain progressive programs are studied; and many other facts concerning learning in the very young are presented. The following is a summary of some of the ideas found in Pines's book and a comparison of them to Suzuki Talent Education.

THE INNOVATORS VS. THE ESTABLISHMENT

Pines says, "A fierce, though largely undeclared, war has been raging since the early 1960's between [the] establishment, which is concerned primarily with children's emotional and social development, and the innovators, who emphasize cognitive, or intellectual growth."[67] Suzuki's Method is an intelligent approach that emphasizes satisfying the desires of both the establishment and innovators; however, Pines would probably place Suzuki more in the category of an innovator. She says, "The innovators include sociologists, linguists, mathematicians, philosophers and computer technicians, as well as many psychologists, all concerned with how young children learn to think and how best to help them."[68] The cognitive educators are concerned with the young child's real desire to know:

> The "cognitive" group feels that by failing to take advantage of young children's real drive to know, the Establishment is wasting something very precious. Once past the sensitive period of their earliest years, children will never again learn with the same naturalness and ease. Teachers who prevent

children from making the most of this period condemn large numbers of them to a downward spiral of failure. They condemn others to years of drudgery spent laboriously learning skills that might have come with ease at an earlier age, and that they might have been using to explore the world around them. Furthermore, happiness does not come from play alone. As one kindergarten teacher wrote—an exceptional woman who taught her five-year-old pupils to write, count, add, subtract, divide, use a simple microscope and play the recorder: "Fun is too weak a word to describe the elation, satisfaction, and inner peace that come from intellectual accomplishment."[69]

BENJAMIN BLOOM, JEROME BRUNER, J. McV. HUNT, MASARU IBUKA, JEAN PIAGET

Jerome Bruner, like Suzuki, believes in the systematic development of abilities from the day of one's birth. But, as Pines summarizes, he and other cognitive psychologists believe that "the idea is not to forget the other aspects of life—the children's vital emotional and social development, which go on simultaneously—but to give intellectual and artistic growth their proper places."[70] As Bruner says, "Half the children in this country [United States] never have a chance to get good at anything, let alone become interested in it. Having failed to master basic skills early in life, they must either beat the system or flee from it."[71]

Cognitive psychologists such as Jean Piaget, J. McV. Hunt, and Jerome Bruner are called "New Mind Builders" by Maya Pines.[72] They believe that "an individual's achievement in life depends very largely on what he has learned before the age of four. If this startling theory is correct, it requires a radical change in society's approach to the years before a child enters school. It implies reversing the present pattern, in which we spend the bulk of our educational resources on more advanced students, and concentrating instead on children during the earliest years."[73] Young children, the cognitives say, can learn any language better than adults can. Suzuki, in *Nurtured by Love*, often talks about the naturalness of language learning in the early years. He compares this naturalness with the difficulty he had in learning German in his adult years and emphasizes the need to teach music and other subjects from the earliest years.[74] Masaru Ibuka's book, *Kindergarten Is Too Late*, is, in part, a summary of Suzuki's educational principles as applied to all subjects at the Sony Foundation–sponsored Early Development Association, Tokyo, Japan: "I have come to the conclusion that man's ability and character are not determined by birth, but are fairly well formed by a certain period in his life . . . the study of cerebral physiology on the one hand and infant psychology on the other has made it possible to show that the key to development of intelligence is in the child's experience of his first three years, that is, during the period of development of the brain cells. No child is thus born a genius and none is born a fool. All depends upon the stimulation of brain cells during the crucial years. Those years are from birth to three. Kindergarten is too late," says Ibuka.[75]

Benjamin Bloom, of the University of Chicago, concludes, through his studies of identical twins separated at birth, that environmental influences are very strong in the development of one's intelligence. Like Suzuki, he does not deny the effects of heredity, but he does place much importance on environment. He says that environment may cause intelligence to vary up to twenty points of IQ. After studying more than a thousand youngsters, Bloom concluded that about half of a person's general intelligence is formed by the age of four and as much as two-thirds by the age of six.[76] In discussing Bloom, Pines summarizes, as surely would Suzuki, "If a child's educational achievements depend so heavily on what he learned before the age of six, the home—not the school—emerges as the major educational institution in the land."[77]

JEAN PIAGET—STAGES OF DEVELOPMENT

The brilliant Swiss psychologist, Jean Piaget, analyzed the intellectual development of children, mainly through observations of the growth of his own children. Piaget categorizes different stages of development: the first stage, the "sensorimotor," lasts roughly from birth to one and half or two years of age. During this stage of growth, there is "interest in prolonging or repeating certain sights and sounds. . . . [The baby] learns to throw objects, pick them up, rattle them, reach them with or without tools, find them when they have disappeared—and discovers that objects have properties of their own. Here lie the origins of children's curiosity and much depends on the fate of these earliest efforts."[78] Genuine intelligence emerges at the end of this sensorimotor period—during approximately the last six months. These months are characterized by the child's ability to begin to invent new methods through mental combination "rather than through groping. It is the take-off point for abstract thought."[79]

The next stage, the "preconceptual," lasts from about ages two to four. The child begins to construct symbols and learns to speak language. "It is also the What's that? stage. . . . As Piaget interprets this question, it indicates not just a wish to know the names of things, but a wish to understand what class of things each one belongs to. It is the beginning of 'classification,' a key element in the child's acquisition of logic."[80] The Suzuki student, after listening to music from infancy (and enjoying the repetition of certain sounds), seems most ready in this preconceptual stage to begin lessons.

The "intuitive" stage, according to Piaget, lasts from about age four to seven or eight. Pines summarizes:

> This is the time of the famous conservation experiments. Although the
> child of two knows that objects exist even when they are hidden under a pillow,

the child of four has not yet learned that a quantity of liquid remains the same regardless of the container into which it is poured. His attention is centered on some particular aspect of the containers—their number, their size or how full they are. He cannot yet think of reversing the pourings; nor can he understand what a reversal would imply. The younger the child, the less reversible his thought. And without full "reversibility" there can be no conservation of quantity, which Piaget sees as a major landmark, occurring somewhere around the age of seven or eight, but sometimes earlier or later.[81]

The Suzuki student, in a stage comparable to Piaget's "intuitive," is most concerned with the sounds and pleasures of the sounds he is making. He is still learning through the naturalness of imitating; he is still exploring, discovering, and investigating. In order to provide the most stimulating intuitive stage for a child, Piaget's motto seems, to be, according to Pines, "The more new things a child has seen and heard, the more he wants to see and hear. . . . The greater variety of things a child has coped with, the greater his capacity for coping. Thus, both curiosity and rate of intellectual development are tied to the variety of situations that have forced the child to modify previous patterns of thought."[82] A music student provided with the kind of environmentally stimulating situation that Suzuki proposes would surely serve as an example for the above motto. Note-reading might be introduced to a Suzuki student during this intuitive stage; if so, it should be taught in a way that will enhance an intuitive, exploring approach—one that emphasizes learning concepts (such as melodic shaping—high or low, lengths of notes—short or long, and so on)—rather than the more specific terminology that can best be introduced in the later concrete and formal operations stages. Piaget believed that "there should be aural, kinesthetic and visual imagery before the symbols of music are introduced."[83]

In Piaget's "concrete operational stage" (about ages seven to fourteen), children begin developing such abilities as the forming of a hierarchy of classes (for example, carnivorous vs. noncarnivorous animals), the understanding of substitution (for example, the use of different combinations of coins to make the same sum), and the understanding of multiplicative operations, that is, relations made in two or more ways simultaneously (for example, a child arranging objects into subclasses by considering simultaneously shape and color will arrive at four subclasses that can be described in terms of both systems at once).

The period of "formal operation" (about age fourteen on) is initiated in children through their cooperation with others. As Ruth Beard summarizes: "Social life enters a new phase of increasing collaboration which involves exchange of viewpoints and discussion of their merits. . . . This obviously has the effect of leading children to a greater mutual understanding and gives them the habit of constantly placing themselves at points of view which they did not previously hold."[84]

Obviously, the concrete and formal operational stages are times when more and more analysis (such as note-reading, technical exercises such as scales, structure and form, and theory) would best occur in music instruction. As the child approaches the formal operation stage, he naturally strives for more independence from his parents and more cooperation with his peers; Suzuki would certainly emphasize that this is the best time for the more theoretical, analytical approach that some other methods place earlier.

Piaget sounds very much like Suzuki when he concludes, "There is pleasure in new accommodations and assimilations, as evidenced by the common urge to repeat new patterns that are almost, but not quite, learned."[85] He gives the maturation of the central nervous system its due: "It simply opens up possibilities. . . . [It] never is sufficient in itself to actualize these possibilities. This actualization requires the child's use of the new form, as well as the influence of both the physical and social environment."[86] And finally, Piaget "agreed that children in intellectually stimulating environments advance more rapidly than others," says Pines. She continues, "His theories also explained why environments that restrict children's opportunities to explore, to test their own hypotheses, to have their questions answered and other questions raised, would retard their development."[87] Talent Education, with its emphasis on individual attention, perfection of each step with the help of teacher, parent, and recordings, and a broad musical environment that encourages concert attendance and continual musical growth, is certainly conducive to "new accommodations and assimilations"—to the intellectually stimulating environment that Piaget encourages.

ERICH FROMM ON CHILDHOOD DEVELOPMENT

Before continuing the summary of Pines's book, it seems appropriate to insert a description by Erich Fromm of childhood development and its relation to learning. Fromm's ideas, even though not completely analogous to those of Suzuki and the cognitives, will help the reader comprehend Talent Education and some of the theories that Pines discusses:

> When an individual is born he is by no means faceless. Not only is he born with genetically determined temperamental and other inherited dispositions that have greater affinity to certain character traits rather than to others, but prenatal events and birth itself form additional dispositions. All this make up, as it were, the face of the individual at birth. Then he comes in contact with a particular kind of environment—parents and other significant people around him—to which he responds and which tends to influence the further development of his character. At the age of eighteen months the infant's character is much more definitely formed and determined than it was at birth. Yet it is not finished, and its development could go in several directions, depending on the influences that operate on it. By the age of six, let us say, the character is still more determined and fixed, but not without

the capacity for change, provided new, significant circumstances occur that may provoke such change. Speaking more generally, the formation and fixity of the character has to be understood in terms of sliding scale; the individual begins life with certain qualities that dispose him to go in certain directions, but his personality is still malleable enough to allow the character to develop in many different directions within the given framework. Every step in life narrows down the number of possible future outcomes. The more the character is fixed the greater must be the impact of new factors if they are to produce fundamental changes in the direction of the further evolution of the system. Eventually, the freedom to change becomes so minimal that only a miracle would seem capable of effecting a change.

This does not imply that influences of early childhood are not as a rule more effective than later events. But although they incline more, they do not determine a person completely. In order to make up for the greater degree of impressionability of early age, later events have to be more intense and more dramatic. The impression that the character never changes is largely based on the fact that the life of most people is so prefabricated and unspontaneous that nothing new ever really happens and later events only confirm the earlier ones.[88] [For a more scientific explanation of Fromm's ideas—a description of how man's brain develops, how the neurons interconnect over the formative years—read *The Universe Within* by Morton Hunt (Simon and Schuster, 1982), pp. 32–47.]

Suzuki, like Fromm, certainly admits that there are hereditary and environmental influences that affect different learning rates in children (see quote by Honda under section 14 on p. 18). But in reference to Fromm's statement, "The individual begins life with certain qualities that dispose him to go in certain directions, but his personality is still malleable enough to allow the character to develop in many directions within the given framework," Suzuki would surely state that potential music talent and appreciation would be within any individual's "given framework," at birth. Also, Suzuki certainly advocates that the earlier the learning situation, the more natural and easier it is for one to take in information for growth and change. Even so, it seems that Suzuki's strongly motivating educational environment (the use of parents in the learning situation, monthly group concerts, classes, emphasis on listening and concert attendance, highly individualized instruction, and so on) would, to some extent, be "more intense and more dramatic" than the normal educational environment and, thus, for the older student, "make up for the greater degree of impressionability of early age" as quoted by Fromm in the previous paragraph. In other words, the Suzuki Method, though basically designed for the use of instruction beginning with the child's earliest years, is organized to serve as a strong motivator of change within the individual into the later years also; it might, because of this factor, serve as a better approach for some older beginners than the traditional methods.

JEROME BRUNER—GROWTH OF MIND

Pines, in her discussion of Jerome Bruner, director of the Harvard University Center for Cognitive Studies, quotes Bruner: "The growth of mind is very strongly dependent on the kinds of tools one uses. . . . Man's development depends on three kinds of tool systems: for manipulation, for looking, and for symbolization. . . . Man is born naked, and culture shapes him."[89] According to Bruner, there are three ways in which the young deal with information—the enactive, the iconic, and the symbolic.[90] The earliest stage, the enactive, lasts from birth to about four years of age; the iconic approximately from five to seven; and the symbolic from seven or eight on. Bruner clarifies these three ways with a description of an experiment with children that involves a board on which electric bulbs are set up to light in any one of three patterns. Children of various ages were asked to find the pattern that had been represented:

> The four-year-old presses all over the board and hardly ever solves the problem. He's in a state of glee when he presses three things in a row and something lights up. At five, a child will check each of the images at once. But only at seven or eight will a child begin to combine these images into an information space, and use the rules of overlap, inclusion, exclusion. He'll stop for a minute, press one bulb, and know that if it doesn't go on, it can only be the third pattern. So, action first; imagery second; symbols third.[91]

Pines summarizes: "Bruner believes [that] the main job of preschools should be to work toward the translatability of one into the other: action into pictures and speech."[92] Suzuki is similar to Bruner in his emphasis on listening first, then learning by imitation in small steps followed by larger and larger steps, then learning more and more through analytic techniques. For example, the postponement of reading until it can be used in a more meaningful way—as a service to the learning of the music rather than as an end in itself—follows this procedure.

And Bruner is similar to Suzuki in his concern with artistry and perfection: "The great question now is not the question of expression, but of how to prepare the child to bring some artistry into whatever he is doing."[93]

J. McV. HUNT, MYRTLE McGRAW, ABRAHAM MASLOW

J. McV. Hunt, a professor of psychology, at the University of Illinois, wrote a revolutionary book, *Intelligence and Experience*, in the early 1960s. In it he concluded that "it is reasonable to hope to find ways of raising the level of intellectual capacity in a majority of the population. . . . It is one of the major challenges of our time."[94] Pines summarizes Hunt's ideas:

> Hunt believes that future generations of human beings can become far more intelligent—gaining an average of perhaps 30 IQ points—through better management of young children's encounters with their environment. The crucial problem is what he calls "the problem of the match"—finding the most stimulating circumstances for each child at each point in his development. Given anything too incongruous, children will withdraw, or ignore it; anything too familiar, and they will have no need to modify existing patterns of thought. The trick is to find circumstances with "an optimum of incongruity,"—just a little beyond what the child already has stored in his brain.[95]

Hunt discusses an experiment by psychologist Myrtle McGraw, who trained an eleven-month-old baby to roller-skate just as he was beginning to learn to walk. She says that "when a child is developing the walking scheme, the addition of roller skates is only a relatively slight variation from the environmental situation he faces in getting up on his own two feet."[96] This child roller-skated skillfully by the age of sixteen months, whereas his twin brother did not begin skating lessons until he was twenty-two months old and did not make progress for a long time. Hunt suggests that this "match" is important and helps explain why a foreign language is best learned at a time children are learning to speak. He "points out that a good match produces such intrinsic motivation and pleasures that it becomes unnecessary to worry about pushing children."[97]

Hunt, like American psychologist Abraham Maslow, believes that there is a hierarchy of motivational needs. Hunt's lists includes pain-avoidance, hunger, thirst, security, sex, plans, and information-processing which includes aesthetic experiences.[98] Maslow refers often to the need for self-actualization—to strive for the highest potential within oneself—"the development or discovery of the true self and the development of existing or latent potential."[99] Suzuki, with his concern for developing "fine human beings, happy people, and people of superior ability" (*Nurtured by Love*, p. 119) is certainly in agreement with these ideas of Hunt and Maslow. And Suzuki's Talent Education, with its strong emphasis on individual pacing and motivation, provides opportunities for the occurrence of the best "matches" for learning; surely Hunt, McGraw, and Suzuki would all agree that, as in the learning of language, roller-skating, and so on, music is best discovered from the earliest months, "matching" the time when sounds are being discovered. And the highly individual attention each Suzuki student receives from his teacher and parent allows this natural interest in discovery to continue as the student progresses. Careful planning to match the child's musical studies with his discoveries and interests will lead him to enjoy learning, and that enjoyment will lead him higher and higher to understand his own true essence.

OMAR MOORE—"TALKING TYPEWRITER"

In Chapter 5 of her book, Pines discusses a most interesting educational innovation—the "talking typewriter" of Omar Moore of the University of Pittsburgh. The requirements of this system include a modified electric typewriter with dictation equipment, an exhibitor, and a human instructor. A more expensive version of the talking typewriter is a $35,000 automated machine called the Edison Responsive Environment. Through the talking typewriter system children as young as three have learned to read and write. Pines says of Moore: "Particularly between the ages of two and five, he believes, children are capable of extraordinary feats of inductive reasoning if left to themselves in a properly responsive environment. Unlike most adults, he says, children can and do enjoy learning."[100] In Moore's method, an individualized program is designed for each child; the child is placed in a special environment where he teaches himself without much immediate adult interference. At first glance, this seems contrary to Suzuki's idea of parental and teacher involvement, but further analysis will show philosophical similarities between the two methods. First, Moore's typewriter, like Montessori's "prepared environment" and Suzuki's Talent Education method, requires careful structuring by a teacher. In each case someone is needed to organize the learning environment. In speaking of Moore's talking typewriter, Pines says that "a machine—like a book—is only as exciting, rigid, provocative, or dogmatic as the ideas of the person who devises its program."[101]

A summary of the talking typewriter approach is given by Pines:

> At Yale in 1959 . . . Moore opened a Responsive Environments Laboratory on the campus of the Hamden Hall Countryday School, a coeducational school for 340 children from nursery to twelfth grade.
>
> The lab [had] six soundproof booths, which some sixty of the youngest children visited voluntarily every day. Its rules were simple: No child could stay longer than half an hour a day, though he could leave sooner if he wished. Since there was room for only six children at a time, they took turns coming, but were always free to pass up their turns.
>
> On their first visit to the lab, the children were shown around by another child—part of Moore's plan to make them feel that the lab belonged to them. Parents were never permitted to see their own child in the lab. Even the regular teachers, whom the children might have wanted to impress or defy, were kept in the dark about their pupils' progress. A separate staff, made up largely of Yale graduate students' wives, was carefully instructed never to praise or blame any child. In Moore's words, "The lab represents thirty minutes away from the significant persons in the child's life—he is on his own, in a new environment, where all activity is carried on strictly for its own sake."
>
> Sitting before a talking typewriter for the first time, the child was given no instructions at all. He soon discovered that this interesting, adult-looking

machine was all his to play with. Whatever key he struck, the machine responded by typing the corresponding symbol in jumbo type, while a voice named the letter. Four days out of five, the voice was simply that of the human monitor sitting beside him, but if he was in the fully automated booth the machine spoke in the voice of whoever had programmed it. . . .

No two children proceeded in exactly the same way. . . . When their interest in this free exploration waned, the monitor switched a control dial and changed the game to a puzzle.

Without warning, a letter would appear on the exhibitor facing the child. The machine—or the monitor—would name the letter. And to the child's amazement, all the keys would be blocked, except the one that had been named. It was now a game of try-and-find-me. Eventually the child would hit the right key. Bingo! The key would go down, the machine would type the letter . . . and after a short interval another letter would appear on the exhibitor.

Urged on by curiosity and a desire to hit the jackpot, the children soon learned to find any letter, number, or punctuation mark that appeared and was named. . . . The children became familiar with various styles and sizes of type—upper-case, lower-case, cursive—as well as with handwritten letters, which could be flashed on the projector's screen. And they learned the sounds of the letters as well as their names.

At the same time, the children effortlessly learned to touch-type. . . .

As soon as the child became expert at this game and the challenge diminished . . . the rules were changed once again. Instead of a single letter, a word would appear on the exhibitor. The word came from the child's own vocabulary, since one of the monitors had previously had him talk into a tape recorder for this very purpose. This insured that the child was interested in this particular word, and also that he understood it. . . .

At no time was the child actually "taught" anything. . . . After periods of varying lengths—days, weeks or sometimes months—the child would suddenly realize that the letters he knew actually made up words that had meaning and that he himself could now write such words. This discovery is so elating that when it happens, children have been known to jump up and down in excitement, or run out of the booth to talk about it. In Moore's opinion, this is the way to introduce learning to children—to make it so exciting that they are hooked for life. . . .

Many details must be planned ahead to make the responsive environments system work. Every afternoon, the lab staff met to discuss the children's progress—an essential step. . . .

The role of the monitor during lab sessions varied with the degree of automation in the booth. Sometimes she took over the voice part, speaking as gently and patiently as the E.R.E. . . . A child was simply left alone with the machine—he might need a handkerchief, or a change of program, or depending on his mood, some human company. . . .

About once a week, each child at the lab played with chalk and a blackboard in the booth which had the least automated equipment. Since the child had formed a mental image of various letters, sooner or later he would try to trace them on the blackboard's horizontal lines. At this point, the monitor would put the appropriate letter on the projector and suggest that he draw one like it. Thus, the child would learn to print as painlessly as he had learned to touch-type.

Moore's plan was to give equal weight to all forms of language—reading, writing, speaking, and listening—so as not to produce speakers who have difficulty in writing, or tongue-tied writers. In many schools the curriculum for the first six grades tends to treat reading and writing as separate subjects, he says.[102]

Moore, like Suzuki, produced results that many would find outstanding. Many of the children in his kindergarten read at first- or second-grade level, many first-graders up to sixth-grade levels (the average around third-grade level), and many of the second-graders at the ninth-grade level (the average around sixth-grade level). (These results are from tests devised by the Educational Development Laboratory of Huntington, Long Island.[103]) "Far more impressive than these figures was the free use of language—spoken, written, typed, or dictated—by many children at the lab. The first-graders actually put out their own newspaper, written and edited entirely by the children themselves. . . . The newspaper contained drawings, riddles, and poems, as well as stories."[104]

Pines, in analyzing the reasons for these chldren's abilities, offers the following possibilities: their high socioeconomic level, their innate ability, their freedom of action, and, mainly, their constant exposure. "Because typing on an electric typewriter is so much easier for little fingers than making letters by hand, the children who came to the lab produced—and were exposed to—many more symbols than would be possible elsewhere. . . . Those who stayed in the booth longer typed an average of 2,000 strokes a week, counting punctuation and spaces. They were surrounded by symbols, just as toddlers must be surrounded by words before they can learn to speak."[105]

Even though the talking typewriter method develops an individualized program for each child, it still follows a structured program that first teaches the child letters, then words—all while providing an environmental learning situation that incorporates language from each child's own environment. The Suzuki Method, if properly taught, uses a similar approach. Although the Suzuki teacher follows a structured program in which all children follow basically the same repertoire, he is free to incorporate other repertoire, technical studies, and creative games according to the needs of the child; and each child is free to develop at his own individual pace. The concern with making learning very exciting is common to both methods. Although Moore's approach does not directly involve the assistance of a parent during the training session, it certainly requires involved, concerned, and responsible parents. The machine-monitor combination also, in a sense, serves some of the same purposes that a parent would serve in the Suzuki lesson (for example, making corrections in a nonthreatening way and pacing the individual development of the child).

Moore, like Suzuki, believes that those who start younger do better. He feels that "they have an easy, natural swing to their behavior. The older ones are more careful and deliberate. But a three-year-old will act as if he weren't paying attention. It's really free exploration, in a relaxed, fluid way. At that age they can also tolerate a great many more errors than older children—or adults—would accept.[106]

Suzuki's and Moore's concerns about patience are similar. In the talking typewriter approach, "In the privacy of a booth, children who don't understand quickly need not be embarrassed or suffer from constant comparisons with fast learners. The talking typewriter has infinite patience. It plays no favorites. It never tires of repeating things. It never gets angry, and no child need feel anxious about losing its love. Thus, the slower children are not deprived of the chance to make their own discoveries, and the brighter ones can proceed without boredom."[107] Similarly, a good Suzuki teacher or parent is sure to provide a learning situation in which the child feels he is not being tested; his mistake will be corrected in a caring manner, and both teacher and parent are as patient as Moore's typewriter.

Moore, like Suzuki, is humanitarian in his concern for the development of all children. Pines discusses Moore's work with mentally retarded children and says that the results are encouraging: "A boy with an IQ of 65, for example, took nine months to learn what the brightest children had learned in three weeks—but eventually he got there, without any pressure, and learned to copy simple words, sentences, and stories."[108] Moore's method, like Suzuki's, holds hope for retarded or handicapped youngsters—not just "normal" children. Dr. Honda's quote (see pp. 18–19) "If a hundred-meter race is carried out by several children, there are some who are faster than others. But even those who are slow will reach the goal if they continue to run"— summarizes a belief common to Suzuki and Moore.

CARL BEREITER AND SIEGFRIED ENGELMANN: "PRESSURE-COOKER APPROACH"

An approach to education referred to by Pines as the "Pressure-Cooker Approach" has been developed at the University of Illinois (Urbana) by Carl Bereiter and Siegfried Engelmann. This program is very controversial because of what some refer to as its "driving approach." Pines says, "So far, it has produced more rapid change in culturally disadvantaged four- and five-year-olds than any other technique can claim, at least in certain specific skills. But it is not a system for the faint-hearted."[109] Bereiter and Engelmann's school has rejected the play-oriented nursery school idea. Instead, it concentrates on a few areas and extensively drills the children for two hours daily. Pines describes a typical class:

> There were fifteen four-year-olds in the first class I visited. . . . Three were newcomers being trained separately to catch up with the others. . . .

"These are blocks. Now listen carefully. Are these blocks? Yes, these are blocks. Listen carefully. What are these?" A little Negro boy who had been listening as though hypnotized replied, "Blocks." "Give me the whole sentence," admonished the teacher. . . .

While one group practiced language, another group of four-year-olds worked on letters and a third learned arithmetic. Standing in front of a blackboard, their teacher wrote, "1 + 0 = 1" and translated it for them, pointing as she spoke: "Start out with one, get no more—get zero more. One plus zero equal one. Say it for me." . . . They sang out with great relish, clapping their hands rhythmically. Catching the youngsters' rollicking spirit, the teacher said, "Real loud now. Talk Big!"[110]

Pines comments that, on first impression, this all seems rather like a noisy and unpleasant version of learning by rote: "The children are steamrollered along, given no chance to slacken their pace or to withdraw from it all. . . . But the majority are very much with it, and they obviously enjoy the chance to make noise. It's an intensely physical kind of teaching: rhythmic movements, clapping of hands, cheers like those of a cheerleader, lots of concrete objects related to the matter at hand, arm and hand movements to illustrate points."[111]

Besides the good feelings that come from being successful (often for the first time in their lives), the children are also rewarded with praise, hugs, and sometimes food. Teachers are conscientious about speaking with each child frequently concerning his progress.

The subjects covered in this "pressure-cooker" school include language (spoken and written) and arithmetic. Times are set aside for drawing, singing, and outdoor sports. Even these activities are structured. No chance to teach is overlooked: "To get his raisins each child must answer the question, 'Which is your right hand?' in the approved manner; 'This is my right hand.' To get his juice he must say, 'My cup is blue,' or whatever color his Dixie cup may be."[112]

About half of the children who enroll in the program are black, the other half white. Many of them are from culturally disadvantaged homes and could barely speak when they enrolled. To make up for the children's deprived backgrounds, Engelmann and Bereiter believe that a tough, no-nonsense, hardworking approach must be used to bring up their level—that these children must be presented with as much environmental stimulation as possible. Pines writes of a math class taught by Engelmann that aptly demonstrates this approach. She describes a noisy classroom in which much shouting is going on between teacher and student—where shouts of praises are abundant when students respond correctly and shouts of encouragement are given when they are not correct.[113] As Pines says, "There is so much activity that no one has time to be bored."[114]

Bereiter and Engelmann formulated their educational ideas through asking two simple questions: What do children need to learn, and how can it be taught in the available time? They believe that "teaching implies, first, that the teacher is convinced the thing is worth doing, whether the child wants to or not, and, second, that the teacher knows how to teach—that his way, if not the best, is at least better than leaving things to happenstance."[115]

Pines summarizes other ideas of Bereiter and Engelmann:

> In Bereiter's opinion, many attempts to allow a child freedom of choice stem from indoctrination in the idea that teachers are not qualified to make these choices. "Teaching is equated with playing God in the eyes of lots of educators, and of most old-style child-development people, but I've finally come to an attitude that's more characteristic of other professional people, like physicians. I'd expect any competent doctor to make me well, whether I wanted to get well or not—and this is particularly true about children! I can quit smoking or not, but a child has got to take his medicine. . . . Not all medicines have to be unpleasant. But if you feel that everything you do must be pleasant or interesting for the child, you've curtailed your freedom. Suppose you design a way to teach arithmetic that is on the whole very pleasant, what do you do when you hit a bad spot? . . . The simplest thing is to go ahead even if it is unpleasant, and get through it and on to something pleasant. Then the teacher has some freedom."
>
> [Bereiter and Engelmann] point out that a little stress is good for children so long as it is not due to fear of failure, concern over pleasing the teacher, or sheer competitiveness, but caused by curiosity or a desire to achieve competence. The idea is to make the children feel they are succeeding at something very tough—when, in fact, the problems are carefully geared to their capabilities.[116]

What about the development of creativity in the child in such a program as that of the "pressure cooker"? Bereiter and Engelmann believe that for creative thinking, one must have the necessary tools, that divergent thinking is not fostered simply by allowing children to do so-called creative activities such as painting or molding clay.

They suggest that "activities can be built into a teaching program that encourages the child to use what he has learned to create new things: inventing new verses for songs, generating explanations for events in stories, thinking up new words that rhyme or alliterate with other words."[117] Those who criticize the Suzuki method by saying that it does not offer enough creative activities might think of the above quote and remember Suzuki's similar ideal—that discipline can lead to freedom and creativity. The good Suzuki teacher knows how to incorporate creative games, listening activities, additional repertoire, improvisation, and composing into the lessons and especially the group classes.

The results achieved by the "pressure-cooker" approach have been almost miraculous. For example, by the end of one year, a group of five-year-olds placed at mid-second-grade level in math and at mid-fifth grade in reading and spelling on the Wide-Range Achievement Test. Four-year-olds gained an average of seventeen points of IQ.[118] This high success rate is probably a result of several factors: a well-organized program, high expectations of and demands on the children, the use of qualified teachers who care, and much individual attention through a low student-teacher ratio. The similarities to Talent Education in these factors are obvious.

What some critics dislike most about Bereiter and Englemann's approach is the seemingly militaristic atmosphere that prevails in their "pressure-cooker" environment. Of course, Bereiter and Englemann would argue that, from a humanitarian standpoint, they are doing deprived children a favor by giving them necessary tools they have never had. With proper Suzuki music education, one should never have to resort to such a high-intensity approach; it is hoped that the child will receive the natural education that Talent Education can provide—education that will occur at appropriate times so that strong pressure techniques will not be needed in later years to make up for deficiencies.

GLENN DOMAN—*HOW TO TEACH YOUR BABY TO READ*

Glenn Doman founded Philadelphia's Institute for the Achievement of Human Potential in 1957 to treat brain-injured children. He devised a highly stimulating program of flashcard educational techniques which he eventually expanded to teach the nonhandicapped young as well. His books include *How to Teach Your Baby to Read*, *Teach Your Baby Math*, and *How to Multiply Your Baby's Intelligence*. He believes that "our individual genetic potential is that of Leonardo, Shakespeare, Mozart, Michelangelo, Edison, and Einstein." His system incorporates the flashing of appropriate cards (pictures, words) at brief periods three times a day—beginning almost at birth.[119] Doman, a strong advocate of Suzuki's philosophy, wrote the foreword for Masaru Ibuka's *Kindergarten Is Too Late*, a book that summarizes Talent Education principles. In this foreword, Doman states, "What Mr. Ibuka's vision could bring about is the destruction of such things as ignorance, illiteracy, insecurity, and uselessness—and who is to say whether that in turn might not reduce poverty, hatred, and killing?" Doman continues,

> All that is required for tiny children to grow up speaking many tongues fluently, reading the most complex of languages, doing instant mathematics, swimming, riding horseback, painting in oils, playing the violin, and doing them all with skill is that we give our children love and joyful exposure to the things we know. . . . Is it difficult to imagine that the world would be a lovelier place if a three-year-old's hunger to see all there is to see were fed with Michelangelo, Winslow Homer, Monet, Rembrandt, Renoir, Leonardo, and Rockwell, as well as Mickey Mouse and Happy the Clown? For in truth, the tiny child has an infinite appetite to learn all that he does not know, and he has not the slightest shred of judgement as to what is good and what is bad. Can one doubt that the world would be a safer place if

a two-year-old's hunger to hear all that there is to hear were fed with Bach as well as rock; with Beethoven as well as "Mary Had a Little Lamb? . . . I have seen newborns swim with the Timmermans in Australia. I have seen four-year-olds speak English with Dr. Honda in Japan. I have seen small children do advanced gymnastics with the Jenkins in the United States. I have seen three-year-olds play the violin and the grand piano with Dr. Suzuki in Matsumoto . . . I have seen three-year-olds read Kanji, the language of the scholars in Japan. I have letters from thousands of mothers the world over who wrote in the most charming of terms to tell me of the wonderful things that happened to their two-year-olds after they taught them to read, using my book *How to Teach Your Baby to Read.*[120]

Dr. Glenn Doman is a true soulmate to Shinichi Suzuki, so similar are their philosophies, particularly their beliefs in the potential of all and the transfer of genius to various subjects. Especially beautiful about Doman's philosophy is his appreciation of the profoundness of such a wide range of reality—from Mickey Mouse to Shakespeare, from Mary Had a Little Lamb to Beethoven; how much this is like Suzuki's almost Zenlike reverence for every note, every human being, his compassion and sympathy for all men.

One word of caution concerning Doman: for his early developmental reading programs to work, the entire environment must be made extremely stimulating; then the flow of learning to read develops out of the need to understand the environment rather than as an end in itself. Similarly, Suzuki students, to develop properly, must have the total music environment for healthy music growth; thus reading and analysis come at appropriate times to help in music-making and appreciation.

MARIA MONTESSORI

Maria Montessori, the famous Italian educator, has had a large impact on American preschool education. Beginning in the early 1900s, Montessori ran day-care centers in Italy for children ages three to six. Though initially these centers were for children from slum areas, Montessori saw them as models for "middle-class" schools: "The elementary classes in the future would begin with children such as ours who know how to read and write . . . who are familiar with the rules of good conduct and courtesy, and who are thoroughly disciplined in the highest sense of the term, having developed, and become masters of themselves, through liberty. . . . [Our children] pronounce clearly, write in a firm hand, are full of grace in their movements . . . and possess the power of spontaneous reasoning."[121] Pines suggests that the main attraction in Montessori's work for American middle-class parents is that children in her program learn to read, write, and count at a very early age.[122] These, however, were not Montessori's ultimate goals;

she, like Suzuki, had lofty ideals and used the "mechanics of education to strive further." Pines says,

> She wanted her charges to become as powerful in their concentration, as independent of spirit, as strong of will and as clear of thought as the world's greatest geniuses. She noted that many major discoveries stemmed from such virtues as independence and persistence. . . . "Culture," she said, "is not the accumulation of knowledge, but the prepared order in the mind which is to receive such knowledge." Her goal, then, was to train children to be like connoisseurs: so sensitive to the specific attitudes of things around them, and so expert in classifying them, that everything would possess interest and value for them.[123]

How did Montessori expect to achieve such results? Children, she said, learn best in a carefully controlled "prepared environment—an environment that uses a rich array of educational toys such as puzzles and games that help the child towards both physical and mental growth and independence. Montessori's wide range of educational equipment allowed the child to work at his own pace and urged him to strive for perfection—virtues that are also found in Suzuki's Talent Education. The Montessori teacher, like the Suzuki teacher, serves as a director for the growth of knowledge from within the child. The teacher must be highly qualified in the power of observation and in the ability to structure a carefully planned motivational learning environment. Montessori said, "Children are really patient and gentle creatures. They have been much maligned. Their overriding aim in life is simply their own self-development—their 'autoeducation.' "[124] She was determined that this "autoeducation" not be left to chance.

Montessori (1870–1952), a physician, was painfully aware of pedagogical causes of retardation in children. Much of the medical community believed in the predominance of physical or medical causes. Montessori, through her studies of the French physician Edouard Séquin, became interested in the education of the retarded; this interest eventually led her to many conclusions that differed from those of the general medical community. At the age of twenty-eight she became the director of a state orthophrenic school for children who were considered educationally hopeless. Through her hard work she proved the soundness of her methods: many of the retarded children she taught passed public examinations for primary certificates just as well as "normal" children did. Proud of her success, she began devoting herself to normal children as well.[125] Her use of didactic materials with these children, many taught at housing projects (in a children's house or Case dei Bambini), showed her that

> when she had used her didactic materials with the retarded, the puzzles and exercises merely made education possible; but when she used this equipment with normal children, she found it stimulated them to teach themselves. . . .

It convinced her of the need to give normal children as much freedom as possible. . . .

After a fruitless search for someone who would manufacture a large and elaborate alphabet for them, similar to the one she had used with retarded children, Montessori decided to cut their own letters out of paper and sandpaper. . . . This was how she stumbled on her famous movable alphabet and sandpaper letters. . . .

As the method evolved, the directress would take two of the sandpaper letters at a time starting with the vowels and present them to a child, teaching only their sounds, not their names. She would also show him in what direction to trace the letters with his fingers. In this way the child learned three things at once: what the letters looked like, how they sounded, and how they felt. This last impression, muscular memory, said Montessori, often superseded that of either sight or sound in small children.

In presenting the consonants, the directress would add a vowel sound and pronounce the syllable as a whole. But no particular rule was followed as to the order in which the letters should be presented, since Montessori wished to let the child's curiosity be his guide.

The next step was to ask the child to find the letters that the directress pronounced: "Give me o! Give me i!" If he failed, he was not told he was wrong, but the lesson was ended for the day. A cardinal rule was never to insist on teaching when the child did not respond readily. . . .

By the time a child could recognize letters by touch alone, even when blindfolded, compose words easily with the movable alphabet, and fill a geometric inset with neatly parallel lines, he was ready for what Montessori called the "explosion into writing." One day he could not write by himself—and the next day he could: It was as simple as that.

Montessori reported countless episodes of the excited joy of a child who wrote a word for the first time: she compared such children to hens who had just laid an egg.[126]

The similarities to Suzuki's approach are obvious: the concern for all children; the belief that the retarded as well as the normal can learn; the idealistic goals; the use of a carefully prepared educational program that allows for development at each child's individual rate; the use of motivating factors such as a prepared environment and caring, well-qualified teachers.

Today, Montessori schools abound in America; some are affiliated with the more orthodox Association Montessori Internationale, some with the American Montessori Society. The latter group tends to be less disciplined and rigid. Unfortunately, as Pines mentions, "There are also some Montessori schools that prosper as business enterprises, without affiliation with either Montessori society. My own first contact with such a school nearly soured me on the whole method because, unfortunately, it was a caricature of what Montessori had intended. . . . Nearly everything (in a class I attended) violated the Montessori spirit: the restriction of movement, the insistence on quiet, the class-wide demonstration, the lack of freedom of choice, and particularly the teacher's authoritarian attitude. . . . It destroyed what

J. McV. Hunt calls Montessori's major contribution, her solution of 'the problem of the match': Letting the child find out for himself what best matches his own particular interests and stage of development.''[127]

The possibility exists that Suzuki instruction in America might suffer some of the same fate. Although the Suzuki Association of the Americas has devised teaching guidelines and pedagogy programs, it is possible for one to claim to be a Suzuki teacher without following these guidelines or attending any pedagogy courses in Talent Education. Even those teachers who have attended some Suzuki seminars may be lacking in a thorough pedagogical background and offer poor instruction; one could perhaps do more harm than good if he does not have the needed caring attitude, pedagogical and philosophical understanding, and Suzuki training. The SAA's guidelines for teacher sanctioning should help maintain standards. (On this point, see my new book for a thorough discussion, *Is Suzuki Education Working in America?*, available in 1985.)

MRS. THOMAS HOPKINS—CULTURAL DIFFERENCES AND SIMILARITIES

Pines summarizes some of the differences between American and European children as noted by Mrs. Thomas Hopkins, director of the West Side Montessori School in New York City: "There is a fantastic difference between the behaviour of European and American children in Montessori schools, according to Mrs. Hopkins. Being more disciplined at home, the European children are much quieter and have more fear of adults; they have been told what to do so often that they see the little rules rather than the big ones, and sometimes won't do anything at all until they know whether it is right. Therefore, the Montessori teacher has to develop their independence.

"American children, on the other hand, come from child-centered homes; as a result, they have plenty of independence, and much more vitality. 'Montessori is especially adapted to American children,' Mrs. Hopkins declares, 'You can give them big rules, and within these they can act—go as fast or as slow as they wish. They have the initiative, and they'll go.' ''[128]

As summarized by Steven Staryk (see chapter 7, p. 131), there are many similarities between Japanese and European cultures in their "seriousness of character, determination and racial qualities sympathetic to the stringed instrument" (refer to footnote 173). *Newsweek* magazine, in referring to Japan's school system as "the world's most successful" gives much of the credit for this high quality to the great respect children accord their teachers. Japanese students are, in general, much more like Europeans than Americans in their respect for authority. But as *Newsweek* points out, "Oddly enough, the Japanese now believe they can improve on the world's most successful school system by making it a bit more American. . . . Says Akio Nakasima, director for upper secondary schools at Tokyo's Ministry of Education: 'The American System is superior in that it treats each child as an individual and offers an opportunity to develop his or her special ability.' "[129]

Perhaps Suzuki is particularly well adapted to American culture for similar reasons. The often heard criticism that American children are too independent for Talent Education to be effective does not seem justified in light of the above observations. American children's early strivings for independence and creativity would, on the contrary, seem to make a thoroughly organized system such as Suzuki's workable—usable, in a sense, as a "taking-off point" for creativity—as a developer of the tools that the child first needs in order to have the means to express what is within him. (For further discussion on cultural aspects, see Chapter 7, point 13, and *Is Suzuki Education Working in America?*)

SUSAN GRAY AND THE EARLY TRAINING PROJECT

Pines describes an interesting program in Tennessee:

> A group of psychologists from the George Peabody College for Teachers in Nashville tried a summer preschool program to counteract the progressive retardation they had seen among Negro children in Murfreesboro. This seemed to work, but by the end of the first grade the results had all washed out—no difference remained between the special group and the controls.
>
> Bravely, the group decided to try a string of summers rather than a single one, and to add a weekly visit to the children's homes all year round as a link between one summer and the next. . . .
>
> The first summer preschool in this series began in 1962, with twenty three-year-olds from poor families in which there was an average of five children. In half the cases, the fathers were absent. The children's mean IQ was 86.
>
> Daily lesson plans were worked out for each child. Although the equipment was the same as that of conventional nursery schools, it was used in a much more deliberate manner, explains Dr. Susan Gray, the psychologist who directed the Early Training Project. For example, one-inch colored cubes served to teach numbers, colors, and position words . . . as well as to develop the children's drive for achievement ("Build the tallest tower you possibly can"). With only five children per adult, immediate rewards were possible.
>
> After three summers of training, the children gained 9 points of IQ. During the same time, the control children lost 6 points. On a preschool test given to all children who entered the first grade, those who had been in the program scored nearly as well as middle-class children.
>
> Then Dr. Gray noted a strange thing: By the end of the first grade, the controls were doing so well they nearly caught up with the experimental group, even though the latter had retained their gains in IQ. However, another control group in a town sixty miles away did not show the same progress. This led her to believe that the local children's gain must have resulted from diffusion—from the influence of the experimental children on

their friends and neighbors. "If what we are finding is indeed diffusion, this is one of the most optimistic findings possible," she said.

Shortly thereafter, evidence of another kind of diffusion turned up—diffusion downward, toward the younger brothers and sisters of children in the program, as a result of the weekly home visits.[130]

As does Talent Education, Gray's program presented a structured course of study taught by qualified, caring instructors; other similarities include the open attitude of expectation—the belief that the children will come up to what is expected of them, the contact with the home environment through a parent, and the fact that other children (friends and relatives) closely associated with those in the special program were "pulled along" as a result of the experimental children's influence. In relation to this last point, observers of Talent Education often comment that Suzuki training affects an entire family. Brothers, sisters, and parents find their own lives becoming more disciplined. Of course, the child who does well cannot help but influence others—he motivates them as well as serves as an example of how one becomes an achiever. Siblings of Suzuki students often progress faster than the original student when they start lessons simply because they have had the good fortune of learning from their sibling's experience. People are naturally attracted to healthy, educated, happy students. It is human nature to grow and to learn from others who are growing. The influence of Suzuki students spreads beyond immediate family members to friends, classmates, and other members of society.

SUCCESSFUL PRESCHOOL PROGRAMS—SUMMARY

Pines also analyzes many other preschool programs that have dealt with disadvantaged children in special ways. She concludes that all such schools that have had success in providing these children with skills they need share the following traits, which are certainly found in the Suzuki approach: "[These schools] deliberately plan sequences that will lead the children to specific goals. They realize that time is their most precious commodity, and that each activity must be selected for its maximum contribution to learning. Last but not least, their teachers work with small groups or individual children."[131]

RENÉ SPITZ AND WAYNE DENNIS—EFFECTS OF DEPRIVED ENVIRONMENTS

To illustrate the tragedy that can happen to babies not given proper love, care, and stimulation, Pines discusses a film made by Dr. René Spitz. Spitz showed how strongly deprived babies that he observed in a foundling home where they received almost no attention began to lose interest in their surroundings. They eventually stopped playing, hoping, and caring. Spitz compared the development of this group with that of a group of infants in a women's prison nursery whose mothers were allowed to take care of them. This second group thrived although many of the mothers were either mentally retarded, delinquent minors, or psychopaths.

In an orphanage in Teheran, described by Wayne Dennis, infants "became so apathetic and retarded that fewer than half of them learned to sit up alone by the age of two years. . . . At the age of four, 85% of them still failed to walk alone. Even the sequence of motor skills which they developed took a peculiar turn, despite the general belief that such sequences are fixed by built-in mechanisms. Instead of creeping before standing up and walking, these children scooted on their rear ends—propelling themselves forward from a sitting position."[132]

Pines concludes that the earlier and longer in life maternal deprivation occurs, the worse the results. If the deprivation lasts for only a few months, the baby, if given excellent care later, might overcome the bad effects. But if the deprivation lasts as long as three years, the damage might never be undone.[133]

The obvious conclusion is that an infant needs love, attention, and stimulation in order to grow. Simply, he needs caring; he needs to be "nurtured by love" as Suzuki says. And Hunt adds that the infant also needs the opportunity to make repeated efforts that will lead him to learn new skills.[134] Talent Education's combination of parental involvement, environmental stimulation through listening and imitation, and caring attitude certainly explains much of its success in early childhood education. Homes that are as void of musically stimulating and caring environments, just as the orphanages described above are void of healthy environments, can do much damage to a child's natural musical development. As Suzuki says, it is no wonder so many children become tone deaf because they grow up in totally deprived musical environments. How many would instead grow up to have the musical genius of Mozart if Talent Education surrounded them?

JAMES BASTIEN AND JOHN KENDALL—SUZUKI'S INFLUENCE ON STARTING AGES FOR AMERICAN MUSIC INSTRUCTION

In concluding our review of Pine's discussion of the cognitive psychologists, it is interesting to note that Suzuki has been advocating many of their ideas for almost forty years. As John Kendall, a violinist and educator who has been a strong advocate for Suzuki's ideas, points out, before Suzuki's influence in America in the 1960s, it had been conceded that the fourth grade (about age ten) was the ideal time to begin string classes. "Yet in Japan, under Suzuki's system, the average 10 year-old is playing the Bach Double Concerto and the Vivaldi A Minor Concerto with ease and security."[135]

Through Suzuki's influence, the beginning ages for many string classes have been lowered; however, even today, many educators still advocate later ages as best for beginning instruction. For example, James Bastien says that instruction in piano traditionally is begun for children "of average ability" between the ages of seven to eleven: "Some children may be ready to begin as early as five, others would do better to wait until they are nine or ten."[136] Suzuki has certainly created much debate in America concerning the best ages to begin music instruction. And he has already had a major influence, not only in the large numbers of students studying musical instruments through his method in the United States and other countries but also in his effects on string programs in America's public schools (see Kendall's book, *The Suzuki Violin Method in American Music Education*) and even in traditional music educators' attitudes toward their own instructional programs. (For example, Bastien states many Suzukilike ideas in his discussion titled "The Advantages of Early Instruction."[137]) Suzuki's greatest contribution in relation to the cognitive psychologists has probably been the proof that his method works and that it works for large numbers. The results have been shown to the public through television, magazines, newspapers, and, most of all, public appearances sufficiently that even the most cynical can see that very young children can and do learn at a rate far exceeding what most of us have been taught to expect.

NOAM CHOMSKY AND PETER FARB—THE MIRACLE OF LANGUAGE

An important premise of the Suzuki philosophy is that the learning of any subject can be just as natural as the learning of language. As Pines says, "A three-year-old who cannot talk arouses grave concern, for good reasons. But the everyday miracle of a toddler's learning to speak tends to be taken for granted—though it is probably the most difficult intellectual accomplishment a human being is ever called upon to perform."[138] Peter Farb expresses similar sentiments:

> A child of four has performed an awesome intellectual feat. He has not merely learned the names of things; he has acquired an entire linguistic system that enables him to create sentences for the rest of his life. If among the words a child knows are hill, water, Jill, fetch, Jack, pail, and go, he may eventually put them together into a sentence like Jack and Jill went up the hill to fetch a pail of water. Think for a moment how remarkable this sentence is. The child has taken a random assortment of words and given them order. Jack and Jill do not appear just anyplace in the sentence, but serve as the subjects of the verb go. Equally important, the child added what are known as "markers" in the form of functor words (and, up, the, to, a, of).[139]

How does a child achieve such a remarkable achievement? Farb states:

> No child is capable of speech until he has heard other human beings speak, and even two infants reared together cannot develop a language from scratch. Nor does any single "natural" language exist. A child growing up anywhere on earth will speak the tongue he hears in his speech community, regardless of the race, nationality, or language of his parents.
>
> Every native speaker is amazingly creative in the various strategies of speech interaction, in word play and verbal dueling, in exploiting a language's total resources to create poetry and literature. . . . This sort of linguistic creativity is the birthright of every human being on earth, no matter what language he speaks, the kind of community he lives in, or his degree of intelligence. . . .
>
> And at a strictly grammatical level also, native speakers are unbelievably creative in language . . . every person constantly creates utterances never before spoken on earth.
>
> Noam Chomsky [of the Massachusetts Institute of Technology] believes that all human beings possess at birth an innate capacity to acquire language. Such a capacity is biologically determined—that is, it belongs to what is usually termed "human nature"—and it is passed from parents to children as part of the offspring's biological inheritance. The innate capacity endows speakers with the general shape of human language, but it is not detailed enough to dictate the precise tongue each child will speak—which accounts for why different languages are spoken in the world . . . instead of learning billions of sentences, a person unconsciously acquires a grammar that can generate an infinite number of new sentences in his language.
>
> Despite very uneven performances that a child hears all around him, in only a few years—and before he even receives instruction in reading and writing in "grammar" school—he puts together for himself the theoretical rules for the language spoken in his community.[140]

The learning of language is truly remarkable, yet most of us take it for granted. It is perhaps the most outstanding example of learning that occurs in humans. There are linguists and others more highly trained in its use; still the amazing fact remains that most of us learn a comprehensive language system and large vocabulary and use it as a vital part of our lives. Why? Perhaps because we learned it in the most natural way possible—under circumstances that were "pure," that is, there was a most important reason to learn it: to communicate and survive. We learned language according to need, not just to have a device to "show off." Learning was taken for granted; we were not under constant stressful situations in which we were "punished" for our mistakes (made to feel bad, given bad grades, given no rewards), but instead we were given much encouragement. (For example, note how the infant just learning to say "mama" is encouraged—he is not punished for not yet being able to say complete sentences!) One is learning language for correct reasons—to make life more useful and happy. One innately realizes the essential need of language.

ALLEN INMAN—"I AM MUSIC"

Analyzing all of this, one is amazed at the naturalness of Suzuki's "mother tongue" approach. So positive does it seem that we find ourselves asking why this language-learning "mother tongue" approach has not been applied on a mass scale to various other subjects throughout history. Some will argue, of course, that music is not a language and that the rules of learning music are not the same as those of language. To them, I reply that music *is* a language. It is, in fact, an extension of man's spoken language: Man can only whimper or whisper so softly and shout so loudly. Because he has memory he retains feelings both good and bad; the intensity of these feelings often calls for expression that the body and man's use of language are too limited for. The arts, in a sense, serve a purpose of helping make up for this limitation in our communication system. Music is heightened feelings, heightened communication, heightened language. The following poem by Allen C. Inman expresses it beautifully:

> *I am Music—most ancient of the arts. I am more than ancient; I am eternal. Even before life commenced upon this earth, I was here—in the winds and the waves. When the first trees and flowers and grasses appeared, I was among them. And when Man came, I at once became the most delicate, most subtle, and most powerful medium for the expression of Man's emotions. When men were little better than beasts, I influenced them for their good. In all ages I have inspired men with hope, kindled their love, given a voice to their joys, cheered them on to valorous deeds, and soothed them in times of despair. I have played a great part in the drama of Life, whose end purpose is the complete perfection of man's nature. Through my influence human nature has been uplifted, sweetened and refined. With the aid of men, I have become a Fine Art. I have a myriad of voices and instruments. I am in the hearts of all men and on their tongues, in all lands among all peoples: the ignorant and unlettered know me, not less than the rich and the learned. For I speak to all men, in a language that all understand. Even the deaf hear me, if they but listen to the voices of their own souls. I am the food of love. I have taught men gentleness and peace: and I have led them onward to heroic deeds. I comfort the lonely, and I harmonize the discord of crowds. I am a necessary luxury to all men. I am Music.*

Music *is* a necessary luxury; it is certainly needed by man. Obviously some men have more need and appreciation for it than do others; perhaps this has to do with the emotional makeup of each individual. People need language throughout their lives in order to survive. We all need music to some degree, but some devote more of their lives to it than do others. This is a factor that Suzuki is very aware of; he realizes that not all of his students will complete the Talent Education course of study or become professional musicians. In fact, only a small percentage will study the course with the intention of using the knowledge gained for a music career. This is not important; much more important is the learned discipline that can be carried through to other areas of endeavor pursued by each individual. Most important of all is the heightened awareness of life that can come through development of the senses through music training. And, of course, even if one does not continue his musical studies through the most advanced levels, he has still achieved a most important objective: the appreciation of music—a universal language.

JOHN KENDALL—MODERNNESS OF SUZUKI PEDAGOGY

The Talent Education philosophy of Shinichi Suzuki is respected so much by some of its advocates that it almost takes on a spirit of reverence in their minds. This spirit may not be understood by some of those who know little about Talent Education and may turn them away from objectively studying the philosophy. I believe that men unfamiliar with the method should first be made aware of the excellent, thorough pedagogical approach of Suzuki, who spent more than three decades of research and study to produce his method. As Kendall emphasizes in his summary of the violin method:

> The pedagogy used by Suzuki is up-to-date and utilizes many of the teaching devices currently favored in America, including exercises for the left hand, rhythmic variants, bowing gymnastics, shifting exercises, and, for the very young, beginning in the middle section of the bow with short strokes, frets taped or marked on the fingerboard, systematic explanation of finger patterns, a key approach geared to these patterns—and many other ideas, games and teaching devices.[141]

Speaking from my own experiences as a piano teacher and performer, I am impressed with the pedagogical approach of the piano method—the use of the whole arm and wrist as well as fingers, the use of excellent repertoire, the involvement of the parent, the use of many motivational devices, and so on. There is a more extensive discussion of this in the chapter on the Suzuki method applied to musical instruction of various instruments and subjects. Here I merely wish to suggest that there is much scientific soundness behind Suzuki's approach and that those who are skeptical might do well to approach the method from a more pedagogical and scientific standpoint. The following discussion of Robert Gagné is presented with this approach in mind.

ROBERT GAGNÉ—THE CONDITIONS OF LEARNING

Robert Gagné's *Conditions of Learning* is an excellent study of what happens when one learns. It provides a summary of necessary conditions for learning to occur: when reading it, one immediately becomes aware of how well Talent Education provides the conditions Gagné considers essential.

Gagné says that in the management of instruction the following five conditions must be established: objectives and structure; motivation; a suitable stimulus situation; proper communication from teacher to learner; and opportunity for learning feedback (confirmation by the teacher of the correctness or incorrectness of the learning).[142] He also offers a similar list of decisions one has to deal with concerning efficient learning: objectives; the structure of the knowledge to be learned; motivation; conditions for learning (how it best happens); the transferability of knowledge; and assessment.[143] The second list, because it deals with efficiency, adds the important concept of transferability.

In summarizing the best instructional situation, Gagné talks about the various ways in which the environment exerts its effect on the learner:

> (1) Presenting the stimulus. Every type of learning requires a stimulus, and usually these stimuli must be located within the learning environment, outside the learner. . . .

> (2) Directing attention and other learner activities. Environmental components also act on the learner by directing his attention to certain stimuli or aspects of stimulus objects and events. . . .

> (3) Providing a model for terminal performance. The importance of the function of informing the learner about the general nature of the performance to be acquired . . . most commonly, the "model" of performance to be expected following learning is conveyed by oral or printed communication.

> (4) Furnishing external prompts . . . cues may be provided in the instructional situation to establish a proper sequence of connections or to increase the distinctiveness of stimuli. . . . For example, they may be auditory, as in emphasizing the differences in sound of such French words as rue and rouge.

> (5) Guiding the direction of thinking. When principles are being learned, and particularly when learning takes the form of problem solving, the direction of recalled internal connections may be guided by instructions from the learner's environment. . . . Generally, instructions having this function of "hinting" and "suggesting" take the form of oral or printed prose statements.

> (6) Inducing transfer of knowledge. Providing for the transfer of learned concepts and principles may be accomplished in a number of ways. . . . The process is usually initiated, however, by verbally stated questions of the "problem-solving" variety. An important alternative method is to place the individual within a problem situation more or less directly, without the use of words to describe it. . . .

(7) Assessing learning attainments. The environment of the learner also acts on him to assess the extent to which he has attained a specific learning objective or subobjective.

(8) Providing feedback. Closely related to assessment of learning outcomes is the provision for feedback concerning the correctness of the learner's responses. The questions that are asked the learner, followed by his answers, must in turn be followed by information that tells him whether he is right or wrong. . . .[144]

The Talent Education approach fulfills the conditions given in the above three lists. For example, in the second list—"decisions one has to deal with concerning efficient learning"—one may note the following: Learning objectives are clearly stated in various Suzuki materials (*Nurtured by Love*, introductions to method books, syllabuses for SAA courses, and so on); the structure of the knowledge to be learned is organized thoroughly in the records or tapes and repertoire books and is outlined in SAA-approved courses; motivation is a strong element of the Suzuki method through the use of parental involvement, listening, and constant performance opportunities; the total environment approach is certainly conducive to providing good conditions for learning; many quotes by Suzuki show his concern with the transfer of the child's musical knowledge to other aspects of life as well as the transfer of concepts learned in one composition to other pieces. Masaaki Honda summarizes, "Our understanding of the phrase 'Talent Education' does not only apply to knowledge or technical skill but also to morality, building character and appreciating beauty. . . . Thus, our movement does not mean to raise prodigies. We must express it in other words as a 'total human education' or enriched environment."[145] Talent Education's emphasis on review of previously learned material is important in the development of transfer of concepts: A student sees similarities in learning techniques, musical phrasing, dynamics, problem solving, and other points between new and old pieces. He learns how to transfer these concepts from one place to another; assessment in Talent Education is a vital factor. The great amount of individual attention allows for constant analysis and assessment of the child's progress by the teacher, parent, and student. The student's greatest feedback comes through his interaction with the Talent Education environment—through his continual opportunity to check his own growth in relation to the recordings, other students, and his teacher and family.

Gagné lists eight different classes of situations in which humans learn:

The implication is that there are eight corresponding kinds of changes in the nervous system which need to be identified and ultimately accounted for. . . . In brief, the varieties are as follows: Type 1—Signal Learning— The individual learns to make a general, diffuse response to a signal; Type 2—Stimulus-Response Learning—The learner acquires a precise response to a discriminated stimulus; Type 3—Chaining—What is acquired is a chain of two or more stimulus connections; Type 4—Verbal Association—The learning of chains that are verbal. Basically, the conditions resemble those for other chains. However, the presence of language in the human being makes this a special type because internal links may be selected from the individual's previously learned repertoire of language; Type 5—Multiple Discrimination—The individual learns to make different identifying responses to as many different stimuli, which may resemble each other in physical appearance to a greater or lesser degree; Type 6—Concept Learning—The learner acquires a capability of making a common response to a class of stimuli that may differ from each other widely in physical appearance; Type 7—Principle Learning—A chain of two or more concepts; and Type 8—Problem Solving—A kind of learning that requires the internal events usually called thinking. Two or more previously acquired principles are somehow combined to produce a new capability that can be shown to depend on a "higher-order" principle.[146]

Gagné says that, for any specific kind of learning to occur, there must be certain prerequisites. In the above list, each type has as a prerequisite the mastery of all of its preceding types; for example, for type 8 learning to occur, type 7 must have been mastered; type 7 requires type 6 as a prerequisite, and so on.[147] Thus any good learning situation must be designed so that one is not being asked to learn a type of advanced learning before mastering earlier types. One of the great dangers of a mass education system such as that of the American public school system, with many students per teacher, is that there is little chance for the instructor to give the individual attention that would assure learning all steps thoroughly. Written examinations certainly are not enough—they basically are not designed to test learning that might be retained over an extended period of time or to test thoroughly such types of learning as problem solving; in other words, many such tests deal with knowledge that can be studied and tested with no assurance that it will be retained in the future. A method like Suzuki's, which involves parents and thus provides for continual supervision from parent and teacher, can be successful in assuring that learning occurs in the correct order and with enough repetition to ensure that real learning occurs. The review system of Talent Education assures that learned knowledge is retained, used, and thus available as a base upon which to build future knowledge.

Applying Gagné's types of learning to music, the following examples can be found: signal learning—the individual's physical-emotional reactions to the sounds of the music (feelings of pleasure, pain, joy, sadness); in an example of stimulus-response learning, the student learns a specific movement (such as thumb movement or wrist movement) through being shown and rewarded (a nod, praise, "yes") by the teacher when the movement is done correctly; chaining—learning of a series of specific physical movements such as those required in putting together several notes; verbal association—the learning of terminology associated with what has already been accomplished. For example, after demonstrating the movements involved in playing a series of notes, the teacher would verbally explain, "This finger goes on this key and the wrist goes up." Learning terminology such as the names of the notes and the word phrase may apply here, but the true understanding of some of the terminology will not come until later with the learning of concepts; multiple discrimination—learning differences (the various rhythms in the Twinkle variations, for example, or endings of phrases that have similar beginnings) found within the compositions and being able to perform the compositions correctly, that is, with the different parts all in the right order; concept learning—the learner is able to demonstrate his understanding of concepts such as phrase, melody, accompaniment, and expression marks. He is not merely able to play or imitate what he has been shown but is able to demonstrate his mental understanding. For example, he would know what to play if the teacher asked for the "third phrase of the right-hand part" of a certain song he has learned; principle learning—the student is able to work with two or more concepts simultaneously or in succession (examples: play the melody and accompaniment together, play the first phrase loud followed by the second phrase soft, play the entire piece, that is, play all of the phrases [concepts] in correct succession); and problem solving—the student develops independent thinking such as occurs in solving technical problems—for example, being able to analyze correctly the movements needed for certain technical passages.

Any educator, Suzuki-trained or otherwise, should constantly question whether he is providing the conditions for learning that Gagné presents. He should give each student enough individual attention to ensure that learning occurs according to a structured order and that enough repetition occurs to maintain the learning—to be sure that each step is mastered.

JOEL KOVEL AND ERICH FROMM—CAUSES OF UNHEALTHY DEVELOPMENT

Many philosophers, psychologists, and other authors have written about the "causes" of healthy or unhealthy human development. To understand healthy growth better, one needs also to analyze what causes unhealthy growth. Here I will quote the ideas of Joel Kovel on the causes of neurosis and Erich Fromm on the existence of social "necrophilia."

In reading Kovel's ideas on the causes of neurosis, one notices a description of environmental causes—conditions almost opposite to those advocated by Suzuki education:

> It is our infancy which is immediately implicated in neurosis. Social forces play a necessary enabling role, yet neurosis remains the unfinished madness of childhood carried forward.
>
> Essentially, neurosis arises because the human mind is forced to undergo

too many intense and contradictory feelings before it is able to deal with them. Although continuous from one moment to the next, the child's experience undergoes many drastic modifications in a relatively brief period of time. Too often there is no other way to deal with the flood of stimuli and the child's vulnerability to these stimuli than to transform them into neurotic experience. The family exists to provide a buffering world of play and protection against infantile hazards; and to the extent the family does its job, the individual is spared neurotic disturbance. Yet that extent is never complete. Because of the inherent contradictions of the infantile situation and the inevitable shortcomings of a family's adult members (who were infants themselves, and live moreover in a society that demands a certain degree of neurosis), the family can never do more than approximate the goals of developing autonomous, free offspring. And generally speaking it does a lot less.

. . . Human infants are creatures of the utmost helplessness and at the same time limitless desire. The two qualities are, moreover, coordinated; the weaker we are, the greater our needs and dependency, and the less we can do about impulse. The little child's need is so great—far in excess of what is biologically required for survival—that real gratifications must often be felt as frustrations. . . . The child freely confuses intentions with actual deeds. . . . There is probably an auto-erotic component to every significant infantile wish. Without built-in control, the body is at first a playground over which desire can flit carefree.

Yet, even without parental interference—through suppression, unavailability, seduction and so forth—these wishes are bound to founder on their own contradictions.

We cannot tolerate the presence of a hate toward those whom we also genuinely love. Yet the child has to deal with such problems. . . . Thus nothing is more real than jealousy, or feeling the impossibility of incestuous wishes. If one is to have one's mother, what will become of father?

. . . While the real trouble sets in if the parents contribute their own disturbance, or if fate somehow intervenes in a destructive way, it is essential that we recognize the great susceptibility of the child-mind to neurotic influence. The course of childhood development contains its measure of reason and its peaks of joy, yet is set round with terror. . . . The child's inherent ambivalence becomes blotted out by the continual reaffirmation of parental regard; fears are put to rest by parental benevolence; and desire is neither squelched nor fanned into uncontrollable flames. There is thus no reinforcement of inevitable fears by the environment. The child's capacity to love is then given away; and the developing personality is allowed to put things together and set aside from consciousness what is impermissible. The demons lack sufficient impetus to break down the barrier, while the structuring agencies gain every day from identification with civilizing influences.[148]

The overwhelming impression one gets from reading Kovel's thoughts on causes of neurosis is his belief that control is important in maintaining a healthy balance for the child—a control that the parent must constantly work for. It is a never-ending quest, and, if a healthy balance is maintained, as stated above, "the child's inherent ambivalence becomes blotted out by the continual reaffirmation of parental regard." For healthy growth, the child needs the kind of caring and attention that one finds in good Suzuki parents—in all good parents who care about the development of their children.

Erich Fromm has brilliantly discussed the causes of destructive or "necrophilous" (love of death) personalities. He concludes that many factors in modern life have created a widespread social "necrophilia," which is often more in evidence than its opposite "bilophilia" (love of life). For a detailed analysis of Fromm's ideas, see *The Anatomy of Human Destructiveness.* Here a summary of one of Fromm's ideas concerning how a society can lose control and endanger its sanity must suffice. According to Fromm, we can be conditioned through watching television to place the appreciation of commercial products on the same level as awareness of our deepest human feelings. Years of conditioning to such stimuli as the following television quote can give us warped values: "Today a terrible tragedy happened but more about that after this commercial" (from a newscast). We can become more concerned with material than with spiritual aspects of our lives and thus become more and more "necrophilous." (See Fromm's *Escape from Freedom* for a discussion of the effects of commercial advertising.[149]) Fromm offers many other ideas about the development of a necrophilous society—running away from reality through misuse of religion, emphasis on materialism, lack of respect for education, lack of compassionate understanding of man that can be gained through historical learning, emphasis on monetary values, fear of the unknown, lack of idealistic leaders, and others. Fromm offers a sign of hope, however: there *are* those in society very concerned with love of life:

> Simultaneously with the increasing necrophilous development, the opposite trend, that of love of life, is also developing. It manifests itself in many forms: in the protest against the deadening of life, a protest by people among all social strata and age groups, but particularly by the young. There is hope in the rising protest against pollution and war; in the growing concern for the quality of life, in the attitude of many young professionals who prefer meaningful and interesting work to high income and prestige; in the widespread search for spiritual values—misguided and naive though it often is. . . . The antinecrophilous tendencies have also manifested themselves in the many politico-human conversions that have taken place in connection with the Vietnam war. Such cases show that although the love for life can be deeply repressed, what is repressed is not dead. Love-of-life is so much a biologically given quality in man that one should assume that, aside from a small minority, it can always come to the fore, although usually only under special personal and historical circumstances. . . . Indeed, the presence and even the increase of antinecrophilous tendencies is the one hope we have that the great experiment, Homosapiens, will not fail. There is no country where the chances for such reassertion of life are greater than in the technically most developed country, the United States, where the

hope that more "progress" will bring happiness has been proved to be an illusion for most of those who have already had a chance to get a taste of the new "paradise." . . . The forces working against it are formidable and there is no reason for optimism. But I believe there is reason for hope.[150]

Certainly Suzuki Talent Education is a great love-of-life movement—a ray of hope in the midst of much stagnation one experiences in society. And, if Fromm is right, the United States, because of its emphasis on freedom of expression, is perhaps *the* country where a positive, life-giving educational force such as Suzuki's can most come to the fore.

BETTY EDWARDS—EVERYONE CAN DRAW

Betty Edward's book, *Drawing on the Right Side of the Brain*, is subtitled *A Course in Enhancing Creativity and Artistic Confidence*. Dr. Edwards, an art instructor at California State University, Long Beach, expresses many Suzukilike ideas:

> My premise is that developing a new way of seeing by tapping the special function of the right hemisphere of your brain can help you learn to draw. [This] model has provided me with a method of teaching that solves the problem I started out with: how to enable *all* of the students in a class instead of just a few to learn the skill of drawing. . . . Because only a few individuals seem to possess the ability to see and draw, artists are often regarded as persons with a rare God-given talent . . . while this attitude of wonder at artistic skill causes people to appreciate artists and their work, it does little to encourage individuals to try and learn to draw; and it doesn't help teachers explain to students the process of drawing. . . . You will soon discover that drawing is a skill that can be learned by every normal person with average eyesight and average eye-hand coordination—with sufficient ability, for example, to thread a needle or catch a baseball. Contrary to popular opinion, manual skill is not a primary factor in drawing. If your handwriting is readable, or if you can print legibly, you have ample dexterity to draw well. . . . Learning to draw is more than learning the skill itself . . . you will learn how to see.[151]

In her book, Dr. Edwards outlines exercise and instructions based on a course of nine lessons: "Nearly all of the students begin the course with very few drawing skills and with very strong anxiety about their potential drawing ability. Almost without exception, the students achieve a high level of skill in drawing and gain confidence to go on developing their expressive drawing skills in other courses or by practicing on their own."[152] Dr. Edwards is a strong believer in the importance of developing both hemispheres of the brain and argues that one of the main reasons that artistic talent is so undeveloped in our culture is that our culture trains the more analytical left hemisphere of our brain much more than the arts-oriented right hemisphere (see pp. 74-75, question 6, for more discussion on this topic). She devotes an entire chapter in her book to a historical analysis of the hemispheres of the brain. Much of the book is geared toward helping the student use both hemispheres of the brain further to develop the right hemisphere: "It's my belief that if persons untrained in art can learn to make the shift to the artist's mode of seeing—that is, the right-hemisphere mode—these individuals are then able to draw without further instruction. To put it another way, you already know how to draw, but old habits of seeing interfere with that ability and block it." Dr. Edwards sums up that "drawing is a teachable, learnable skill that can provide a twofold advantage. By gaining access to the part of your mind that works in a style conducive to creative, intuitive thought, you will learn a fundamental skill of the visual arts: how to put down on paper what you see in front of your eyes. Second, you will gain the ability to think more creatively in other areas of your life."[153]

Dr. Edwards not only believes that everyone can learn to draw in the right environment, but she also believes it is essential that "we begin to build a school system that will teach the whole brain. Such a system will surely include training in drawing skills—an efficient, effective way to gain access to right brain functions." She expresses sadness that "the right brain—the dreamer, the artificer, the artist—is lost in our school system and goes largely untaught."[154]

Betty Edwards and Shinichi Suzuki share many beliefs: given the right environment, all have talent; manual skill is not the primary factor, rather, it is learning to see, in the case of art, and learning to listen, in the case of music; the arts are essential to education in order to develop the "whole" person; those who become skilled in seeing and drawing or listening and playing musical instruments gain confidence to continue developing skills more and more independently; arts training can and should be used by individuals to help them think more creatively in other aspects of their lives; and our educational systems are inadequate and could benefit from a change of emphasis to include more arts programs and more optimism about human nature.

I highly recommend that everyone involved in Talent Education read Dr. Edward's book. As you discover through her genuis and your own ability to see and draw, you will surely believe more and more in the true potential of the Suzuki philosophy.

ROGER M. WILLIAMS—LINK BETWEEN ART AND LEARNING: IDEAS OF HOUSTON, PLATO, SHAW, MASLOW, AND MASTERS

To illustrate similar ideas of another author, quotes from the article "Why Children Should Draw—The Surprising Link between Art and Learning" by Roger M. Williams follow. Williams discusses all the arts (dance, theater, music, art, and so on) in his article and believes that they are essential for the full development of the human potential:

> For the past decade or so, budget-cutters and back-to-basics zealots have been hacking away at the "frills" in America's schools. Inevitably, the arts are among the first victims. But now a countermovement is under way. Important new evidence shows not only that the arts are beneficial in themselves but also that their introduction into a school's curriculum causes marked improvement in math, reading, science, and other subjects that the educationists pronounce "essential." Indeed, some researchers are now saying that the absence of art programs can retard brain development in children. . . .
>
> . . . Arts have far more than an "enrichment" role to play in the schools. They appear to stimulate a child's natural curiosity and—perhaps literally—to expand the capacity of his brain. The arts even help children discover their own worth and identity and thereby point the way to future happiness. . . .
>
> . . . Jean Houston, director of the Foundation for Mind Research in Pomona, New York, . . . criticizes the way the arts have been "encapsulated" in the typical school curriculum and declares, "A person needs to think in terms of images as well as words. He needs whole-body thinking—to evoke more of his entire mind-body system. Verbal-linear-analytical intelligence is a small part of the intelligence spectrum. There is also visual—aesthetic—plastic (working with the hands) intelligence, but that is not acknowledged in the schools. . . .
>
> The arts have always been related to a peripheral role in American cultures, including American education. They have established perfunctory and unimaginative "art courses" that barely scratch the surface of a wondrously varied subject area and, worse, fail to encourage students to let their creative instincts guide them.
>
> Nonetheless, plaintive voices have long been raised in support of the arts as a basic component of education: Plato perceived that the natural laws governing the structure of the universe—harmony and proportion, balance and rhythm—also govern music, dance, painting, poetry, and so on: he therefore urged making these art forms a foundation of the educational method. . . .
>
> Bernard Shaw [said]: "I am simply calling attention to the fact that fine art is the only teacher except torture." The American psychologist, Abraham Maslow, postulating "learning one's identity" as an essential part of education, believed that the arts are far closer to the core of education than are the more exalted subjects. Education emphasizing art, music, and dance, Maslow said in 1967, "can be a glimpse in the infinite, into ultimate values." . . .
>
> How do the arts help children learn? It is known that before the age of about six the brain increases in "gray-matter"; that is, in cells or neurons. After that, throughout life, the neurons make countless interconnections, associations based on such sensory perceptions as sight, touch, and sound. By an as yet undiscovered process, these associations are stored in the brain

as learning. They are critical to our ability to recall events from our past
. . . If these connections and associations are not made at an early age,
it is probable that the brain's neurons suffer something analagous to muscular
atrophy, and the development of the entire organ is, to that extent, stunted.

The differentiation of the brain into left and right hemispheres certainly
plays a role in arts-centered learning. According to the widely accepted
theory, the left hemisphere is the seat of analysis and sequential learning,
including verbal and mathematical skills, while the right is superior in visual-
spatial abilities. Says Robert Masters, Houston's husband and coresearcher:
"If the current thinking is correct that the arts come out of the right, or
visual, side, you are obviously damaging the brain if you don't cultivate
that side as well as the analytic side."

Doctors Houston and Masters shy away from making specific claims
about the arts stimulating physical growth of the brain. But they believe
firmly in the arts' far-reaching effects on bodily and intellectual development. As Dr. Masters puts it, "The arts stimulate greater body awareness
and less muscular inhibition. Lack of stimulation of that sort leads to in-
hibitions in the motor cortex and in the ability to think certain kinds of
thoughts and feel certain kinds of feelings." . . .

The child without access to a stimulating arts program, Dr. Houston
adds, "is being systematically damaged. In many ways he is being
de-educated."[155]

This excellent article expresses many fine ideas about the importance of
the arts in society and its educational system. Williams summarizes many
philosophical points that are similar to those of Suzuki; their reverence for
the arts is similar. Educators involved in the arts should strive for the comprehensive understanding of their value that Williams has; they will better
understand the importance of their vocations and present stronger cases for
art programs to those (certain public school administrators, for example) who
might doubt their importance.

BENJAMIN BLOOM—TRAITS COMMON AMONG
OUTSTANDING PEOPLE

It seems appropriate to conclude this chapter with a summary of the findings of a special University of Chicago research team led by Benjamin Bloom.
This team studied the life histories of one hundred outstanding people—
concert pianists, Olympic swimmers, tennis players, and research
mathematicians—who "reached the top of their fields between the age of
17 and 35."[156] Dr. Bloom and his associates wrote a report that offered a list
of several common traits or conditions that seemed prevalent among the one hundred outstanding people they studied. The reader is asked to review mentally the
ideas of all the authors discussed in this chapter while he reads the following summary of Bloom's report; note how many factors found in the report have been
discussed over and over by the various authors—especially by Shinichi Suzuki.

The University of Chicago investigation identified several conditions that "appear crucial in producing excellence" traits that are common among outstanding people: "As the data emerge from the study, they seem to show that most human beings are born with enormous potential—in one area or another—and also demonstrate the extraordinary power of parents." The following factors are prevalent in outstanding people's childhoods: "parents who greatly value and enjoy either music, sports or intellectual activity and view it as a natural part of life, so that the child learns its 'language' as easily as he learns to speak; parents who believe in the work ethic; a first teacher who is warm and loving, who makes the lessons seem like games and lavishes rewards; this teacher need not be highly skilled . . . but the instruction must be given on a one-to-one basis, and the parents must take great interest in it; a second teacher who emphasizes skill and self-discipline. Again the instruction must be individualized; a gradual change in the child and his family as both realize the progress the child has been making. They now begin to focus their resources on the developing talent; access to . . . a 'master teacher' . . . no sacrifice in time, money or effort seemed too great; although many of the people . . . were unquestionably more talented than average as children, none was a 'child prodigy'; the children developed their ability because of the instructions and attention."

In analyzing the above conditions Bloom concluded that the key factors in motivating children are the value system found in the home and the encouragement received at an early age. For example, the parents of the successful pianists from the study provided a musical environment through recordings, musical toys, concert attendance, singing together, teaching the children to play and read notes, and providing instruments and music books in the home. Some parents attended music lessons, and most supervised their child's practice; some took music lessons themselves. As the pianists grew and expressed a desire to excel, other activities often took second place with practicing sometimes taking twenty to twenty-five hours weekly.

Bloom concluded, "Some form of dedication to a talent is good for the child and good for society. . . . There is a great satisfaction in excelling, and such efforts are the source of most human achievements."

CONCLUSIONS—GAIL SHEEHY'S PATHFINDERS

This chapter has been presented to provide the Suzuki teacher with more insights into the great scientific and spiritual achievements (can they be separated?) of Shinichi Suzuki and others—insights the teacher can fall back on for support during those times when negative aspects of society and its educational systems loom more in the foreground than seems comfortable—at those times when the great life-giving ideas of Dr. Suzuki appear so positive that we wish to share them with others. Talent Education has a universal appeal, but to grow, it needs healthy leadership—caring, innovative persons such as those this chapter has discussed. As Gail Sheehy says in her book *Pathfinders*, "If we wish to focus on these people who have refreshed their society after a period of individual withdrawal and comeback, where do we begin looking? . . . to the artist who imagines new possibilities, to the observer who sees, the sentinel, who warns, the witness who testifies. These are the often unlikely and sometimes even quiet but transcendent pathfinders who offer the fresh blood of their own rebirths to transfuse their society."[157]

7

A Defense Against Often-Heard Criticisms of Talent Education: The Universality of the Suzuki Method

The Talent Education philosophy and method have been subject to controversy. This concluding chapter presents a defense against some of these criticisms and a summary of the possible strengths and benefits that Suzuki education might bring to music and general education in the United States and other countries.

CRITICISMS OFTEN MENTIONED

1. *The Suzuki Method does not develop individuality.* Some believe that because the method emphasizes that all of its students learn the same repertoire in chronological order, Talent Education does not encourage the development of each student's individuality. The charge is that the students all play like "robots." As stated earlier (see p. 18), Masaaki Honda asserts that just the opposite is true—that Suzuki training encourages individuality by allowing each student to develop at his own pace and by presenting thorough, well-organized, disciplined training that allows more freedom through the development of each student's abilities.

On the contrary, the individuality of the typical American student, in my estimation, can be greatly limited through an educational system that requires students of similar age to study at the same grade levels. The Suzuki method allows for individual differences in student development and, through its monthly group recitals in which students of various ages play similar repertoire, students become less conscious of their age differences in relation to their learning levels.

The Suzuki repertoire serves as a basic language. Just as we can expand our basic spoken and written language to express our own individual thoughts (through learning words indigenous to our own environment and needs), Suzuki students can use and expand the basic repertoire for the expression of their own musical individuality. Even while the basic repertoire is being

121

learned, individuality is emphasized through the student's listening to and playing different interpretations. As the student matures, he develops more and more desire to hear other interpretations and to formulate his own interpretive ideas. He begins to find interest in other music besides that of the basic repertoire and helps his teacher in the selection of repertoire for study after completion of all the volumes or for incorporation between certain pieces found in the volumes.

Although Talent Education does not emphasize improvising, written theoretical games, and extensive verbal expression of feelings about music as do some American methods, it does incorporate creative games and teaching approaches; a good Suzuki teacher is extremely creative and innovative in finding the best motivational and pedagogical approaches for each student. The method offers enough flexibility within its framework to encourage creative teaching and responses. American students are taught to be independent much earlier than Japanese students; they ask many more questions about why and how they do something. Some American teachers "Americanize" the Suzuki approach by incorporating more creative approaches (see p. 57, Motivation and p. 76, Question 8). Japanese students, because of their respect for authority, tend to ask fewer questions but may learn more; the more one knows, the more free he is to use his knowledge (see Chapter 6, p. 110 for a discussion of independence in American children). A combination of the strong discipline of the Japanese and the independent strivings of the Americans will lead to a healthy educational philosophy for American Talent Education.

2. *Learning by imitation and listening rather than by reading in the beginning years will cause students to be poor sight-readers later.* This is one of the most frequently heard criticisms and one that has proved invalid. As Suzuki explains, the pupil is naturally slow at reading when he first starts but, because he has already learned the basic mechanics of playing the instrument, he is freer to develop reading later, when it is needed. He eventually becomes a good reader. As in reading of language, when music reading is first introduced the student is naturally not able to read at the level of his playing ability. Eventually his reading ability improves. Because he is learning to read mainly so as to assist himself in learning his music, the reading does not become an end in itself that could possibly hinder music-making. Because the student is already used to sounds and concepts associated with creating music by the time he starts to read, he learns to read in long, horizontal lines rather than vertically; for example, he learns to associate the appearance of a phrase as notated with the sound of a phrase he has been playing and hearing. Learning to read in large units is very beneficial to later sight-reading.[158]

George Kochevitsky, in *The Art of Piano Playing: A Scientific Approach*, offers a philosophy on note-reading similar to Suzuki's:

Usually, in traditional pedagogy, the pupil seeing the note sign, finds the corresponding [note], [plays] it, and looks for the next note sign, next [note] and so on. The scheme is: visual impression—search for a note—movement. Alas, the result of this movement is very seldom heard. There is not time for listening, the next note must be found and played. . . . Rather, from the beginning the teacher should strive to establish and develop the following scheme: auditory stimulus [the inwardly heard tone]—anticipation of motor act [Suzuki's "stop and prepare" technique]—motor act resulting in actual sound—auditory perception and evaluation of the actual sound. . . . In the initial period of study, the pupil should concentrate on tone production, starting from single, separate tones, with attention on tone quality, proprioceptive sensations and form of movement; all three closely united. Soon he should be given simple tunes to play by ear. At first the teacher plays sample tones as well as short tones, and the pupil reproduces them by direct imitation. . . . The introduction of note signs as symbols of things already experienced comes later. How much later depends on the individual pupil's capacity.[159]

In the United States and most countries the teaching of written language is not usually started until the fifth or sixth year of a child's life. The critic of the Suzuki reading approach should bear this in mind.

Good sight-reading develops through opportunities for students to read new music. Many Suzuki schools have regular ensemble or orchestral performing groups, which are associated with the school or are located nearby. These groups offer students opportunities for reading music other than that found in the method.

The often heard criticism of Suzuki students, "But can they read?" is mentioned less and less as the method has become better known. When Suzuki students first performed in the United States, many of them were at very advanced performance levels (above, Volume 4 in violin) but had not yet thoroughly pursued note-reading. Some educators, impressed with these students' playing skills but shocked with their lack of reading ability, failed to understand the simple Suzuki concept that, as with language, reading should and would be taught later. These educators' reaction would be equivalent to responding with dismay to the fact that five-year-olds can speak fluently but cannot yet read. Now that more and more Suzuki string students are performing in school, college, and conservatory orchestras, and many are concertmasters or first chair performers, musicians and educators are recognizing that not only do Suzuki students learn to read but, if given the proper time and development, they greatly surpass most of their traditional peers. Talent Education students can and do become excellent sight-readers because they are trained so well to see and hear the music "linearly"—to hear the whole, to hear the sound of the entire phrase, not just one note at a time. The ability to hear accurately and naturally transfers to the ability to read if the Suzuki concept of teaching reading through making associations with previously learned sounds is followed. (See Question 3, p. 68, for further discussion.)

3. *The Suzuki Method is a "mass" teaching method and therefore does not deal with the individual child.* This misconception is partially the result of numerous photographs, published in newspapers and periodicals, and television programs that show large numbers of students at monthly group classes or recitals. As John Kendall summarizes:

> The performances of large groups is really a by-product of individual lessons and small group work. . . . A more flexible arrangement between group and private work exists, but . . . each student does get individual attention not only from the teacher but from the parent as well.[160]

The Suzuki student actually gets much more individual attention than the typical American student; this is a great part of the success of the method. In addition to the weekly supervision by the teacher, the Suzuki student receives constant supervision from a parent in his daily practice and is given much more opportunity to perform, thus receiving much more attention than his traditional counterpart.

4. *The Suzuki Method is really a "speed formula" approach that develops ability fast but is weaker overall than a method that stresses slower development.* Many American students start violin study at about age ten, but, as Kendall pointed out in 1966, "In Japan, under Suzuki's system, the average ten-year-old violinist is playing the Bach Double Concerto, the Vivaldi A minor Concerto, etc. with ease and security."[161]

At the 1983 International Suzuki Teachers' Conference in Amherst, Massachusetts, Dr. Suzuki commented that the standards have greatly improved since 1966 in Japan and that many ten-year-olds have already completed all of the volumes of repertoire music that is equivalent to our college Master of Music level of study.[162]

Many Americans, seeing the contrast between the average American and Suzuki students, assume that the Suzuki student has learned through a "trick" system. Yet, the Talent Education philosophy stresses slow, careful development; some beginners take as long as a year to learn the first piece. Because of careful initial preparation, the Suzuki student usually develops much faster later. With language development, one takes months to utter the first word, then eventually one day of learning may equal that of an entire previous month or even a year. One may learn as many words in one day as in the entire previous year at the age of two or three. Talent Education is similar. A Suzuki student may take several months to learn to bow, to stand or sit correctly, to play the first note. He may take a year to perfect the first piece. But during this slow initial stage, something much more comprehensive is happening inside his brain as he listens to recordings and concerts and watches parents, siblings, and other students learn—his real learning occurs inside. At first, the exterior results—the ability to play—seem slow, but as the student grows, the results begin showing more and more. Eventually, a student may take about the same amount of time or even less to learn an entire volume as he took to learn to perform his first note or piece.

5. *Because the Suzuki Method requires the attendance at lessons and practice supervision by one of the parents, it may find acceptance difficult in a country such as the United States, which does not emphasize such close parental cooperation.* Talent Education does require much involvement of the parents. The rapid growth of the Suzuki movement in America (in numbers of students, schools, teachers, and institutes) proves that the United States has many caring parents who seek alternate and effective methods of education. In teaching Suzuki students at numerous institutes throughout America, I have found that very few Suzuki teachers complain that parents are unwilling to attend lessons. There are more complaints of less than full cooperation in home supervision, but even these are few. The main criticism I hear from teachers is the lack of quality and total involvement in much of the home supervision of listening and review, a subject that is discussed in more detail in *Is Suzuki Education Working in America?*

6. *Because the small Suzuki student is introduced to music study before he is mature enough to decide for himself if he wishes to learn to play, the direction of his life is unfairly being determined by his parents and teacher.* Dr. Suzuki says: "I just want to make good citizens. If a child hears good music from the day of his birth, and learns to play it himself, he develops sensitivity, discipline and endurance. He gets a beautiful heart."[163]
Suzuki emphasizes that no student should be encouraged to study against his wishes. In fact, only about 5 percent of the beginning Talent Education students in Japan complete their courses and become professional musicians. Suzuki believes that those who do not have learned a sensitivity and discipline that can be transferred to other areas of study. Any culture, of course, socializes its children in areas such as religion, dress, morality, politics, ethics, and aesthetics. Suzuki presents a healthy "socialization," which allows for choice, discipline, sensitivity, and knowledge that can be beneficial in other areas of life.
Inherent in the Talent Education philosophy is the belief in music's great contribution to society and an awareness of the universality of music. Only the most cynical observer would fail to notice the joyous, life-giving force of music; it exists in many forms—folk, popular, rock, jazz, classical—and helps to make man's life happier. Music is open-ended; it leads inward and outward to awareness. All mankind is surrounded by sounds and by man's organization of sounds into music. Talent Education helps to heighten this

awareness and, at the same time, teaches man abilities that transfer to other aspects of life. I suspect that those who are most critical of Talent Educator's early start have failed to experience the true joy of music. Many who criticize also fail to see how they indoctrinate their children into various traditions, often without questioning these traditions' values. Many such people are content to surround their children with the mediocrity of television or inadequate school systems. I find such criticisms sad because what the people are really expressing is their own fear of inadequacies for growth within themselves. (My new book *Is Suzuki Education Working in America?* presents a comprehensive summary of the 1983 National Commission on Excellence in Education report that, in part, analyzes causes of some of America's negative attitudes toward education.)

7. *Because of the emphasis on repetition, the student can easily become bored.* Because the student is made aware of why he is repeating a certain passage—to improve it or to make it more secure—and because repetition is usually not identical, it is not boring to the student if taught correctly. In Talent Education, repetition is used in a creative way—the child is shown its purpose.

Repetition is an extremely important aspect of life. How many millions of times do we eat, sleep, say the same words? How often do we express the feeling, "I am hungry"? Yet it does not bore us because it has meaning each time. The Talent Education teacher seeks to find meaning in each repetition. He understands the importance of having students repeat compositions enough times so the music becomes a natural part of their systems, just as walking. The teacher also understands the importance of meaningful review and teaches techniques that emphasize repetition of already learned material as well as the learning of new concepts (for example, new interpretations, new dynamics, tempi, touches, emotions, and so on).

8. *Children as young as two or three years of age do not have the mental or physical capacity to begin music instruction.* The proof that this idea is incorrect lies in the overwhelming evidence of the large numbers of young children who *are* able to play accurately under Talent Education. Numerous modern educators advocate early childhood education. (See Chapter 6, especially the discussion of the cognitive psychologists on pp 83-87.)

Those who offer this criticism fail to see the Talent Education analogy to language development. They do not recognize the amazing abilities in speech and language comprehension that the average two- or three-year-old demonstrates, and they are unaware of the physical capacities of the very young. When they do see an example of an outstanding young talent, they are inclined to think that such a child is a "prodigy"—not the norm. If they could see the amazing number of "prodigies" in Japan at the annual Suzuki graduation concerts or in America at numerous festivals and institutes, maybe they would understand that man's great potential begins at birth.

9. *The Suzuki Method does not emphasize competition enough to be, in certain aspects, effective in a competitive society such as the United States.* This is one of the most often heard criticisms of Talent Education. Many writers have noted, however, that in various ways such as education Japan has become much more competitive since World War II and is, in certain aspects, even more competitive than the United States. Talent Education has been very successful in both countries—proof that a noncompetitive educational approach can be used even in competitive surroundings. (See *The Japanese* by Edwin Reischauer.[164] The August 1, 1983, issue of *Time*, "Japan—A Nation in Search of Itself," is also recommended. These sources will increase the reader's awareness of similarities in both cultures in relation to competition.) Even so, many American teachers whom I have consulted believe that activities emphasizing competition such as honor convocations, practice-a-thons, play-a-thons, contests, and graduation ceremonies can be incorporated into Suzuki instruction. The Suzuki ideal, however, is that the student compete with the potential within himself; he should strive for goals that the environment provides and learn from, rather than compete with, his fellow students. Talent Education emphasizes growth, with no end to learning. The student who pursues the goal naturally has no need to compete with another; such competition would imply a need to be better than the other. Those striving to grow wish to learn from those with superior abilities and to help their superiors in their growth, for, in return, they can learn more from them in the future.

10. *Photographs of performing Suzuki students often show them with very serious expressions; they look as though they are not enjoying themselves.* Suzuki students are very serious and disciplined in their approach to study. Their serious aspect does not mean that they are not enjoying their studies. The Suzuki student is given much opportunity to have fun through games and through a relaxed atmosphere at lessons. Many students express joy and elation after performances; Dr. Suzuki and other Talent Education teachers often use humor as a means to relax students. I suspect that many Americans are so conditioned to our "smiling culture"—advertisements, television commercials, and newscasts, among other things, constantly emphasize the "eternal grin"—that we do not realize that a smile is not always needed to indicate enjoyment. In performing, Talent Education students are merely expressing the same devotion and intensity that any other serious performing artist would.

11. *The repertoire found in the method is limited—it contains little romantic and no contemporary music.* As discussed earlier (see pp. 17, 40, 68), the Suzuki method does not attempt to present a thorough introduction to all literature; rather, it serves as a "basic alphabet" that presents a comprehensive technical and musical approach through excellent baroque, classical, and some romantic literature. Students are encouraged to incorporate additional

repertoire within the method and at the completion of the volumes. Often they learn all the volumes by age nine or ten. Therefore, many years remain in which to add further repertoire. A good teacher will encourage the student to balance his studies with music from various periods but will also be guided by the student's interests in emphasizing certain eras or composers.

12. *The early start encouraged by Talent Education does not guarantee that the advantages of the early development will continue into adulthood.* The March 28, 1983, issue of *Newsweek* magazine contained a cover story entitled "Bringing Up Superbaby—Parents Are Pushing Their Kids to Learn Earlier Than Ever. Does It Help or Hurt?" The article discusses many programs including Head Start and those of Glenn Doman and Shinichi Suzuki. It objectively analyzes the often-heard question: Are early starts advantageous in the long run? *Newsweek* offers some positive conclusions about the Head Start program:

> The earliest Head Start programs tried to give poor children a leg up on the middle-class competition, and at first glance the results are heartening. Irving Lazar of Cornell University found that 2,100 Head Start children who attended preschools in the 1950's and 1960's were up to 10 times more likely to get through school without failing than peers who didn't receive the early push. . . . Even if early education lets a toddler leapfrog ahead of her peers, will she stay at the head of the class? In studies at the University of North Carolina, Craig Ramey is following 175 children, half of whom were reared as their parents ordinarily would, and half of whom were enrolled in preschool from the age of three months. When he tested the children an average of 15 months after they entered the program, he found that those who attended preschool outscored the others on IQ tests by about 15 points. He warns, however, that it is too soon to conclude that the differential is permanent. Head Start children usually lost their advantage by the fourth grade and students at progressive schools often catch up to peers who were taught to read early. It seems that children whose parents care about education will catch up to playmates who start learning earlier. . . . Intense early learning is drawing fire from psychologists not only because it doesn't live up to its claims but also because it may impede other skills—"Pressure from academic achievement can take away something from other agendas such as the development of social skills," warns Ramey. [From another viewpoint] although society loses "an enormous amount of cognitive talent by not encouraging it," says Lazar, "even a stimulating environment of books, museum visits and nature lessons can only help a child reach his potential. . . . Yes, early education can save children who would founder in impoverished homes. But it does no more for young intellects than interesting caring parents can. Says Jerome Kagan of Harvard University, "It is not the activity per se but the melody behind the words—not what one teaches but how one demonstrates to a child that learning is important."[165]

The *Newsweek* article discusses both sides of the issue but concludes that what counts most is "interested, caring parents" and "how one demonstrates to a child that learning is important." My own conclusion is that all the advantages of the early start can and will continue into adulthood if the stimulating, caring environment continues. To keep growing, one must continually be stimulated to want to grow. The knowledge gained through early stimulation can fade if not used or encouraged to grow, just as muscles gained through a weight-lifting program can atrophy if the program is discontinued. The Suzuki student who quits growing, who does not follow the tenets of the Talent Education philosophy (particularly those dealing with listening and review), who does not expand his musical environment to include more and more motivating and interesting aspects, who does not realize that there is never an end to education—yes, this student may lose some advantages of an early start. But the student who keeps growing, studying, and learning can only benefit from an early start so that his outstanding abilities become more and more superior as he develops. As Glenn Doman says, "The World would be a richer, saner, safer, lovelier place if all children had mastered languages, arts, and basic sciences before they had grown to be teen-agers, and could then use their teen years to study semantics, philosophy, ethics, and comparative religion as well as advanced arts and advanced science or whatever else they'd like to learn."[166] Similarly, in Talent Education, the comprehensive early start can only help lead one to the wide, wide world of never-ending knowledge as long as the search continues.

13. *Because of the great culture differences between the United States and Japan, the Suzuki Method will not be beneficial to American education.* According to Charles Parker, who taught in Japan for several years:

> Suzuki's influence is due in large measure to the fact that in oriental thought there is a positive—one might almost say dynamic—reverence for the teacher and master. Suzuki has achieved the status of a great teacher and master and that is why he has thousands of disciples. He has established a way of life—a new way of life for the younger generation. . . . Japanese psychology demands that one play a role and follow a way of life. This is what the Japanese understand by personality; hence the utter devotion of Suzuki's violin students and the extraordinary musical feeling which so many of his young disciples have shown. . . . These Japanese children are not taking music lessons. They are living.[167]

Clifford Cook discusses a connection between Talent Education and Zen Buddhism:

> Daisetz Suzuki (a leading writer on Zen) summed up all that he had written, experienced, or said—"The most important thing of all is love." (Shinichi Suzuki titled his autobiographical and educational book *Nurtured by Love*.) A sudden, instantaneous quality to the view of the world gives

total presence of the mind; there is no other time than "this instant." The "eternal now" does not come from anywhere, is not going anywhere. So it is with the training of concentration in Talent Education, and the refusal to the clock.[168]

Dr. Cook continues with other observations:

> West: Divide and conquer. East: Unify and live. Zen's pursuit of psychological wholeness aims to achieve a thoroughly integrated man without a divided mind. Egolessness, non-interference by the conscious mind, an immovable center with great motility all around it, immediateness of action, an uninterrupted movement of life-energy—these concepts were taught in fencing and applied to violin playing also. . . . Zen is a depth religion of the here and now, "this moment"—not a horizontal, expansionist religion emphasizing a future life and always new experiences. Many parallels can be drawn between Talent Education as contrasted with western education and Zen Buddhism as contrasted with Christianity. . . . Zen gives importance to beauty and art in life, emphasizes quality rather than quantity, feeling more than technique.[169] [See also Chapter 5, Question 9, p. 78.]

Suzuki's reverence for every single note is analogous to Zen's respect for every aspect of life—for all that exists. To gain more understanding of this reverence, the reader is advised to read D. T. Suzuki's books on Zen Buddhism.

Theodore Normann, in his introduction to Kendall's book about Suzuki discusses certain aspects of Japanese tradition:

> One should note how basic to the Suzuki system of instruction are those ways of learning which go far back into Japanese tradition: the atmosphere of sharing in the education of children by members of the family, an environment that encourages naturally the kind of development desired by the group, the virtues of review and repetition until mastery and security are firmly gained, the stress placed upon the development of the senses (in this case the art of hearing), the satisfaction of the young child's need for imitation through providing desirable models—always accompanied by courtesy, kindness, and infinite patience. . . . Certainly, the Suzuki system of instruction, western though it may be in its musical orientation, is deeply rooted in traditional Japanese culture with its respect for beauty, its veneration for the past, and, in its traditional music, a centuries-old dependence upon learning through the medium of imitation.[170]

The following quote from a *Newsweek* magazine article illustrates another possible cultural difference between Japan and America:

> Could you learn all the words [of Japanese], you could not make yourself understand in speaking unless you learned to think like a Japanese—that is to say, to think backwards, to think upside down and inside out. . . .

Language plays a rather unusual role in Japan. Americans set great store by the literal meanings of words; Japanese are much more interested in the relationships and introductions that go unspoken. . . . The Japanese have virtually a contempt for literalism.[171] [See also Chapter 5, Question 1, p. 67.]

A discussion of cultural differences between the United States and Japan could be the subject of a book in itself: whatever cultural differences the reader has discovered in this study or a more comprehensive volume, he will also note many similarities; the differences are not so great as to make Suzuki education ineffective in the United States. (See Chapter 6, pp. 101-2, for Mrs. Thomas Hopkins's conclusions about education in relation to cultural differences.) And obviously there are enough similarities for the method to work—as proved by the large numbers of American children studying under the Talent Education system. Suzuki himself would dismiss much discussion of the matter, for he studied in Europe for eight years and was thoroughly introduced to Western culture. The repertoire of the method is Western, and as Kendall emphasizes in his summary of the violin method:

> The pedagogy used by Suzuki is up-to-date and utilizes many of the teaching devices currently favored in America, including exercises for the left hand, rhythmic variants, bowing gymnastics, shifting exercises, and, for the very young, beginning in the middle section of the bow with short strokes, frets taped or marked on the fingerboard, systematic explanation of finger patterns, a key approach geared to these patterns—and many other ideas, games and teaching devices.[172]

Professor Steven Staryk of Oberlin College suggests that certain traits of one culture can be found in another:

> The success [of the Suzuki Method in Japan] is due largely to the social, economic and cultural environments of the Orient, an atmosphere not unlike that of Eastern Europe which produced the majority of the last generation of violinists, and still continues to produce the vast majority of those of the present. Whether by heritage or by necessity, East Europe, Japan, and other Far East nations share a seriousness of character, determination and racial qualities sympathetic to the stringed instrument.[173]

Dr. Suzuki, in *Nurtured by Love*, emphasizes his own belief in the similarities of people the world over. He tells of an occasion when he performed a Bruch Concerto at a dinner party attended by Albert Einstein. A guest who heard Dr. Suzuki play was impressed with the "Germanness" of his performance. Einstein commented, "People are all the same, Madam."[174] In his books, articles, and lectures Suzuki constantly emphasizes the universality of people's strivings. (The reader is advised to consult *The Japanese* by Edwin Reischauer for a thorough discussion of Japanese culture. The *Time* issue, "Japan—A Nation in Search of Itself," August 1, 1983, mentioned earlier, is very comprehensive in its coverage of differences and similarities between Japan and other countries. The articles on education, culture, art, music, and language are especially recommended.)

CONCLUSION

Is the Suzuki Talent Education philosophy beneficial to the United States and other countries? Already hundreds of thousands of American students have studied under the Suzuki Method. With the growth of the Suzuki Association of the Americas and with continued publicity, the Suzuki philosophy should rapidly reach more Americans. How many people eventually will study under the Suzuki Method, or the quality of the teaching of the method, or the influence of the philosophies of the method all depend upon numerous factors. One of the most important is the structure and quality of organizations such as the Suzuki Association of the Americas that encourage the growth of Suzuki education. Perhaps the most important is the simple fact that man's basic need is to grow, and growth leads to health.

I believe that Talent Education has many positive traits that should be incorporated into music education and general education throughout the world. I have pointed out many strengths throughout this book. A system that offers such a well-organized repertoire of teaching materials and a thorough philosophical approach should be given careful consideration by all educators. A system that offers hope to even the most slowly developing child raises great optimism for the growth and education of greater numbers of people. When encouraged by leaders as optimistic as Suzuki, Talent Education could benefit mankind greatly, just as it has already greatly influenced music education. Certainly, educators in other fields should consider adapting Suzuki principles. I believe that those who will benefit most from Dr. Suzuki's ideas are those who share in his general optimism and hope:

> People say that I am trying to do the impossible and am expanding my energies for nothing. But I know that what I conceive is possible, and I believe that one day the human race will create the kind of world in which everyone will realize that children have the potential [to be] fine human beings, happy people, and people of superior ability.[175]

This book has discussed the history, the philosophy, and the method—in essence, the potentials of Talent Education. The next volume, *Is Suzuki Education Working in America?* will ask if the potentials are being fully realized and will answer with a strong "yes." This "yes," however will be qualified with concerns over some new directions needed in America's view of Talent Education as well as music and general education.

Appendix 1
Starting Young Pianists with the Suzuki Method

by Constance Starr*

After American string teachers were introduced to the Suzuki Talent Education method for the violin at the Music Educators National Conference in Philadelphia in 1964, it was natural that teachers of other instruments should become curious about its application to their field of teaching. Piano teachers, in particular, wanted to know if this method was being used by piano teachers in Japan. It was then discovered that the study of piano using Suzuki principles had been in existence almost as long as the string program, although there had been so little publicity about the work and its highly successful results that very few people were aware of the program's existence.

Suzuki's ideas germinated with his recognition of what he calls "mother-tongue" learning. If any normal child in any country is able to learn his native language, no matter how difficult that language may be, without textbook or teacher, then this surely proves that every normal child has a great sensitivity and ability to learn at a very early age, provided his environment is favorable. This discovery was the beginning of Talent Education.

Assisting Shinichi Suzuki in the development of the piano program were Mrs. Haruko Kataoka and Mrs. Shizuko Suzuki, sister-in-law of Mr. Suzuki. Both are excellent piano teachers, who have proven the efficiency of the method by the many competent students they have trained in Japan.

There are three important factors that must be present for young children to acquire the skill of playing a musical instrument, following Talent Education principles: listening and rote learning, the mother as home teacher, and the specific technical beginning. These factors, accompanied by slow, careful work, guarantee a high degree of success.

Suzuki says listening should begin at birth. The ideal climate is an environment saturated with music, perferably concentrating on a specific piece of music from the

*Reprinted from *Clavier*. (April 1972): 7–13, © The Instrumentalist Company, used by permission of The Instrumentalist Company. (The original article was reprinted in *Suzuki Piano School*, Volumes 1–2, 3–4, 1973 edition. The revised version, printed below, was included in the 1976 edition, published by Summy–Birchard Music Division of Birch Tree Group Ltd., Princeton, N.J. Used by permission.)

Baroque period. This is repeated again and again. Music from this period is harmonically simple and rhythmically vivid and identifiable. Even a very small infant shows recognition of a piece of music after he has heard it repeatedly. This, of course, is the ideal, and not always achieved in reality.

When the actual study of the piano begins, most frequently at age three or four, the child receives a recording of the music in *Suzuki Piano School*, Vol. 1. His instructions are to listen to the recording as often as possible. This listening may take place while the child plays, during his meals, or at bedtime as he is awaiting sleep. He absorbs the music without conscious attention, and it soon assumes the status of an old friend—perhaps in the category of a much-loved blanket or stuffed animal! As he begins to play the music he has been listening to, he will have an aural memory to aid his physical learning and a built-in error recognition system that should be infallible.

Now he is simulating his language learning experience. He has not been hampered by learning to read first. He has learned to use the language of music before he learns to read it. He has heard and been made aware of good tone quality, sensitive musical phrasing, and fine rhythmic execution. These will become part of this learning, as well as the musical ideas and notes. He will have the confidence of truly knowing the music—intellectually and musically.

Later, after his advancement into difficult classical repertoire, he will listen to many recordings made by different artists so that he may mature creatively in his own interpretation and execution.

The role of listening cannot be overemphasized. It is a unique departure from traditional teaching procedures. Talent Education success is greatly attributable to this listening and rote learning at the beginning of study. Mr. Suzuki has called listening "the most important training of musical ability." He can easily tell, he says, whether a student is doing the prescribed listening. It is difficult to impress the mothers, even Japanese mothers, with its importance. When Suzuki emphasizes that their children's progress depends upon the amount of listening they do, the mothers become more conscientious. The rapid progress made by the children enrolled in Talent Education in Japan (for example, five year olds playing Beethoven Sonata Opus 49, No. 2, and the two Minuets in Gigue from the B flat Partita of Bach) is traceable to this emphasis. This early training helps to make not just a skillful technical performer, but a fine and sensitive musician as well.

Rote learning, as used by Suzuki, comes from the listening and from the guidance of the mother. Through her intelligent attention at lessons and her referral to the Suzuki books, she is able to show notes and fingering to the child. The child should be allowed to pick out the tunes by himself if he is able and wants to do this. Then the mother must be a director of the learning, calmly pointing out notes, putting the proper finger in the right place, etc. Many Japanese mothers were observed with notebooks and copies of the music at the lessons and were making written notes of all the teacher's directions and suggestions.

THE MOTHER AS HOME TEACHER

The mother's role is a vital part of the necessary environment. Without adult supervision of the home practice between lessons, a young child or even an older beginner cannot progress as rapidly or as well as he is potentially able. The mother may not have had any formal music training, but she attends every lesson and listens attentively, trying to understand everything that the teacher requests of the student. In this way she can supervise all home practice. Rarely does the child practice alone until he has reached an advanced stage.

The Japanese teacher requests that the mother attend every lesson, and that she undertake seriously her role as a "home teacher." This, of course, includes the obligation to see that the child listens to his recording each day. Many Japanese mothers find the practicing and lesson attendance very enjoyable. Those who know little about music often spend time learning and studying so that they can give better assistance to their children.

It is the mother's job to find ways of motivating her child and keeping the practice times pleasant and rewarding. Many Western parents do not have a good general relationship with their children in other areas, so they don't find it easy to work well with them in the area of practice. This is an unfortunate situation. It can be overcome by effort and understanding; the rewards are gratifying and worthwhile.

BEGINNING TECHNIQUE

The beginning technical instruction, while certainly of primary importance in the learning of a skill, is postponed until the proper preparation has been accomplished.

First, it is necessary that the child be taught good posture. In Japan an adjustable chair is used for the student, but it is possible to use an artist's bench or any adjustable stool. The child must also have a footstool on which to rest his feet. The soles of the feet should rest comfortably on the stool. Stools of different heights are available for the Japanese students, so that each child can be accommodated. The child's posture must allow for maximum freedom and relaxation in his playing. He must not have unnecessary strain in any part of the body. For this reason he should sit with back straight and far enough away from the keyboard to allow him to lean slightly forward with arms hanging comfortably at his sides. The adjustment of height of chair and footstool is one of the ways the young pianist can compensate for not having a quarter or half-size piano available to him.

"Preparation" is a key word in this beginning training. Not one note is played during beginning instruction without careful preparation of posture and hand position. The teacher expects or hopes that there will also be mental preparation. (Suzuki often uses picturesque language when instructing children. "Don't start the car until the door is closed," he says.) When the teacher observes that the student is ready to play, she says "hai"—"yes" in Japanese.

The American child often finds this slow beginning difficult. He tends to be more impatient and eager to get on with playing. The teacher must realize that this preparation is important for the pupil's future development.

The small child delights in big motions. He likes to feel rhythms with his body. This is obvious in his love of action games involving music and motion. With this in mind, the use of arm action to achieve a tone when beginning at the keyboard answers the needs of the child as well as the demands of tone quality. The fingers of a four-year-old are too small and too weak to produce a tone of adequate volume and quality.

FIRST KEYBOARD EXPERIENCE

[note by R. L.—see Question 1 on p. 67 before reading the next section.]

The first variation of "Twinkle, Twinkle Little Star" in Suzuki Piano School, Vol. 1 is the child's introduction to the keyboard. The right hand begins first, most often using only the thumb at the first lesson.

The teacher plays   with the thumb on C above middle C (= 72–76). The teacher should play this variation at this brisk tempo when presenting it and the student should be expected to play at this tempo when performing it himself. From the beginning he must be encouraged to develop quick, fast movements. If he is allowed to play slowly and heavily, his movements become sluggish and he loses rhythmic feeling. The short, quick movements required to play this variation correctly are building the ability to think and move quickly. The hand should be relaxed and the thumb positioned so that it will touch the key on the spot at the side of the thumb next to the fingernail. It is important that the teacher keep the wrist straight, using the forearm and hand as a unit so that the tone is produced by the weight of the arm. Since the child's first action at the keyboard should be arm action, he will be confused if the teacher illustrates with only finger or wrist action.

Even though the curved position of the hand is ideal, some children will at first play with stiff and straight fingers. The teacher helps the child assume a better position by shaping the hand and placing it on the keyboard in a relaxed position in preparation for playing each individual note of "Twinkle." Soon his finger joints will become more firm. He will become more at ease at the keyboard and be able to relax his hand and retain the relaxed position without help while playing. Also, since the fifth finger is weak and in need of support, Japanese teachers allow beginners to play on the side of this finger. This must be corrected as soon as possible. The four-year-old often has a very weak fifth finger, but with encouragement to work on keeping it in an upright position like the other fingers, he will gradually be able to accomplish this important step.

Some children may be able to imitate the teacher's arm action, tone, rhythm, and tempo after observing the teacher demonstrate a few times. If the child needs further help, the teacher may take the child's right hand in her right hand, holding his thumb between her thumb and middle finger and guiding his forearm with her left hand. In this way she may guide his hand and arm as he plays. She may do this a few times, then allow him to rest while she plays for him again. If his tone is harsh, he is probably "pushing" as he depresses the key instead of allowing the weight of the arm to help produce the tone. This may sometimes be explained to an older child, but he can best achieve the desired result solely by listening and watching. This procedure may have to be repeated again and again. Each effort should be preceded by careful preparation as mentioned above.

This same instruction should be given each time a new finger is introduced, second finger on D, third finger on E, etc.

A soon as the child can do this with some ease, he may practice the interval at the beginning of the "Twinkle" melody. He plays the 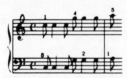 with the thumb on C. Then the teacher moves the child's hand so that the fourth finger is poised above G, and he plays the same pattern on G. He may then try this by himself, but always with the stop and preparation between the notes. If necessary the teacher may point to the G key from beneath the child's hand until he is able to find this easily by himself. Following this he may be instructed to play the entire first phrase, taking time before playing each note to prepare and poise the hand properly. With a very young child this may take many lessons. The student may practice the five-finger exercise and the first phrase of "Twinkle" for some time before advancing. He may then play the entire first variation, with a stop before each change of note. Only after this preparation does he play the first variation continuously as it is written.

As the child begins Variation II, which features legato touch, he may need more guidance. The teacher again shows the student how to hold the hand in a relaxed position, fingers rounded, hand, wrist, and arm level.

Variation II

A flexible wrist is used on the quarter note. As the finger depresses the key, the wrist and arm flex downward until they are approximately on a level with the key, then raise slightly as the key is held. On the following eighth note, the wrist and arm return to the previous level position and are played with the same action as that of Variation I. The child may be asked to rest his hand on top of the teacher's hand as she plays, so that he will be able to feel the slight rise and fall that occurs.

Variation III

When the student begins Variation III he plays it similarly to the first variation with forearm action, no motion in the wrist. He is usually asked to play with a softer tone using less arm action than in Variation I. As he advances he may begin to use a flexible wrist action in this variation, but should not be expected to do so in the beginning.

"TWINKLE MELODY"

The "Twinkle" melody comes at the end of the variations. Here the student uses the previously mentioned technique of Variation II, which will apply to all legato playing. Once again the wrist flexes and the arm moves downward as the key is depressed and rises slightly while it is held; the next key is depressed on the following downward motion to produce a smooth line with a consistent tone quality.

It is the extensive use of relaxed arm action in the early period of instruction that enables the small hand to move around the keyboard with ease. As the student matures physically and advances musically, he uses less arm motion. The large motion is no longer needed, but natural arm weight with the wrist as the shock absorber to achieve tonal beauty and power remains an important element of the advanced student's technique.

It should be noted here that writers on piano technique have pointed out the many sins committed in the past in the pursuit of weight and relaxation at the keyboard. This use of arm weight must not be exaggerated or developed without accompanying emphasis on strong independent finger action. It is only the intelligent combination of the two techniques that will produce the desired results—fine tone and facile fingers.

Those who have heard performances by Japanese children are well aware of their fine, clean passage work. It is obvious that there has been emphasis in their training on firm finger joints and strong finger action.

CONTINUED STUDY OF THE FIRST PIECE

A small child should continue studying these right hand variations for as long as he needs to accomplish the requirements. He may then add the variations for the left hand to be learned in the same manner. The student may go on to learn more of the right hand melodies of the pieces following "Twinkle" while he continues to do only the variations with the left hand. The review and continued practice of these variations should go on as he is progressing into more advanced work so that he will improve and reinforce his previous learning.

As the variations are presented in Volume I, it would seem that beginning students are required to play with two hands together immediately. In fact, this is not the case. Begining students play all of the "Twinkle" variations at the lesson with only one hand, often accompanied by the teacher. (This is the general procedure with all students.) After the child has become proficient with each hand separately, he may then play hands together.

After "Twinkle" a few pieces are presented with two hands playing the same melody, two octaves apart. From then on the little pieces are simple five-finger melodic lines with simple left-hand accompaniment. The standard procedure is to allow the child to begin as many of these melodies as he desires, with the mother's assistance as needed for correct notes, fingering, etc. He may be able to pick out the melodies by himself, or the mother may play small sections of the melody for him so that he can watch and imitate. If necessary she may point out the correct keys to him. He practices the right-hand melodies many times after he has learned the notes and fingering, often with mother or teacher playing the left-hand along with him. In that way the learning of the sound the two parts together is reinforced. The child is carried along by the secure accompaniment of the other part. Now the left hand follows the same learning pattern.

The average child's first effort at playing hands together is laborious and very slow. Most children soon overcome this difficulty and progress more rapidly after successfully playing a few pieces hands together. It is important that parent and child understand that the part of each hand must be known very well before the two parts are played together. If the child practices slowly and carefully when first putting the two parts together, already knowing each line well separately, there will be a minimum of difficulty. This is a time for much encouragement from both parent and teacher.

GRADUATION PIECES

The students are expected to study all of the music in the order given. As goals throughout this study there are "graduation" pieces. In Japan, when a student has completed the study of a graduation piece, he makes a tape recording of his performance which is sent to Mr. Suzuki, who listens to it and returns it to the teacher with recorded instructive comments.

The graduation pieces used in Japan are:

I.   Minuet No. 2, Bach—Vol. II
II.   Two Minuets and Gigue, B flat Partita, Bach—Vol. IV
III.   Turkish Rondo from Sonata, A major, K. 331, Mozart—Vol. VI
IV.   Italian Concerto, Bach
V.   "Coronation" concerto, Mozart, or Sonata, F minor ("Appassionata"), Beethoven [Note by R. L.: See updated list on p. 39.]

Any teacher can adopt this graduation idea as a motivational aid if he wishes, using these pieces of music or working out his own plan.

TIMING OF GRADE LEVELS

In Japan quite a few five-year-old students submit graduation tapes of the Bach B flat Partita after having studied one and a half to two years. Since this music is at the end of Vol. 4, the rate of advancement seems fantastic.

Similar examples of fast progress were observed—a seven-year-old who had studied three and a half years, playing the Turkish Rondo; an eight year old, who had studied three years and eight months played the Italian Concerto.

Enough children progress at a fast rate to be quite impressive. If only one or two students showed such ability, they might be called prodigies and the matter dismissed, but when many students make comparable progress, it is certainly noteworthy.

Not only the difficulty of the pieces but the quality of the performance is impressive. Many of these children play with as much or more sensitivity and technical facility than students far more advanced in years. One college teacher, upon viewing a video-tape performance by a five-year-old said, "How I wish some of my students could play as well!"

LESSON SCHEDULE

In the very beginning it is considered necessary for the student to have two short lessons per week. When the teacher observes that the student has established good practice habits and the mother has established good practice habits and the mother has become a reliable home teacher, twice a week supervision is not necessary. The time to change to one lesson a week must be decided by the teacher.

The lessons are arranged so that parent and child are present at the lessons of other students. Each student must consider attending lessons of others as part of his own lesson. Students spend the waiting time watching and listening to other students, sometimes reading or doing homework but in a spot where it is possible to absorb from the environment. This kind of atmosphere accustoms the child to playing in the presence of others and helps to motivate him through hearing the performance of more advanced students.

There is a disadvantage for the first group of beginning students of a teacher using the Suzuki method. There are no advanced students to stimulate the beginners to want to play. Mr. Suzuki places great stress on the importance of this part of the environment. He suggests, therefore, that the beginning group of students should be varied ages. If they are all four-year-olds, for example, their rate of progress will often be similar. But if the ages are varied, some four, fives, sixes and sevens— perhaps even eights and nines—the older children, who may naturally make more rapid progress, will soon begin to provide some of the necessary motivational environment.

The length of the lesson is variable. A very young child may have only a two or three minute lesson if his attention span is short; even an older child may not be able to concentrate more than five minutes. Of course, at the beginning the lessons of each child must be short because the material studied is limited. It is most necessary to have the parent understand this variability in the lesson period from the start. The American parent is accustomed to measuring the value of the lesson by the time spent. He may feel that he is paying for, and should receive, a certain amount of the teacher's time. However, if the student shows a lack of concentration and attention, nothing is to be gained by spending longer time with the teacher. Teacher, student, and parent are accomplishing nothing.

Since the studio is always full of students and parents during the lesson time of each child, the atmosphere is more relaxed than in the usual private music lesson. Yet in Japan, when it is the child's turn to take his lesson, his concentration is so intense that activity can be going on in the studio and he shows no sign of distraction!

Actually, most American children can develop more concentration than is usually thought possible. Mr. Suzuki believes this is a gradual process and that concentration periods become progressively longer as the child, even a very young child, progresses in his study.

The mother's role has already been described in some detail. At the lesson she is seated at the left of the student, as the teacher sits at the right. The mother should consider that she is taking a lesson, a lesson to teach her what her "homework" will be. Not one Japanese mother was ever observed reading a magazine or doing needlework during her child's lesson. In fact, the mothers also always watch other children's lessons closely.

HOME PRACTICE

It is the tendency of mothers to try to prolong the home practice beyond the length of the child's concentration ability. Just as the teacher terminates the lesson when concentration stops, so must the mother terminate home practice. It is better to plan two, or three, or more short periods of careful practice during a day than one long period which might result in careless work.

REPETITION—REINFORCEMENT

An important Suzuki principle is that of repetition or reinforcement. After a child has learned a piece, he does not drop it when he is able to play it acceptably. Indeed, quite the opposite, for only when he knows the notes and fingerings can he improve his musicianship and tone quality. So as he goes on to play new music, he continues to use the past music for this development. This includes the development of speed and greater facility. In this way, he always has a performing repertoire of many pieces, and he plays them well enough to enjoy playing them.

Some teachers have questioned the ability of the student to do this repetition without getting bored. This will not usually be a problem, even with American students, unless the parent or teacher first expresses such boredom.

All of the students, especially the young ones, are pleased by repetition. Besides, they are not just repeating, they are trying to improve! There is a marvelous feeling of security in being able to do something well and being aware of it. It is an excellent way to build confidence in one's ability.

MOTIVATION

Motivation is almost always a problem for the teacher and parent. Japanese teachers and parents often meet together to discuss and share ideas about motivation. There are some parents whose creative approach is very helpful to their child. They are naturally excellent home teachers who are able to find ways to stimulate their child's desire to practice and play well. In these meetings they are able to share their ideas with other parents. This can be a great help to all.

Mr. Suzuki feels that natural motivation is provided by the recordings and by the attendance of the child at lessons of other children. The standardized repertoire is also a source of motivation, because the child often wants to play a certain piece of music that he has heard. If this piece is some distance ahead in the book, he may work hard to study the music that precedes it so that he may be able to play the desired piece.

Although competition permeates every facet of life, it is not considered a source of motivation in Suzuki training. Teacher or parent should never compare one child with another. The child should be taught from the beginning that any competition is only with himself, that he must practice and work hard to play as well as he possibly can. If he is listening to the recordings, the high standards set for him also provide necessary goals.

PLAYING FOR THE STUDENT

The Suzuki teacher does a great deal of playing both for the child and with the child. It is better when working with a young child to limit the amount of verbal explanation and emphasize the demonstration. The Japanese teachers do much playing alongside of the child because they feel that he is more apt to understand and copy a relaxed way of playing if he sees it done than if it is explained to him. With a beginner, playing in the upper register of the same piano by the teacher is most effective.

SPEED AND FACILITY

American teachers have expressed amazement at the speed and facility displayed by the young Japanese Suzuki piano students. Mr. Suzuki says that teachers must change their idea that young children cannot play fast. "Don't make special compensations for children," he says. "They can do what most adults can do." He feels that teachers have kept children from playing fast because they felt it could not be done.

It is true that slow, careful practice is required while learning, but this is to insure that the student will have the preparation necessary to play the piece at the proper tempo for performance. If the student has a relaxed, well-established technique and has done much listening, his background should be excellent. Once he is able to play a piece at a slow, careful tempo, then a fast, accurate performance will result naturally as he continues to practice this same piece, gradually increasing the tempo.

RATE OF ADVANCEMENT

Naturally, there is no prescribed length of time it will take to complete any of the volumes. A child of four will probably progress more slowly than one of seven or older. Some three- and four-year-olds work on only "Twinkle" for as long as a year! Most of the students observed progressed more rapidly.

The rate of progress depends on many things. How much correct practicing a child does or is capable of doing will be most important. The maturity of the child will be the deciding factor, regardless of age. Good home teaching by the mother and extensive listening to the recordings by the pupil have a great effect on speeding up progress.

READING MUSIC

It is essential that the child not begin reading music until he has mastered the beginning technique, until his ear has been trained to recognize good tone quality, and until he has become sensitive to musical phrasing. If the reading is begun too soon, a good foundation may never be built, or it may topple if it is not yet well established.

Usually by the time the pupil reaches Volume 2, he should have a good foundation in technique, tone, and musicianship; then note reading may be begun.

Music reading can be introduced by using books ordinarily given to the beginning piano student who is taught in a traditional manner. There are no special books designated for this purpose in Suzuki training. The most important factor in the choice of materials for this purpose is the size of the printed notes and symbols. These must be large for the small child or he cannot easily differentiate between line and space notes, etc. As he progresses, he may also use the music he already knows in Book I to associate signs and symbols with their sound and duration.

Reading is not taught by finger number because this creates problems and habits that must be broken later if one is to become a proficient reader. Even after the student becomes a capable reader, he performs all music from memory at his lessons. Because of his previous training, this is not difficult for him. It is just considered normal procedure.

PEDALING

Since the Suzuki student has been taught to produce a smooth legato line in his beginning training, it is not necessary to consider pedaling until his advancement beyond Volume 4. When pedal is required, a very young child must use a pedaling device that allows him to pedal without strain. This is only a problem with the student who progresses so rapidly that his physical growth does not match his musical advancement.

TONALIZATION

The word "tonalization" was coined by Mr. Suzuki a few years ago. He wanted to apply to instrumentalists the same kind of training that vocalists receive in their vocalization exercises.

The pupil's ear must be trained to recognize beautiful tone quality and then he must constantly be instructed in the method of producing fine tone. This is the goal of tonalization instruction.

Lines (||||||||||) appear between the notes in many of the early pieces. These stress the need for continuing good tone quality from note to note, the continuous "singing" of the tone. When these lines occur across phrases they do not mean that phrasing is to be ignored, but only that the tone must continue a singing quality from phrase to phrase. This is a visual reminder of the much mentioned "tonalization."

PATIENCE AND PRAISE

Mr. Suzuki has said that the word "patience" should never be applied to the learning experience by either teacher or parent. Patience has the connotation of controlled frustration; yet the parent, in particular, should enjoy the learning process. He must be helped to understand that the learning process of a small child is often very slow, but that every effort, every step, no matter how small, should be a pleasure to watch.

Very few parents show impatience when an infant is learning to walk or to talk. They realize that the child has an inner timetable and that he will progress at his own rate. Yet when the child begins the learning of a skill, the attitude changes. Many parents become overanxious and impatient, and want to push their children. This is no pleasant experience for either child or parent. The parent is usually irritable and quick-tempered and the child is tense and loses confidence.

In place of criticism, praise should be plentiful. Mr. Suzuki says that all mothers seem to find it difficult to praise their children. Yet no matter how bad a performance may be, there is always some small aspect of it that can be praised. Perhaps his posture was good, his rhythm steady, or may be he struggled to complete the piece. A sincere "good" in response to even this small effort can build confidence and, perhaps most important of all, stimulate a desire to do better. Mr. Suzuki often says "Good. Now let's try to do better!" or "Good. Now let's try to do it this way." This positive response makes a student feel able and eager to improve.

Even though the mother or teacher may find it difficult to change her natural negative responses, she will find any effort to do this well-rewarded by the student's improved cooperation.

SUZUKI AND WESTERN CULTURE

As with all innovative educational ideas, there is disagreement among educators about the merits of Suzuki training. But since creative and sincere teachers are always on the lookout for new ideas to make teaching more effective, they shouldn't dismiss any without thorough investigation and evaluation.

One such idea, that of rote learning, is a source of concern to many teachers. They fear that the student's ability to read music will never develop or will suffer because of this beginning period of playing by rote, yet can it be truthfully said that most children taught to read at the outset of study become excellent sight-readers? If the reading of music is begun seriously after the student has acquired beginning skills, and if reading is made an integral part of study from then on, the possibility of the child's becoming an excellent sight-reader should be as good as that of the student who has read from the beginning.

There are those who say that the ethnic difference in the Oriental and Western cultures make adoption of these ideas difficult in the United States. It is true that a direct transplant is not always feasible. American children are not as quick to accept the teacher's requests or instruction without question, they are more easily distracted, and their diverse activities make serious work and rapid progress less possible.

These negative observations may have some validity. But that does not discount the fact that, in spite of these seeming handicaps, many American children taught according to Suzuki principles have been able to develop into fine musicians and skillful performers—with greater ease and more enjoyment than when taught by traditional procedures.

As a teacher, I found these ideas so exciting that, even with limited time available, I could not wait to experiment. Here I found the most gratifying, enjoyable teaching experience that I had ever had the opportunity to know. Since we are not preoccupied with note-reading, we can concentrate on establishing a solid technique and on training the ear to listen to tone. Too many piano students do not seem to be aware of the existence of "good" or "bad" piano tone. At the same time, it is possible to teach music-phrasing and dynamics—the vital parts of musical expression—very early in the student's career. Also, since the child continues to use well-learned pieces for his musical and technical refinement, he has the advantage of having a playing repertoire at all times. With features such as these, the Suzuki method deserves serious consideration by our Western world!

* * *

Constance Starr formerly taught at the University of Tennessee, Knoxville. She received her degree in piano from the Eastman School of Music. In 1968,

Mrs. Starr, with her husband and children, went to Matsumoto, Japan, where the family spent thirteen months at Shinichi Suzuki's Talent Education Institute. While there, she prepared a series of videotapes showing both piano instruction and performance. Mrs. Starr is co-author of the college text, *Basic Piano Technique for the Classroom Teacher*.

Mrs. Starr has recently published *The Music Road*, a series of three books designed to teach theory, ear-training, and sight-reading as a supplement to the Suzuki piano books. Available from Kingston Ellis Press, 1014 Freemason Street, Knoxville, Tennessee 37917.

Appendix 2

Suzuki Piano Method—New and Effective Education in Music

Introductory Remarks by Dr. Suzuki, Presented at the Beginning of Volume 1 of the *Suzuki Piano School*

Through the experience I have gained by conducting experiments in teaching young children for over thirty years, I have come to the definite conclusion that musical ability is not an inborn talent but an ability which can be developed. Any child, properly trained, can develop musical ability just as all children in the world have developed the ability to speak their mother tongue. Children learn the nuances of their mother tongue through repeated listening, and the same process should be followed in the development of an ear for music. Every day children should listen to the recordings of the music which they are studying or about to study. This listening helps them to make rapid progress. The children will begin to try their best to play as well as the performer on the recording. By this method the child will grow into an adult with fine musical sense. It is the most important training of musical ability.

Tonalization: The word "tonalization" is a new word coined to apply to violin training as an equivalent to vocalization in vocal training. Tonalization has produced wonderful results in violin education. It should be equally effective in piano and all instrumental education.

Tonalization is the instruction given the pupil, as he learns each new piece of music, to help him produce a beautiful tone and to use meaningful musical expression. We must train the pupil to develop a musical ear that is able to recognize a beautiful tone. He must then be taught how to reproduce the beautiful tone and fine musical expression of the piano artists of the past and present.

IMPORTANT POINTS IN TEACHING

(1) What is the best way to make a pupil enjoy learning and practicing? This is the principal problem for the teacher and parents, that of motivating the child properly so that he will enjoy practicing correctly at home. They should discuss this matter together, considering and examining each case in order to help the child enjoy the lessons and practice. They should be sensitive to the state of mind of the child. Forcing the child every day, saying "Practice, practice, practice," is the worst method of education and only makes the child hate practicing.

(2) In addition to daily practice at home, the pupil should listen to the recording of the piece he is learning every day and as often as possible. This should be habitual. Progress will be very rapid. Six days a week of practice and listening at home will be more decisive in determining the child's rate of advancement than one or two lessons a week.

(3) The pupil should always play without music at the lessons. This is the most important factor in improving the pupil's memory. It also speeds the pupil's progress.

Instruction in music reading should be given according to the pupil's age and capability. It is very important for the pupil to learn to read music well, but if the child is forced to read music at the very outset of this study, and always practices with music, he will, in performance, feel quite uneasy playing from memory and therefore will not be able to show his full ability.

In acquiring a skill, ability grows through daily habit. In learning his mother tongue, the child begins to read only after he is able to speak. The same approach should be followed in music. Music reading should be taught only after the child's musical sensitivity, playing skill, and memory have been sufficiently trained. Even after they have acquired the ability to read music, however, the children as a rule play from memory at all lessons.

(4) When a pupil gets to the stage where he can play a piece without a mistake in notes or fingering, the time is ripe for cultivating his musicianship. I would say to the child, "Now you are ready. We can start very important work to develop your ability," and then I would proceed to teach a beautiful tone, fine phrasing, and musical sensitivity. The quality of the pupil's performance depends greatly on the teacher's constant attention to these important musical points.

The following point is very important. When the child can perform piece A satisfactorily and is given a new piece, B, he should not drop A but practice both A and B at the same time. This procedure should continue as new pieces are added. He should always be reviewing pieces that he knows well in order to develop his ability to a higher degree.

(5) Mothers and children should always watch private lessons of other children. This is an added motivation. When the child hears music played well by other children, he will want to be able to play as well, and so his desire to practice will increase.

Lessons should vary in length according to the need of the child. The attention span of the child should be taken into account. If the small child is able to concentrate only for a short time, it is better to shorten the lesson time until he is more adaptable. At one time the lesson may be only five minutes, at another, thirty minutes.[176]

Explanatory Note about the Suzuki Piano Method as formerly presented by Summy-Birchard Company at the beginnings of Volumes 1–2 and 3–4 of the *Suzuki Piano School*. (These notes are no longer included in the International Editions.)

Shinichi Suzuki's philosophy of Talent Education, first developed in relation to the violin, can apply to the study of any instrument. The basic idea is that children learn to make music as they learn their mother tongue, through hearing it spoken, imitating the sounds, and gradually attaching meaning to them. Learning is based on listening.

The preface to Suzuki Piano School sets forth these general principles and offers helpful suggestions to teacher, parent, and child. The suggestions are not detailed and specific, however, since Suzuki does not believe in confining the teacher to a rigid plan of instruction. But many piano teachers, especially those who know little, if anything, about Suzuki violin teaching, are puzzled by certain aspects of the Suzuki piano books and may have questions which they don't find answered in the text.

We undertook to obtain answers from sources who had been able to observe Suzuki piano teaching at firsthand as it is carried on in Japan. These included Constance Starr, University of Tennessee, whose husband William worked closely with Dr. Suzuki during the year they were in Japan, and Julian Leviton, DePaul University, Chicago. Both interviewed Mrs. Kataoka, who with Shizuko Suzuki, sister-in-law of Dr. Suzuki, developed the piano method under his guidance. We also spoke with Misako Yanagida, accompanist for the 1971 Talent Education tour of Suzuki Japanese children, who participated in the Suzuki Institute teacher training program.

Q. Do Japanese children trained in the Suzuki piano method start lessons at a very early age as do Suzuki violin students?
A. Yes, as early as the age of three or four.

Q. How can a three-year-old handle the piano? Outside of toys, there aren't small-scale pianos as there are fractional-size violins.
A. By using arm action rather than finger action. Like the "mother-tongue" approach, this too is according to natural development. The infant makes large movements at first and only gradually learns to make finger movements with small muscles.

Q. Granted that a small child can play isolated notes with arm action, how can he manage stretches? For instance, the very first piece, "Twinkle, Twinkle, Little Star," requires a stretch of a 5th between thumb and 4th finger.
A. By moving his arm sideways to position his fingers for the interval.

Q. Is there any other purpose in using arm-action exercises?
A. Yes. Such exercises are excellent for developing firm finger joints.

Q. But won't this type of practice cause percussive sounding tone?
A. No, for two reasons. First, listening is the heart of all Suzuki teaching. The student constantly listens to the reference recordings, which are models of good tone. He also practices tonalization exercises in which he concentrates on producing a beautiful singing legato.

Q. While it is possible to teach a beginner to play single melodies by ear and imitation, how can he learn to play hands together when the left-hand pattern is different from that of the right?
A. He learns the right-hand melody and left-hand pattern separately, then puts them together, always helped by listening to the recordings.

Q. When should reading be introduced?
A. In the Suzuki violin method, reading instruction begins by the end of Vol. 4. Because of the differences between single-line violin music and more complex piano music, however, reading is introduced earlier for piano students—by the end of Vol. 1.

Q. If reading isn't introduced until the end of Vol. 1, why does the child need to have the book at all?

A. Reading isn't introduced abruptly. The child learns the names of the keys at the outset. Then after he learns a piece by ear and imitation, he is encouraged to look at the symbols for what he has played. Gradually, he begins to associate these symbols with the keyboard. In this way he teaches himself to read—far more successfully than if a method of reading is imposed on him that he doesn't find natural.

Q. Is reading ever taught by finger numbers?

A. No. Fingering is given for technical purposes only. This is obvious, since in the very first piece, "Twinkle, Twinkle, Little Star," the 4th finger is used on two different keys.

Q. What is the meaning of the lines connecting notes (I I I I I I I) found in Vols. 1, 2, and 3?

A. These are to bring out the idea of tonalization.

Q. Why do these lines sometimes not coincide with the phrase marks?

A. Because the idea of legato often carries over to the next phrase, especially at the half cadence, and there shouldn't be an abrupt break between phrases. Occasionally, the connecting lines suggest alternate phrasings.

Q. Does every student have to study everything in each volume and in the order given?

A. Yes. The sequence is very carefully planned for development of the child's technical and musical expression. However, after the student finishes Vol. 1 and has some reading ability, he may be given additional material to supplement the basic method.

Q. When should pedal be introduced?

A. Not until Vol. 6. All pieces in the earlier books sound well without pedal. By not using pedal, the child learns to play cleanly and to produce legato with his hands rather than with the pedal.

Q. How long should it take to complete Vol. 1?

A. This depends entirely on the maturity of the child. Obviously, a three-year-old is going to progress far more slowly than an older child.[177]

These notes are reprinted by the kind permission of Summy-Birchard Music Division of Birth Tree Group Ltd., Princeton, N.J. Copyright 1978, Zen-On Music Co., Ltd., Tokyo. Summy-Birchard Music holds the copyright for the entire world (except Japan) for all existing works for the violin, piano, cello, flute, and viola, each written, arranged, or compiled by Dr. Suzuki or the Talent Training Research Institute (of which Dr. Suzuki is chairman) and published under the trademark the Suzuki™ Method. Summy-Birchard Music will acquire rights upon creation of each work for the copyright for the entire world (except Japan) for additional musical works or works of music guidance composed or written by Dr. Suzuki intended for inclusion in the Suzuki™ Method.

Notes

1. Shinichi Suzuki, *Nurtured by Love*, trans. Waltraud Suzuki, (Smithtown, N.Y.: Exposition Press, 1969), p. 8.

2. Ibid., p. 85.

3. Ibid., p. 73.

4. Ibid., p. 74.

5. Ibid., p. 75.

6. Ibid., p. 38.

7. Masaaki Honda, *A Program for Early Development* (Tokyo: Early Development Association Press, 1972), pp. 50–51.

8. Elizabeth Mills and Murphey, Therese, Sister, ed., *The Suzuki Concept* (Berkeley: Diablo Press, 1973), jacket notes. It is difficult to make an accurate estimate because of the lack of centralized records.

9. Cary Beth Hackett, "From the Editor's Desk," *American Suzuki Journal*, Institute Issue, Volume 8, No. 2, 1980, p. 3.

10. Honda, *Early Development*, p. 3.

11. Ibid., p. 3.

12. Ibid., p. 2.

13. Ibid., p. 4.

14. Suzuki, *Love*, pp. 27–29.

15. Ibid., pp. 101–2.

16. Ibid., p. 75.

17. Ibid., p. 95.

18. Shinichi Suzuki, *Where Love Is Deep*, trans. Kyodo Selden, (St. Louis: Talent Education Journal, 1982), pp. 33–34.

19. Ibid., pp. 11–13.

20. Suzuki, *Love*, pp. 106–7.

21. Clifford Cook, *Suzuki Education in Action* (Smithtown, N.Y.: Exposition Press, 1970), pp. 31–32.

22. Constance Starr, "Starting Young Pianists with the Suzuki Method," *Clavier* 9 (April 1972): 6–13. Revised and published in *Suzuki Piano School*, Volumes 1–2 and 3–4 (1976), p. 10. Page numbers here and in subsequent references to this article are to the revision as found in Volumes 1–2, *Piano School* (1976). (After 1976, this article was no longer published in the *Piano School*.)

23. Suzuki, *Love*, pp. 110–11.

24. Honda, *Early Development*, p. 23.

25. Ibid., p. 28.

26. Ibid., p. 20.

27. Starr, "Suzuki Method," p. 15.

28. Ibid., p. 14.

29. Suzuki, *Love*, p. 56.

30. Honda, *Early Development*, p. 32.

31. Lorraine Fink, "The Suzuki Graduation System: A Unique Process," *Suzuki World*, March–April, 1983, p. 6.

32. Quoted in Honda, *Early Development*, p. 34.

33. Ideas of Mrs. Kataoka's that are mentioned are based on observations and question-answer periods held with her while I was in Japan in 1972; or at the American Suzuki Institute, University of Wisconsin at Steven's Point, 1978–80; or at the Third International Suzuki Convention, San Francisco State University, California, 1978.

34. Starr, "Suzuki Method," p. 9.

35. For example, group classes have been attempted at the American Suzuki Institute, University of Wisconsin, Steven's Point.

36. See Michiko Yurko, *No H in Snake: Music Theory for Children* (Sherman Oaks, Calif: Alfred, 1978).

37. Haruko Kataoka, Shizuko Suzuki, and Shinichi Suzuki, *Suzuki Piano School* (Tokyo: Zen-On Music Publishers, 1970, and Evanston: Summy-Birchard Company, 1973 and 1976: revised International Edition, 1978).

38. All page numbers refer to the 1978 International Edition.

39. Starr, "Suzuki Method," pp. 10–11. This article is printed in its entirety in the Appendix, pp. 133–44.

40. Ibid., p. 10.

41. Letter from Mrs. Starr to the author, September 27, 1973.

42. *Suzuki Piano School*, Volume 3–4, 1970–73 editions, p. 9.

43. Starr, "Suzuki Method," p. 12.

44. Nancy Greenwood Brooks, "Toward a Deeper Understanding of Suzuki Pedagogy," *American Music Teacher*, September/October, 1980, p. 20 and November/December, 1980, p. 26.

45. Evelyn Hermann, *Shinichi Suzuki: The Man and His Philosophy* (Athens, Ohio: Ability Development Press, 1981), pp. 226–27 (quoted from an address that Dr. Suzuki delivered to the Congress of the United States in 1978).

46. Ibid., pp. 171–72 (quoted from an article, "The Law of Ability," by Dr. Suzuki).

47. Ibid., pp. 146–47 (quoted from an address that Dr. Suzuki delivered to the Music Educators National Conference in 1964).

48. Write the Suzuki Association of the Americas (Batterson Building, 319 E. Second St., Suite 302, Muscatine, Iowa 52761), for the brochures, *Would You Like to Start a Suzuki Program?* and *Suzuki Teaching: A Career for You?* (1978). The philosophy and attitudes are quoted from the second brochure.

49. These requirements and the evaluation forms on the next page are from the By-Laws of the Suzuki Music Academy of Chicago. The requirements and teacher evaluation were written by Ray Landers with the assistance of board members.

50. Suzuki Music Academy of Chicago By-Laws, 1980.

51. Edwin Reischauer, *The Japanese* (Cambridge, Mass: Belknap Press of Harvard University Press, 1977), pp. 383–84, 386.

52. Betty Edwards, *Drawing on the Right Side of the Brain* (Los Angeles: J. P. Tarcher, 1979), p. 40.

53. See also Julian Jaynes, *The Origin of Consciousness in the Breakdown of the Bicameral Mind* (Boston: Houghton Mifflin Co., 1976).

54. Reischauer, *The Japanese*, pp. 138–39.

55. This lecture, originally published in the Nagoya Chapter Suzuki Newsletter, is published in *Where Love Is Deep*, pp. 35–36.

56. Jeanne Luedke, "Unit A–Again," *American Suzuki Journal*, April 1983, p. 7.

57. For the authors discussed in this chapter, refer to the general index on p. 183.

58. John Gardner, *Excellence: Can We Be Equal and Excellent Too?* (New York: Harper & Row, 1971), p. 191.

59. Ibid., pp. 191–93.

60. Ibid., pp. 100–2.

61. Ibid., p. 120.

62. Ibid., p. 163.

63. Ibid., pp. 178–80.

64. E. F. Schumacher, *A Guide for the Perplexed* (New York: Harper & Row, 1977), p. 122.

65. Ibid., p. 122.

66. Ibid., p. 124.

67. Maya Pines, *Revolution in Learning (The Years from Birth to Six)* (New York: Harper & Row, 1967), p. 16.

68. Ibid., p. 16.

69. Ibid., p. 17.

70. Ibid., p. 22.

71. Ibid., p. 22.

72. Ibid., p. 46.

73. Ibid., p. 46.

74. Suzuki, *Love*, pp. 9–11.

75. Masaru Ibuka, *Kindergarten Is Too Late* (New York: Simon and Schuster, 1977), p. 19.

76. Pines, *Revolution*, pp. 47–48.

77. Ibid., p. 52.

78. Ibid., p. 55.

79. Ibid., p. 55.

80. Ibid., p. 56.

81. Ibid., p. 57.

82. Ibid., p. 57.

83. Sister Cecilia Schmitt, "The Thought-Life of the Young Child," *Music Educators Journal*, December 1971, p. 24.

84. Ruth M. Beard, *An Outline of Piaget's Developmental Psychology* (New York: Basic Books, 1969), p. 117. The preceding paragraphs on Piaget's developmental stages were summarized in part from chapters 5 and 6 of Beard's book.

85. Pines, *Revolution*, p. 58.

86. Ibid., p. 58.

87. Ibid., p. 59.

88. Erich Fromm, *The Anatomy of Human Destructiveness* (New York: Fawcett Crest Books, 1973), p. 412.

89. Pines, *Revolution*, p. 61.

90. Ibid., p. 62.

91. Ibid., pp. 62–63.

92. Ibid., p. 63.

93. Ibid., p. 63.

94. J. McV. Hunt, *Intelligence and Experience* (New York: Ronald Press, 1961).

95. Pines, *Revolution*, p. 64.

96. Ibid., p. 64.

97. Ibid., p. 65.

98. Ibid., p. 66.

99. Frank Goble, *The Third Force* (New York: Simon and Schuster, Inc., 1971), p. 26.

100. Pines, *Revolution*, pp. 94–95.

101. Ibid., p. 96.

102. Ibid., pp. 97–102.

103. Ibid., p. 107.

104. Ibid., p. 107.

105. Ibid., p. 109.

106. Ibid., p. 111.

107. Ibid., pp. 114–15.

108. Ibid., p. 115.

109. Ibid., p. 69.

110. Ibid., pp. 69–70.

111. Ibid., p. 70.

112. Ibid., p. 71.

113. Ibid., pp. 75–77.

114. Ibid., p. 79.

115. Ibid., p. 81.

116. Ibid., pp. 81, 82, 84.

117. Ibid., p. 85.

118. Ibid., p. 91.

119. This summary of Glenn Doman's ideas is based on the article "Bringing Up Superbaby" *Newsweek*, March 28, 1963, p. 62.

120. This and following quotes from Doman are from the Foreword to Ibuka, *Kindergarten Is Too Late*, pp. 8–11.

121. Pines, *Revolution*, p. 128.

122. Ibid., p. 129.

123. Ibid., p. 129.

124. Ibid., p. 132.

125. Ibid., pp. 132–34.

126. Ibid., pp. 134–36.

127. Ibid., pp. 141–43.

128. Ibid., pp. 145–46.

129. Charles Leerhsen and Aynko Doi, "How the Japanese Do It," *Newsweek*, May 9, 1983, p. 54.

130. Pines, *Revolution*, pp. 174–75.

131. Ibid., p. 185.

132. Ibid., p. 205.

133. Ibid., p. 206.

134. Ibid., p. 207.

135. John Kendall, *The Suzuki Violin Method in American Music Education* (Washington: Music Education National Conference Press, 1973), p. 13.

136. James Bastien, *How to Teach Piano Successfully* (Park Ridge, Ill.: Neil Kjos Co., 1973), p. 131.

137. Ibid., see chapter 5.

138. Pines, *Revolution*, p. 217.

139. Peter Farb, *Word Play—What Happens When People Talk* (New York: Bantam Books, 1973), p. 284.

140. Ibid., pp. 251-55.

141. Kendall, *Violin Method*, p. 11.

142. Robert Gagné, *The Conditions of Learning* (New York: Holt, Rinehart and Winston, 1964), p. 227.

143. Ibid., p. 263.

144. Ibid., pp. 268-71.

145. Honda, *Early Development*, p. 4.

146. Gagné, *Conditions*, pp. 57-59.

147. Ibid., p. 60.

148. Joel Kovel, *A Complete Guide to Therapy—From Psychoanalysis to Behavior Modification* (New York: Pantheon Books, 1976), pp. 19-21.

149. Erich Fromm, *Escape from Freedom* (New York: Avon–Holt, Rinehart & Winston, 1969), p. 276.

150. Fromm, *Anatomy*, pp. 397-98.

151. Edwards, *Drawing*, pp. vii, 2-4.

152. Ibid., pp. 6-7.

153. Ibid., pp. 7, 14-15.

154. Ibid., p. 37.

155. Roger M. Williams, "Why Children Should Draw—The Surprising Link between Art and Learning," *Saturday Review*, September 3, 1977, pp. 11-14.

156. Any quotes in this section are from an article by Maya Pines in the *Rapid City* (S.D.) *Journal*, April 6, 1982, p. 11: "Some Key Factors Common among Outstanding People." This section is a summary of the ideas presented in the article.

157. Gail Sheehy, *Pathfinders* (New York: Bantam Books, 1981), p. 463.

158. This summary is based on a question-answer seminar that Dr. Suzuki conducted for American teachers in Matsumoto in August 1972, which I attended.

159. George Kochevitsky, *The Art of Piano Playing* (Evanston: Summy-Birchard Co., 1967), pp. 30-31.

160. John Kendall, *Talent Education and Suzuki* (Washington: Music Educators National Conference Press, 1966), p. 16.

161. Ibid., p. 15.

162. Private interview with Dr. Suzuki.

163. "Fiddling Legions," *Newsweek*, March 23, 1964, p. 73.

164. Reischauer, *The Japanese*.

165. Sharon Begley with John Carey, "How Far Does the Head Start Go?" *Newsweek*, in "Bringing Up Superbaby," March 28, 1983, pp. 64-65.

166. Foreword by Glenn Doman, in Ibuka, *Kindergarten*, p. 9.

167. *Berkshire Eagle* (Pittsfield, Massachusetts) quoted in Cook, *Suzuki Education in Action*, p. 92.

168. Cook, *Suzuki Education in Action*, pp. 93-94.

169. Ibid., pp. 93-94.

170. Kendall, *Talent Education*, p. 4.

171. Bernard Krisher, "Why Can't We Understand Japan?" *Newsweek*, August 6, 1973, p. 35.

172. Kendall, *Talent Education*, p. 13.

173. Steven Staryk, "String Shortage," *Oberlin Alumni Magazine*, November 1969, p. 2.

174. Suzuki, *Love*, p. 87.

175. Ibid., p. 119.

176. Kataoka, Suzuki; Suzuki, Shizuko; and Suzuki, Shinichi, *Suzuki Piano School, Volume 1*, introductory pages.

177. Ibid. (1970-73 edition only), pp. 6-7.

General Bibliography

BOOKS AND BROCHURES ABOUT TALENT EDUCATION

Bigler, Carole, and Lloyd-Watts, Valery. *Studying Suzuki Piano: More Than Music*. Athens, Ohio: Ability Development Associates, 1979.

Brandt, Jean, and Merrill, Kathryn. *The Pre-Twinkle Book*. Yellow Springs, Ohio: October Press, 1980.

Cook, Clifford. *Essays of a String Teacher: Come Let Us Rosin Together*. Smithtown, N.Y.: Exposition Press, 1973.

      Suzuki Education in Action: A Story of Talent Training from Japan. Smithtown, N.Y.: Exposition Press, 1970.

Fink, Lorraine. *A Parent's Guide to String Instrument Study*. San Diego: Kjos, 1977.

Graham, Beverly. *Suzuki Pianists' List for Supplementary Material: An Annotated Bibliography*. Athens, Ohio: Ability Development Associates, 1981.

Hermann, Evelyn. *Shinichi Suzuki: The Man and His Philosophy*. Athens, Ohio: Ability Development Associates, 1981.

Honda, Masaaki. *A Program for Early Development*. Tokyo: Early Development Associates, 1972.

      Suzuki Changed My Life. Princeton, N.J.: Summy-Birchard Co., 1977.

Ibuka, Masaru. *Kindergarten Is Too Late*. New York: Simon and Schuster, 1977.

Kendall, John. *The Suzuki Violin Method in American Music Education*. Washington, D.C.: Music Educators National Conference, 1978.

      The Suzuki Violin Method in American Music Education: What the American Music Educator Should Know About Shinichi Suzuki. Washington, D.C.: Music Educators National Conference, 1973.

      Talent Education and Suzuki. Washington, D.C.: Music Educators National Conference, 1966.

Kendall, John; Goldberg, Milton; and Suzuki, Shinichi. *Today's Youth and the Violin: A Trilogy on Talent Education*. Lincolnwood, Ill.: William Lewis and Son, 1971.

Kenneson, Claude. *A Cellist's Guide to the New Approach*. Smithtown, N.Y.: Exposition Press, 1974.

Koppelman, Doris. *Introducing Suzuki Piano*. San Diego: Dichter Press, 1978.

      Teaching Suzuki Piano (Volumes 1-2, 3-4, 5-6). San Diego: Koppelman, 1971.

Landers, Ray. *Is Suzuki Education Working in America?* Smithtown, N.Y.: Exposition Press, 1985.

      The Talent Education School of Shinichi Suzuki—an Analysis: The Application of Its Philosophy and Methods to All Areas of Instruction. 3rd ed., Smithtown, N.Y.: Exposition Press, 1984.

Mills, Elizabeth, ed. *In the Suzuki Style: A Manual for Raising Musical Consciousness in Children*. Berkeley: Diablo Press, 1973.

Mills, Elizabeth, and Murphey, Sister Therese, ed. *The Suzuki Concept: An Introduction to a Successful Method for Early Music Education*. Berkeley: Diablo Press, 1973.

Slone, Key Collier. *They're Rarely Too Young and Never Too Old to Twinkle*. Lexington, Ky.: Life Force Press, 1982.

Smith, Leon, ed. Montzka, Art, photographer. *Suzuki: A Gift of Love*. Stevens Point, Wis.: ASTEC, 1976.

Starr, William. *The Suzuki Violinist: A Guide for Teachers and Parents*. Knoxville, Tenn.: Kingston Ellis Press, 1976.

Suzuki, Shinichi. *Ability Development from Age Zero*. Translated by Mary Nagata. Athens, Ohio: Ability Development Press, 1981.

　　　　Developing Children's Ability Using the Suzuki Method: How We Are Doing Now. Matsumoto, Japan: Talent Education, 1977.

　　　　How to Teach Suzuki Piano. Matsumoto, Japan: Talent Education, 1983.

　　　　Nurtured by Love: The Classic Approach to Talent Education. Translated by Waltraud Suzuki. Smithtown, N.Y.: Exposition Press, 1973.

　　　　Where Love Is Deep. Translated by Kyoka Selden. St. Louis: Talent Education Journal Press, 1982.

Suzuki Teaching—a Career for You? Arlington, Tex.: Suzuki Association of the Americas, 1978.

Wickes, Linda. *The Genius of Simplicity*. Princeton: Summy-Birchard, 1982.

Wilson, Charlene. *Teaching Suzuki Cello: A Manual for Teachers and Parents*. Berkeley: Diablo Press, 1980.

Would You Like to Be a Suzuki Parent? Arlington, Tex.: Suzuki Association of the Americas, 1978.

Would You Like to Start a Suzuki Program? Arlington, Tex.: Suzuki Association of the Americas, 1978.

Young, Phyllis. *Playing the String Game*. Austin: University of Texas Press, 1977.

Zathilla, Paul. *Suzuki in the String Class: An Adaption of the Teachings of Shinichi Suzuki*. Evanston, Ill.: Summy-Birchard Co., 1972.

SUZUKI METHOD MUSIC BOOKS AND RECORDINGS

Kataoka, Haruko; Suzuki, Shinichi; and Suzuki, Shizuko.

　　　　Suzuki Piano School. Books: Volumes 1-6. Corresponding disc and cassette recordings (Volumes 1-4 only), performed by Meiko Miyazawa. Princeton: Summy-Birchard Co., 1971, 1973, 1976. Revised International Edition, 1978.

Suzuki Cello School. Books: Volumes 1-6. Corresponding disc and cassette recordings performed by Ronald Leonard. Princeton: Summy-Birchard, 1983.

Suzuki, Shinichi. *Suzuki Violin School*. Books: Volumes 1-10. Corresponding disc and cassette recordings performed by Shinichi Suzuki and Kuji Toyoda. Princeton: Summy-Birchard Co., 1978.

Preucil, Doris. *Suzuki Viola School*. Books: Volumes 1-4. Corresponding disc and cassette recordings performed by William Preucil. Princeton: Summy-Birchard Co., 1983.

Takahashi, Toshio. *Takahashi Flute School*. Books: Volumes 1-5. Corresponding cassette recordings performed by Toshio Takahashi and Marcel Moyse. Princeton: Summy-Birchard Co., 1971.

Note: The following materials use a Talent Education approach but are not official publications of the Suzuki Method.

Smith, Douglas. *Classical Guitar for Young Children: A Rote Learning Approach.* (Book only) Mendota Heights, Minn.: Cavata, 1979.

Landers, Ray. *Second Piano Accompaniments for Piano Students and Teachers.* Volumes 1 and 2 (Books and cassettes). Chicago: Daniel Press—Suzuki Music Academy of Chicago, 1982, 1984.

Anderson, Sandra. *Viola Volumes.* Volumes A and B (Books and cassettes). (Level 4 and 5 Suzuki levels.) Boulder, Colo.: PS Press, Ltd., 1982.

Cerone, David. *Violin Varieties* and *Dances and Concertos.* (Two stereo disc or cassette recordings of the Suzuki violin repertoire for volumes 1-4.) Athens, Ohio: Ability Development Associates, 1979; Princeton, N.J.: Summy-Birchard Co., 1984.

Lloyd-Watts, Valery. *Recital Favorites*, *Minuets and Musettes*, and *Classics.* (Three stereo disc or cassette recordings of the Suzuki piano repertoire for all 6 volumes.) Athens, Ohio: Ability Development Associates, 1978; Princeton, N.J.: Summy-Birchard Co., 1984.

Note: The above listings are available in America and Europe. Write The Talent Education Institute (address on p. 166) concerning materials available in Japan. For example, the *Suzuki Piano School* volumes are available in Japan in excellent recordings by Klaus Hellwig, Dinu Lupatti, and Walter Geisiking.

SELECTED ARTICLES ABOUT TALENT EDUCATION AND RELATED SUBJECTS

The page numbers listed are the first page of each article.

Applebaum, Samuel et al. "A String Teacher's Roundtable." *Music Educators Journal*, February 1979, p. 31.

Baskin, Yvonne. "Interview with Roger Sperry—the Bold Debunker of Split Brain Research." *Omni*, August 1983, p. 68.

Beal, Mary and Gilbert, Janet Perkins. "Music Curriculum for the Handicapped." *Music Educators Journal*, April, 1982, p. 52.

Beer, Alice; Bellows, Natalie; and Frederick, Anna Mae. "Providing for Different Rates of Music Learning." *Music Educators Journal*, April, 1982, p. 40.

Begley, Sharon. "Redefining Intelligence." *Newsweek*, November 14, 1983, p. 123.

Brimelow, Peter. "What to Do about American Schools." *Fortune*, September 19, 1983, p. 60.

Brooks, Nancy Greenwood. "Toward a Deeper Understanding of Suzuki Pedagogy." *American Music Teacher*, September–October 1980, p. 20, and November–December 1980, p. 26.

Brunson, Theodore R. "A Visit with Dr. Suzuki." *Music Educators Journal*, May 1969, p. 54.

"Can the Schools Be Saved?" *Newsweek*, May 9, 1983, p. 50.

Carr, Rachel. "All Children Are Musical." *Woman's Day*, March 1963, p. 44.

Chapman, D. "Every Child a Prodigy." *Look*, November 28, 1963, p. 24.

Chapman, Elizabeth. "The New Approach in the Violin Class." *American String Teacher*, Spring 1979, p. 3.

"Concert at the U.N.: Child Violinists." *Elementary School Journal*, December 1965, p. 148.

Cook, Clifford. "An Oberlinian's View of the 25th Anniversary of Suzuki Talent Education in the United States." *American Suzuki Journal*, November–December 1983, p. 26.

"Composite Report from the American Suzuki Institute." *American String Teacher*, Summer 1972, p. 31.

"Genius by the Gross." *Oberlin Alumni Magazine*, May 1959, p. 1.

"Japanese String Festival." *Music Educators Journal*, November–December 1959, p. 41

"Suzuki in Oberlin." *Music Educators Journal*, April 1965, p. 80.

Cross, Bob. "Checking Up on Suzuki's Little Musicians." *Chicago Tribune Magazine*, October 6, 1981, p. 63.

Dervin, Nancy. "Building Orff Ensemble Skills with Mentally Handicapped Adolescents." *Music Educators Journal*, April 1982, p. 35.

Eagle, Charles and Lathom, Wanda. "Music for the Severely Handicapped." *Music Educators Journal*, April 1982, p. 30.

Faust, D. E. "An Administrator's View on the Suzuki-Kendall Method of String Instruction." *American String Teacher*, Summer 1963, p. 18.

"Fiddling Legions." *Newsweek*, March 23, 1964, p. 73.

Fink, Lorraine. "The Suzuki Graduation System: A Unique Process.: *Suzuki World*, March–April 1983, p. 6.

"Understanding the Suzuki System." *Instrumentalist*, January 1977, p. 58.

Fischer, B. "Suzuki: Teaching and Philosophy." *American Music Teacher*, Volume 15, no. 4, p. 23.

Freed, Richard. "Making Real Music with Three-Year-Olds." *Hi-Fi Stereo Review*, December 1966, p. 61.

Friedrich, Otto. "What Do Babies Know? More Than Many Realize and Much Earlier." *Time*, August 15, 1983, p. 52.

Garfinkel, Perry. "The Best 'Jewish Mother' in the World: Mamasan Is the Force behind the Japanese Advantage in Education." *Psychology Today*, September 1983, p. 56.

Garson, Alfred. "Learning with Suzuki: Seven Questions Answered." *Music Educators Journal*, February 1970, p. 64.

"Suzuki and Physical Movement." *Music Educators Journal*, December 1973, p. 34.

Gavzer, Bernard and Michaels, Marguerite. "The Good News About our [American] Public Schools." *Parade: The Sunday Newspaper Magazine*, January 1, 1984, p. 4.

Gerard, Sister Jane Elizabeth. "Some Thoughts on Suzuki." *American String Teacher*, Summer 1966, p. 3.

Gilbert, Gail, and Talcott, Margaret. "Why Teach Preschoolers?" *Clavier*, February 1978, p. 37.

Gliedman, John. "Interview with Noam Chomsky." *Omni*, November 1983, p. 113.

Gordon, John. "The Young Masters Art Program." (About a Suzuki-oriented art curriculum for children.) *Suzuki World*, September–October 1983, p. 12.

Gordon, Philip. "Thoughts on Suzuki." *American String Teacher*, Summer 1965, p. 30.

Haderer, Walter. "Suzuki String Workshop at San Francisco State College." *American String Teacher*, Fall 1966, p. 37.

Harley, Frances Alexander. "Modern Pied Piper." *American String Teacher*, Fall 1966, p. 20.

Herman, Jan. "Music Magician Suzuki's Success Is Worth Imitating." *Chicago Sun-Times*, October 17, 1982, p. 20.

Hermann, A. "A Japanese Approach to the Violin." *Strad Magazine*, June 1965, ⁻ p. 49.

Hermann, Evelyn. "The Suzuki Philosophy—Fallacies and Facts." *American String Teacher*, Spring 1971, p. 41.

"Invasion from the Orient." *Time*, November 3, 1967, p. 46.

"Japan—a Nation in Search of Itself." *Time*, August 1, 1983, entire issue.

Junkerman, John. "The Japanese Model." *Progressive*, May 1983, p. 21.

Kendall, John. "The Resurgent String Program in America." *Music Educators Journal*, September–October 1967, p. 45.

    "Violin Teaching for Three-Year-Olds: Ten Stereotypes Re-examined." *Instrumentalist*, March 1960, p. 64.

Krisher, Bernard. "Why Can't We Understand Japan?" *Newsweek*, August 6, 1973, p. 35.

Lam, Rita and Wang, Cecilia. "Integrating Blind and Sighted through Music." *Music Educators Journal*, April 1982, p. 44.

Landers, Ray. "The Importance of Arts Education—A Comparison of the Ideas of Betty Edwards, Jean Houston, and Shinichi Suzuki." *American Suzuki Journal*, September 1983, p. 30.

    "Two or More Can Play." *Suzuki World*, July–August 1982, p. 2.

    Response to Review of "Studying Suzuki Piano—More Than Music." *American Suzuki Journal*, Fall 1982, p. 44.

    "Talent Education in Australia." *Suzuki World*, January–February 1984, p. 12.

Langway, Lynn. "Bringing up Superbaby." *Newsweek*, March 28, 1983, p. 62.

Leerhsen, Charles, with Doi, Aynko. "How the Japanese Do It." *Newsweek*, May 9, 1983, p. 54.

Lehr, Joan. "Teacher Training Programs for Exceptional Classes." *Music Educators Journal*, April 1982, p. 46.

Lekberg, C. "Suzuki: Pied Piper of Fiddledom." *Music Journal*, May 1968, p. 20.

Ludke, Jean. "Unit A—Again." *American Suzuki Journal*, April 1983, p. 7.

Matesky, Ralph. "Journey to Japan." *American String Teacher*, Part I, Winter 1974, p. 22; Part II, Spring 1974, p. 50; Part III, Summer 1974, p. 24.

McDonald, Marjorie. "The Suzuki Method, Child Development and Transitional Tunes." *American String Teacher*, Winter 1970, p. 24.

McGrath, Ellie. "To Stem a Tide of Mediocrity." *Time*, May 9, 1983, p. 62.

McManis, Virginia. "Fiddling Is a Family Affair." *American String Teacher*, Spring 1965, p. 10.

McRae, Shirley. "The Orff Connection . . . Reaching the Special Child." *Music Educators Journal*, April 1982, p. 32.

"National Concert in Japan." *School Musician*, August–September 1965, p. 36.

Nickels, Carroll. "Who Is Suzuki?" *American String Teacher*, Fall 1968, p. 4.

Ostrow, Isaac. "String: Suzuki and Rolland, Two Modern Pedagogues." *Instrumentalist*, May 1977, p. 79.

Pastor, Leslie Purcell. "Dalcroze Eurhythmics." *Suzuki World*, May–June 1983, p. 2.

Paul, Anthony. "Music Is Child's Play for Professor Suzuki." *Reader's Digest*, November 1973, p. 269.

Pines, Maya. "Some Key Factors Common among Outstanding People." *Rapid City* (S.D.) *Journal*, April 6, 1982, p. 11.

"Playing by Ear." *Time*, August 24, 1959, p. 36.

Powell, Mary Craig. "Ten Points on Practice." *Suzuki World*, March–April 1983, p. 4.

Raccoli, Susan. "Why Do Piano Lessons Fail?" *American Music Teacher*, April–May 1983, p. 40.

Reuning, Sanford. "The Suzuki Method and American Mothers." *Instrumentalist*, December 1968, p. 47.

Roach, Donald. "Dalcroze Eurhythmics: Active Musicianship Training." *American Music Teacher*, January 1980, p. 42.

Roche, Mary. "How to Lead Your Child to Music." *House and Garden*, September 1964, p. 82.

Sarch, Kenneth. "The Pied Piper of Japan." *Juilliard News Bulletin*, April 1964, p. 1.
        "The Suzuki System: A Critical Evaluation." *American String Teacher*, Summer 1970, p. 6.

Schmidt, Sister Cecilia. "The Thought–Life of the Young Child." *Music Educators Journal*, December 1971, p. 22.

Schultz, Carl. "Shinichi Suzuki: The Genius of His Teaching." *American String Teacher*, Winter 1966, p. 19.

Silberman, I. "On Importing Japanese Violinists." *High Points Magazine*, December 1965, p. 28.

Simka, Arvi. "The Gifted Child and the Piano: The Elementary Years." *American Music Teacher*, February-March 1982, p. 16.

Smith, Douglas. "Classic Guitar for the Young Student: The Advantages of Starting with Rote Teaching." *American String Teacher*, Winter 1980, p. 18.

Smith, Gretchen. "Not for Pianists Only: Haruko Kataoka, Co-founder of the Suzuki Piano School." *American Suzuki Journal*, November–December, 1983, p. 9.

Smith, Herbert. "Some Conclusions Concerning the Suzuki Method of Teaching Violin." *American String Teacher*, Winter 1965, p. 1.

Smith, Jean. "The Suzuki Tradition—Facts and Fallacies—An Interview with Hiroka Primrose." *American String Teacher*, Winter 1980, p. 10.

Starr, Constance. "Starting Young Pianists with the Suzuki Method." *Clavier*, April 1972, p. 7.

Staryk, Steven. "String Shortage." *Oberlin Alumni Magazine*, November 1969, p. 2.

Steck, Sue Ann. "Piano Lessons for the Very Young Child." *Clavier*, February 1976, p. 35.
        "Selecting Methods for the Very Young Child." *Clavier*, November 1978, p. 29.

Steg, Olaf. "The Suzuki Violin Demonstration-Recital." *American String Teacher*, Spring 1964, p. 8.

Stringham, Mary. "Suzuki: If Not in Method, Then in Principle!" *American String Teacher*, Fall 1971, p. 24.

"Suzuki at Chicago Festival." *Time*, October 18, 1982, p. 70.

"Suzuki Conducts Experiment in Teaching Children to Play Instruments before They Can Read Music." *New York Times*, August 7, 1966, Section II, p. 13.

"Suzuki Presents Performances by Ten Children He Taught to Play the Violin." *New York Times*, October 10, 1966, p. 50.

Suzuki, Shinichi. "Talent Education's Ten Points." *American String Teacher*, Summer 1967, p. 23.

Suzuki, Waltraud. "As a Child, Could You Read before You Could Talk?" *American String Teacher*, Summer 1965, p. 23.

Thompson, Keith. "Music for Every Child: Education for Handicapped Learners." *Music Educators Journal*, April 1982, p. 25.

Tress, Lester Van. "Piano Study in Japan." *Piano Quarterly*, Spring 1976, p. 20.

Wassell, Albert. "A Visit with Shinichi Suzuki in Japan." *American String Teacher*, Summer 1964, p. 9.

Wassell, Robert. "Suzuki Answers Questions Again." *Instrumentalist*, August 1966, p. 14.

Waters, Harry F. "What TV Does to Kids." *Newsweek*, February 21, 1977, p. 63.

White, John. "Suzuki—the Master and His Children: Happiness Through Music." *Chicago Sun-Times*, January 2, 1983, p. 60.

White, Linda Darner. "How to Adapt for Special Students." *Music Educators Journal*, April 1982, p. 49.

"Why Public Schools Fail." *Newsweek*, Part One, April 20, 1981, p. 62; Part Two, April 27, 1981, p. 78; Part Three, May 4, 1981, p. 66.

Williams, Dennis. "Can the Schools Be Saved?" *Newsweek*, May 9, 1983, p. 50.

Wilson, James. "Raising Kids." *Atlantic*, October 1983, p. 45.

Winn, Joni. "Boosting Baby's I.Q." *Saturday Evening Post*, November 1983, p. 46.

Woody, Robert. "Wind Instruments in Early Childhood: Guidelines for Teaching." *School Musician*, March 1978, p. 58.

Zelig, T. "Can Toddlers Be Fiddlers?" *Music Journal*, Volume 1, no. 4 (1967), p. 19.

SELECTED UNPUBLISHED MATERIALS ABOUT TALENT EDUCATION AND RELATED SUBJECTS

Behrend, Louise. "Rosin in the Left Hand." New York: Music School of the Henry Street Settlement, 1967.

Brunson, Theodore. "An Adaptation of the Suzuki-Kendall Violin Method for Heterogenous Stringed Instrument Classes." Master's thesis, University of Illinois, 1969.

Carey, Tanya. "A Study of Suzuki Cello Practices as Used by Selected American Cello Teachers." Doctoral dissertation, University of Iowa, 1979.

Cliatt, Mary J. "Criteria for the Selection of Music Activities for the Very Young Children." Doctoral dissertation, University of Mississippi, 1975.

Dawley, Robert. "An Analysis of the Methodological Orientation and the Music Literature Used in the Suzuki Violin Approach." Doctoral dissertation, University of Illinois, 1979.

Gerber, Linda. "An Examination of Three Early Childhood Programs in Relation to Early Childhood Music Education." Doctoral dissertation, University of Illinois, 1975.

Gerren, Nicholas. "A Study of the Relationship between Intelligence, Musicality, and Attitude toward Music." Doctoral dissertation, University of Kansas, 1953.

Hartman, Virgil. "Parental Desires for the Music Education of Children." Doctoral dissertation, University of Southern California, 1970.

Hight, Katherine. "The Suzuki Talent Education Program in the Public School Elementary String Class." Master's thesis, Northwestern University, 1976.

Hoover, Patricia. "A Synthesis of the Findings of Research Related to the Process of Listening to Music, the Status of the Research and Implications for Music Education." Doctoral dissertation, University of Oregon, 1974.

Jenkins, Jeanette. "The Relationship between Maternal Parent's Musical Experience and the Musical Development of Two- and Three-Year-Old Girls." Doctoral dissertation, North Texas State University. 1976.

Kendall, John. "Observation and Report." Carbondale: Southern Illinois University, 1959.

Landers, Ray. "The Talent Education School of Shinichi Suzuki and Application of Its Philosophy and Method to Piano Instruction." Doctoral dissertation, Indiana University, 1974.

Letts, Richard. "Creative Musicianship and Psychological Growth: Bases in Some Theories of Personality, Creativity, Instruction, Aesthetics, and Music." Doctoral dissertation, University of California at Berkeley, 1972.

Neilson, Sally. "Effects of Parent Consultation Seminar Sessions on Academic Achievement of Kindergarten Children." Doctoral dissertation, University of New Orleans, 1977.

Price, Constance. "A Model for the Implementation of a Suzuki Violin Program for the Day-Care Center Environment." Doctoral dissertation, University of Michigan, 1979.

Spert, John. "Adaptation of Certain Aspects of the Suzuki Method to the Teaching of the Clarinet." Doctoral dissertation, New York University, 1970.

Tanner, Jerald. "Expectations of Japanese and American Parents and Teachers for the Adjustment and Achievement of Kindergarten Children: A Cross-Cultural Study." Doctoral dissertation, Michigan State University, 1977.

Thomas, Pheeroba Ann. "Music with the Preschool Child: A Manual of Methods and Materials for Music with Preschoolers, Babies through Kindergartners for Early Childhood Teachers and Administrators." Doctoral disseration, New Orleans Baptist Theological Seminary, 1975.

Tillson, Diana. "The Suzuki Violin Method Adapted for Class Teaching in the Bedford Public Schools." Bedford, N.Y., 1967.

———. "A Developmental Approach to the Suzuki Repertoire." Bedford, N.Y., 1968.

———. "Orff-Kodaly-Suzuki, Three Major New Developments in Elementary School Music Education: Their Interrelationships, and Their Application to Public School Music Education." Bedford, N.Y., 1968.

Trammell, Peggy. "An Investigation of the Effectiveness of Repetition and Guided Listening in Developing Enjoyable Music Listening Experience for Second-Grade Students." Doctoral dissertation, Texas Woman's University, 1977.

Wensel, Virginia. "Project Super Talent-Education News." Vol. 1, Nos. 1, 2, 3, 4. Rochester, N.Y.: Eastman School of Music, 1968.

AUDIO-VISUAL MATERIALS ABOUT TALENT EDUCATION

"Chicagoland Suzuki Music Festival." A 4 hour videotape of the 1982 Festival which Dr. Suzuki attended. Features play in concert with 1,000 violinists, 100 cellists, and several piano soloists, as well as soloist-orchestra concerto program. (Contact Ray Landers for further information.)

"Every Child Can Be Educated." A 35 minute 16mm color film that features Shinichi Suzuki teaching the Suzuki Violin Method Book 1.

"Happy Children of Japan." A 20 minute 16mm black and white film made in Japan in 1962; shows groups and students at different levels.

"1976 All-Japan Conference." Videocassette tape featuring highlights of Tokyo Suzuki Concert at Budokan Hall.

"Starr Piano Video Tapes." A set of videotapes (made in Japan) of Haruko Kataoka teaching piano students. Recorded by Constance Starr.

"Starr Video Tapes." A set of 6 reel-to-reel violin videotapes produced by William Starr—provides a comprehensive overview of the Suzuki Method.

"Suzuki Instruction in Winnetka Public Schools." A 10 minute videocassette of the Suzuki Method as applied in the public schools of Illinois.

"Suzuki Method Video Guidance Series." A set of seven 1 hour videocassettes produced in 1975 in Japan. A definitive reference.

"Suzuki Performing Strings" of Winnetka, Illinois. A videocassette of performances of music by Khachaturian, Vivaldi, Breval, and Paganini.

"Suzuki Piano Pre-Twinkle and Book I Video Tape" with Haruko Kataoka in Matsumoto, Japan. Translation by Huub de Leeow also available, Recorded by Lorraine Landefeld in 1981.

"Suzuki Teaches American Children and Their Mothers." A 27 minute 16mm color film showing Suzuki teaching and explaining his philosophy to children and parents in America.

"Talent Education in Winnetka." A 26 minute 16mm black and white film in three sections: (1) concert performance by Suzuki students of Vivaldi A Minor Concerto for Two Violins; (2) games and techniques used by Dr. Milton Goldberg; (3) the seventh and eighth grade performing Suzuki orchestra performs the Schubert C Major Symphony.

"University of Wisconsin Video Cassettes." 12 tapes of Dr. Suzuki lecturing—demonstrating philosophy, tonalization, finger flexibility, posture, bowing, tone, tempo, and so forth. Available for rental or purchase. Contact American Suzuki Institute, University of Wisconsin, Stevens Point.

"Violin and the Child." 30 minute 16 mm black and white film produced for the 1967 "Montage" television series; features John Kendall and twelve young Suzuki performers.

Many of the above and other materials are available for rental from the Suzuki Association Audio-Visual Library. Contact the S.A.A. for a brochure and information about how to order films.

THE SUZUKI ASSOCIATION OF THE AMERICAS

For membership information, write the Executive Secretary, Suzuki Association of the Americas, Inc., c/o Batterson Building, 319 E. 2nd Street, Suite 302, Muscatine, Iowa 52761. Write the association for information about teacher training programs, national institutes, schools, and teachers throughout the world, subscription to the *American Suzuki Journal*, brochures, and articles.

THE INTERNATIONAL SUZUKI ASSOCIATION

For membership information and application write the International Suzuki Association Office Headquarters, 7922 Northaven Road, Dallas, Texas 75230.

THE TALENT EDUCATION INSTITUTE, JAPAN

For information about the Japanese Suzuki Schools and about their publications, write the Talent Education Institute, 3-10-3 Fukashi, Matsumoto-shi, Nagano Ken, Japan 390.

Annotated Bibliography
Other Suggested Books for Parents, Teachers, and Students

The selections annotated are especially recommended by R. L.

COMMUNICATION WITH CHILDREN

Beck, Helen. *Don't Push Me: I'm No Computer*. New York: McGraw-Hill, 1973. Presents arguments against a high-pressure approach to child rearing.

Bessell, Harold, and Kelly, Thomas Jr. *The Parent Book*. Harbor City, Calif.: Jalmar, 1977. A program to help children in four areas: awareness, relating, competence, and integrity.

Biller, Henry, and Meredith, Dennis. *Father Power*. Anchor Books, 1975. Special challenges of fathers as child rearers.

Briggs, Dorothy. *Your Child's Self-Esteem*. Garden City, N.Y.: Dolphin–Doubleday, 1970. How to help children attain self-confidence, a productive and meaningful life, and, most of all, happiness. The author focuses on issues such as growth stages, sex, discipline, intelligence, creativity, and communication in the light of each's impact on the child's sense of identity.

Church, Joseph. *Understanding Your Child from Birth to Three*. New York: Pocket, 1973. We forget what a child's world is really like. This book will help us remember how large all the "small steps" were and are.

Cline, Victor. *How to Make Your Child a Winner: Ten Keys to Rearing Successful Children*. New York: Walker and Co., 1980. Discusses self-image, social skills, I.Q., moral values, sibling rivalry, school problems, and other issues.

Dobson, James. *Dare to Discipline*. Wheaton, Il. Tyndale House Publishing, 1970. Discipline done positively and for right reasons can lead to freedom.

Dodson, Fitzhugh. *How to Parent*. New York: Signet, 1970.
How to Father. New York: Signet, 1974.

Dreikers, Rudolf, and Soltz, Vicki. *Children: The Challenge*. New York: Hawthorne, 1964. Discusses raising children in ways that are neither permissive nor punitive.

Dreikers, Rudolf, and Grey, Loren. *A Parent's Guide to Child Discipline*. New York: Hawthorne, 1968. A discussion of the differences between "reward and punishment" and "encouragement and consequences."

Dresher, John. *Seven Things Children Need*. Scottdale, Pa.: Herald Press, 1976.

Ginott, Haim. *Between Parent and Child*. New York: Avon, 1967.

       Between Parent and Teenager. New York: Avon, 1969. Two books that discuss communication between parents and children.

       Teacher and Child. New York: Avon, 1972. Written to help the teacher find the right feelings and language to communicate with his student.

Gordon, Dr. Thomas. *P.E.T. (Parent Effectiveness Training)*. New York: Plume, 1970.

       P.E.T. in Action. New York: Bantam, 1976.

       L.E.T. (Leader Effectiveness Training). New York: Bantam, 1977.

       T.E.T. (Teacher Effectiveness Training). New York: McKay, 1975. Ways to communicate so that no one loses; contains chapters such as "Changing Unacceptable Behavior by Changing the Environment"; discusses non-threatening communication through the use of proper "I or You Messages," active listening, and "no-lose" techniques.

James, Muriel. *Transactional Analysis for Moms and Parents*. Reading, Ma.: Addison-Wesley Pub. Co., 1974. How to turn negative feelings into positive ones in family communications.

Jersild, A.T. *In Search of Self: An Exploration of the Role of the School in Promoting Self-Understanding*. New York: Teachers College Press, 1952. Ways for a parent to help children discover themselves.

Lehane, Stephanie. *The Creative Child*. Englewood Cliffs, N.J. Prentice-Hall, 1979. Ways to encourage creativity in pre-school children.

Johnson, Eric. *How to Live Through Junior High School*. New York: Lippincott, 1959.

Lenz, Elinor. *Once My Child: Now My Friend*. New York: Warner Books, 1981. An analysis of problems associated with a child's growing up into independence.

Lepman, Jella, ed. *How Children See Our World*. New York: Avon–Equinox Books, 1971. A presentation of writings and drawings of children.

Rozman, Deborah. *Meditating with Children*. Boulder Creek, Calif.: University of Trees Press, 1975.

Salk, Lee. *What Every Child Would Like His Parents to Know*. New York: Warner Books, 1972.

Spock, Benjamin. *Raising Children in a Difficult Time*. New York: Norton, 1974.

Strommer, Merton. *Five Cries of Youth*. New York: Harper and Row, 1974. Helps parents and teachers understand more the feelings of children and teenagers.

Szasa, Suzanne. *The Unspoken Language of Childhood*. New York: Norton, 1978. Through the analysis of photographs in this book, one learns to understand better what children are communicating through their facial and body expressions.

Zimbardo, Philip, with Radl, Shirley. *A Parent's Guide to the Shy Child*. New York: McGraw-Hill, 1981. Insights into overcoming and preventing shyness from infancy to adulthood.

PSYCHOLOGY OF CHILDHOOD, GROWTH, AND EDUCATION

Arnof, Dorothy and Davis, Bertha. *How to Fix What's Wrong With Our Schools: A Toolkit for Concerned Parents*. New Haven, Ct.: Ticknor and Fields, 1983. Chapter titles include Educational Malpractice in Reading, Improving the Odds on Hiring Good Teachers, Prescription for a New Kind of Leadership, What Makes Kids Bad, and others.

Baker, Sarah. *The Alexander Technique: The Revolutionary Way to Use Your Body for Total Energy*. New York: Bantam Books, 1978.

Barzun, Jacques. *The House of Intellect*. New York: Harper & Row, 1959.

Beard, Ruth. *Piaget's Developmental Psychology*. New York: Mentor, 1972. A thorough discussion of the French psychologist and his developmental theories.

Berends, Polly. *Whole Child: Whole Parent*. New York: Harper and Row, 1975. Studies the first four years of life in relation to child and parent interaction.

Brameld, Theodore. *The Use of Explosive Ideas in Education*. Pittsburgh: University of Pittsburgh press, 1965.

Brown, George Isaac. *Human Teaching for Human Learning*. New York: Viking Press, 1971.

Bruner, Jerome. *On Knowing: Essays for the Left Hand*. Cambridge: Harvard, 1979.
    The Process of Education. New York: Random House, 1960.

Chall, Jeanne. *Learning to Read*. New York: McGraw-Hill, 1967.

Dennison, George. *The Lives of Children: A Practical Description of Freedom in Its Relation to Growth and Learning*. New York: Random House, 1969.

Dychtwald, Ken and Villoldo, Alberto, ed. *Millennium: Glimpses into the 21st Century*. Boston: J.P. Tarcher-Houghton Mifflin, 1981. Original essays by 20 authors explore the future. Includes an essay on education by Jean Houston.

Dewey, John. *Experience and Education*. Woodridge, Ill.: Collier-Macmillan, 1963.

Farb, Peter. *Word Play: What Happens When People Talk*. New York: Bantam, 1975.

Fromm, Erich. *Escape from Freedom*. New York: Discus-Avon, 1965.
    The Anatomy of Human Destructiveness. New York: Fawcett-Crest, 1973. A comprehensive analysis of aggressive and destructive tendencies in society. Fromm concludes that man is not genetically aggressive—that there is hope through positive leaders.
    The Heart of Man: Its Genius for Good and Evil. New York: Harper and Row, 1964.

Gagné, Robert. *The Conditions of Learning*. New York: Holt-Rinehard-Winston, 1965. Gagné presents a scientific analysis of eight types of learning. The chapter on how one learns a language can be related, step by step, to Suzuki's method.

Gallwey, W. Timothy. *The Inner Game of Tennis*. New York: Bantam, 1979. Through a game that takes place within the mind, the performer in life learns to play gracefully and fearlessly.

Gardner, Howard. *Frames of Mind: The Theory of Multiple Intelligence*. New York: Basic Books Inc., 1983. Gardner identifies six types of intelligence—language, mathematic—logical, musical, spatial—visual, body talents (e.g., dance), personal feelings—abilities. Talent Education theories are discussed in the context of the book.

Gardner, John. *Excellence: Can We Be Equal and Excellent Too?* New York: Harper and Row (Perennial), 1961. Can a democratic society such as the United States create an educational system that maintains uniform excellence? Gardner, like Suzuki, believes so and offers many optimistic insights.

Gaylin, Willard. *Caring*. New York: Avon, 1976.

Goble, Frank. *The Third Force: The Psychology of Abraham Maslow*. New York: Pocket, 1971. Many of Maslow's ideas are similar to those of Suzuki. Maslow is very concerned with helping man find his true essence—his self actualization.

Grady, Tom, ed. *Free Stuff for Parents*. Deephaven, Mn.: Meadowbrook, 1981. A listing of the best materials available through the mail for parents—descriptions of a variety of booklets and pamphlets on many subjects of concern about all ages of children. Lists 250 items, ranging in cost from free to $1.00.

Hampden-Turner, Charles. *Maps of the Mind*. New York: Macmillan, 1981. A plea for "the revision of social science, religion and philosophy to stress connectedness, coherence, relationship, organicism, and wholeness, as against the fragmenting, reductive and compartmentalizing forces of the prevailing orthodoxies" (as stated in the introduction).

Hart, Harold, ed. *Summerhill: For and Against*. New York: Pocket, 1970. Fifteen highly qualified authors (including Max Rafferty, Ashley Montagu, John Holt, Bruno Bettelheim, Goodwin Watson, Sylvia Ashton-Warner, Paul Goodman, and Erich Fromm) offer their views on A. S. Neill's philosophy and, in doing so, often summarize their own educational perspectives.

Holt, John. *Escape from Childhood*. New York: Ballantine Books, 1974.
  How Children Learn. New York: Dell, 1970, revised 1983
  How Children Fail. New York: Dell, 1964.
These books discuss the failures of our school system and offer many alternatives. Holt is a strong supporter of Suzuki and discusses him in *Escape from Childhood*.

Houston, Jean. *The Possible Human: A Course in Enhancing Your Physical, Mental, and Creative Abilities*. Los Angeles: J. P. Tarcher, 1982. Contains exercises to awaken the body, senses, brain, and memory.

Hunt, J. McV. *Intelligence and Experience*. New York: Ronald Press, 1961.

Hunt, Morton. *The Universe Within*. New York: Simon and Schuster, 1982. A highly readable account of the latest theories of cognitive science—with special references to right-left brain developments.

Hymes, J. L. Jr. *Teaching the Child Under Six*. Columbus, Ohio: Merrill Pub. Co. 1981.

Jaynes, Julian. *The Origin of Consciousness in the Breakdown of the Bicameral Mind*. Boston: Houghton Mifflin, 1976. A study of the development of the two hemispheres of the brain that will improve the educator's understanding of the role of arts and music in the development of the creative right hemisphere.

Johnson, Robert. *Super Babies: A Handbook of Enriched and Accelerated Childhood Development*. Smithtown, N.Y.: Exposition, 1981. A meticulous record of the development of a four-year-old who speaks four languages, skis, skates, plays the violin, and has encyclopedic knowledge of many subjects.

Jones, Richard. *Fantasy and Feeling in Education*. New York: New York University, 1968.

Jung, C. G. *Psychology and Education*. Princeton: Princeton Press, 1920.

Kohl, Herbert. *The Open Classroom*. St. Paul: Vintage, 1970.

Kohlberg, Lawrence. *The Philosophy of Moral Development: Essays in Moral Development*. New York: Harper and Row, 1981.

Kovel, Joel. *A Complete Guide to Therapy: From Psychoanalysis to Behavior Modification*. New York: Pantheon, 1936. Most important in its definition of neurosis in human nature and modern life.

Kozol, Jonathan. *Death at an Early Age*. New York: Bantam, 1968. In this discussion of the Boston public schools one discovers many reasons why the school systems often destroy creativity and prevent learning.
  Free School. New York: Bantam, 1972.

Lawrence, Sidney. *Behavioral Profile of the Piano Student*. West Hempstead, N.Y.: Workshop Music Teaching, 1978. A look at the cause and prevention of premature dropouts.

Leonard, George. *Education and Ecstasy.* New York: Dell, 1968.

McCandless, Boyd. *Children and Adolescents, Behavior and Development.* New York: Holt, Rinehart, and Winston, 1963.

Mander, Jerry. *Four Arguments for the Elimination of Television.* New York: Morrow-Quill, 1978. Suggests that television is so dangerous to personal health and sanity that it should be eliminated forever.

Maritain, Jacques. *Education at the Crossroads.* New Haven, Conn.: Yale Press, 1943.

Maynard, Olga. *Children and Dance and Music.* New York: Scribner and Sons, 1968.

Mitchell, J., and Teves, H. *Love, the Language of Caring.* Minneapolis: Winston Press, 1977.

Montessori, Maria. *The Absorbent Mind.* New York: Dell, 1967.
        The Montessori Method. New York: Schocken, 1912.
        The Secret of Childhood. New York: Ballantine, 1966.
Perhaps the best of Montessori's books. The philosophy presented is very similar to that of Suzuki and will help one understand the universal appeal of both educators.
        Spontaneous Activity in Education. New York: Schocken, 1965.

Munn, Norman. *The Evolution and Growth of Human Behavior.* Boston: Houghton Mifflin, 1965.

A Nation at Risk: The Imperative for Educational Reform. Washington: National Commission on Excellence in Education, 1983. A scathing report on inadequacies in American education with many positive suggestions for change.

Neill, A. S. *Freedom—Not License.* Williston, Vt.: Hart, 1966.
        Summerhill: A Radical Approach to Child Rearing. Williston, Vt.: Hart, 1977. A highly controversial approach to education that will help the reader to think deeply about freedom versus discipline in education.

Ostrander, Shelia, and Schroeder, Lynn. *Super-Learning.* New York: Dell, 1979. Stress-free, fast learning methods to develop "super memory." Includes a wide range of subjects such as sophrology, autogenics, suggestology, biogenics, and numerous others. Of special interest to Suzuki teachers is the analysis of the theories of Bulgarian educator, Georgi Lozanov, who presents many arguments for the use of Baroque music for learning situations.

Pearce, J. C. *Magical Child.* New York: E.P. Dutton, 1977. Discusses the importance of learning from children and analyzes some of the myths adults have about children. Piaget's ideas are analyzed.

Peele, Stanton with Brodsky, Archie. *Love and Addiction.* New York: Taplinger, 1975. Addiction can be found in many areas including education, relationships and love. Social forces that nurture in vulnerable people feelings of incompleteness are examined by the authors.

Piaget, Jean. *The Child's Conception of the World.* Totowa, N.J.: Littlefield, Adams, and Co., 1965.
        Judgement and Reasoning in the Child. Totowa, N.J.: Littlefield, Adams, and Co., 1968.

Pines, Maya. *Revolution in Learning: The Years from Birth to Six.* New York: Harper & Row, 1967. An excellent summary of many modern educational methods and philosophies including those of Montessori, Piaget, Bruner, Moore, Hunt, Engelmann, Gagné, Bereiter, Head Start programs, Skinner, and others.

Powledge, Fred. *To Change a Child.* New York: Quadrangle, 1967.

Pulaski, Mary Ann Spencer. *Your Baby's Mind and How It Grows: Piaget's Theory for Parents.* New York: Harper and Row, 1981. A clear description of Piaget's theories on child growth, written especially for the layman.

Read, Herbert. *The Redemption of the Robot.* New York: Simon and Schuster, 1966. Emphasizes the importance of arts in education.

Richardson, Ken, and Spears, David, ed. *Race and Intelligence—the Fallacies behind the Race I.Q. Controversy.* Gretna, La.: Pelican, 1972. Several authors discuss intelligence in its relation to development in different environments.

Rogers, Carl. *On Becoming a Person.* Boston: Houghton Mifflin, 1961. Understanding Rogers' "client-centered" ideals will help one strive to reach the individual child even more.

Rossi and Biddle, ed. *The New Media and Education: Their Impact on Society.* Garden City, N.Y.: Doubleday, 1967.

Schreiber, Daniel, ed. *Profile of the School Dropout.* New York: Random House, 1967.

Schumacher, E. F. *A Guide for the Perplexed.* New York: Harper-Colophon, 1978. A philosophical look at human potential through an analysis of traditional values. Includes four chapters on "fields of knowledge."

Schwebel, Milton. *Who Can Be Educated.* New York: Grove Press, 1968.

Sheehy, Gail. *Passages.* New York: Bantam, 1976.
   Pathfinders. New York: Morrow, 1981. Well-researched books that discuss man's development from birth through his most advanced years. Through striving to understand our stages of growth we become more aware, sympathetic, empathetic, and sensitive educators.

Silberman, Charles. *Crisis in the Classroom: The Remaking of American Education.* New York: Vintage-Random, 1970. Chapter titles include What's Wrong with The Schools, How the Schools Should Be Changed, and How to Improve Teacher Education.

Skidelsky, Robert. *English Progressive Schools.* New York: Penguin, 1969.

Smith, Lendon. *Improving Your Child's Behavior Chemistry.* New York: Pocket, 1976. A child psychologist analyzes problems such as hyperactivity. Aspects of heredity, environment, and, particularly, diet are discussed.
   Feed Your Kids Right. New York: Dell, 1979

Thibodeau, Lynn, *Childhood Is.* New York: Carillon Books, 1977. An anthology of essays on various aspects of childhood.

Torrence, E. Paul. *Education and the Creative Potential.* Minneapolis: University of Minnesota Press, 1969.

Vaizey, John. *Education in the Modern World.* New York: McGraw-Hill, 1967.

Vandenberg, Donald. *Teaching and Learning.* Champaign: U. of Illinois Press, 1969.
   Theory of Knowledge and Problems of Education. Champaign: U. of Illinois Press, 1969.

Warner, Sylvia. *Teacher.* New York: Simon and Schuster, 1963.

Weiss, Paul. *The Making of Men.* Carbondale: Southern Illinois Univ. Press, 1967.

Wickes, Frances. *The Inner World of Childhood: The Crucial Relationship Between Parent and Child.* New York: Signet, 1966.

CULTURAL SIMILARITIES AND DIFFERENCES BETWEEN EAST AND WEST

Buscaglia, Leo F. *Love.* New York: Fawcett, 1982.

Personhood. New York: Fawcett Columbine, 1982.

The Way of the Bull. New York: Fawcett Crest, 1973. Well-written, caring thoughts by a California professor who has traveled extensively throughout the world. He talks of man's discovery of self and, in doing so, teaches us much about Asian and Oriental philosophies.

Campbell, Joseph. *Myths to Live By.* New York: Bantam Books, 1973. An analysis of how we re-create ancient legends in our daily lives. Various myths of East and West are studied and compared.

Carr, Audrey and Sohl, Robert, ed. *The Gospel According to Zen.* New York: Mentor, 1970. Brings together the most enlightening parables of East and West with commentaries by Erich Fromm, D.T. Suzuki, Alan Watts, J. Krishnamurti and others.

Cox, Harvey. *Turning East: The Promise and Peril of the New Orientalism.* Austin, Tex.: S and S, 1979.

deMente, Boye. *What the West Can Learn from the East.* Japan: Simpson Doyle and Co., 1963.

Earle, J. V.; Lehmann, Jean-Pierre; Katzumie, Masaru; Tanaka, Ikko; and Yoshida, Mitsukuni. *Japanese Style.* New York: Kodansha International Ltd., 1980. A beautiful book that analyzes, through essays and photographs, Japanese life. Topics discussed include style of Japanese art, aesthetic ideals, and an analysis of Western perceptions and stereotypes of Japan.

Fromm, Erich, with Suzuki, D. T., and DeMartino, Richard. *Zen Buddhism and Psychoanalysis.* New York: Harper-Colophon, 1960. A thorough introduction to Zen Buddhism and how its tenets may be applied in the West.

Hamel, Peter Michael. *Through Music to the Self.* Boulder, Colo.: Shambhala, 1979. Chapter titles include Old and New Paths in Western Music, Encounter with Non-European Music, and Music Between the Worlds.

Hesse, Herman. *Magister Ludi: The Glass Bead Game.* New York: Bantam, 1970.

Narcissus and Goldman. New York: Bantam, 1971. Two philsophical novels that question values of both East and West and discuss the search for balance between discipline and freedom.

Pirsig, Robert. *Zen and Art of Motorcycle Maintenance: An Inquiry into Values.* New York: Bantam, 1974. A wonderful story of a man and his son on a cross-country trip through the United States. This book contrasts many American and Eastern values in education, growth, religion, and quality. The author concludes that the essence of quality is caring.

Reischauer, Edwin. *The Japanese.* Cambridge, Mass.: Belknap-Harvard, 1977. A former ambassador to Japan analyzes Japanese culture in relation to its children, education, attitudes, religion, and other aspects. Various differences and similarities with American culture are analyzed.

Suzuki, D. T. Foreword by Jung, C. G. *An Introduction to Zen Buddhism.* New York: Grove Press, 1964. Through gaining more insight into the Eastern religions, one also learns more of the Eastern cultures and philosophies.

What is Zen? New York: Perennial, 1972.

Suzuki, Shuryu. *Zen Mind, Beginners Mind.* Salem, Mass.: Weatherhill, 1970.

Watts, Alan. *Beyond Theology: The Art of Godmanship.* New York: Vintage-Random, 1964. An analysis of Eastern mysticism and modern science and how understanding their relation to each other can help man prepare for a more unified life.

The Meaning of Happiness: The Quest for Freedom in Modern Psychology
and the Wisdom of the East. New York: Harper & Row, 1979. A discussion of happiness as an elusive but tangible reality, gathered from the wisdom of both East and
West.

Nature, Man and Woman. New York: Vintage-Random, 1970. Mr. Watts
discusses the origins of alienation from nature in Western thought as contrasted
with the Chinese Tao's vision of nature as an organic whole.

The Two Hands of God: The Myths of Polarity. New York: Collier, 1963.

AESTHETICS

Doczi, Gyorgy. *The Power of Limits: Proportional Harmonies in Nature, Art, and
Architecture*. Boulder, Co.: Shambhala, 1981. A discussion of order and form
throughout nature as compared with the arts.

Edwards, Betty. *Drawing on the Right Side of the Brain: A Course in Enhancing
Creativity and Artistic Confidence*. Boston: Tarcher-Houghton Mifflin, 1979.
Applying recent discoveries in brain research, Dr. Edwards presents basic exercises to develop the right hemisphere of the brain and teach anyone to draw
well. A good discussion of left and right brain functions and how they help
one to see and appreciate beauty.

Einstein, Alfred. *Greatness in Music*. New York: Da Capo, 1976. Deals with problems of establishing universal standards of excellence for the evaluation of music,
with reference to composers throughout Western history.

Rudhyer, Dane. *The Magic of Tone and the Art of Music*. Boulder, Colo.: Shambhala,
1982. A panoramic survey of the development of music that shows its relation
to the evolution of the mind. A study of how sound can transform
consciousness.

Yanagi, Soetsu. *The Unknown Craftsman: A Japanese Insight into Beauty*. New York:
Kodansha, 1978. Yanagi, a founder of Japan's folkcraft movement, challenges
the conventional ideas of art and beauty. Chapter titles include "Seeing and
Knowing," "The Beauty of Irregularity," "The Buddhist Idea of Beauty," and
"The Way of Tea."

ART BOOKS

Note: The author believes in the interrelatedness and importance of all arts. A home
that provides excellent books of art will help develop a sensitivity to the importance of the arts in general. Especially recommended are the following titles:

Argan, G. C.; Francastel, P.; Hetl-Kuntze, H.; Jaffé, Hans; Kahane, P.P.; Levey,
Michael. *20,000 Years of World Painting Series*. New York: Dell-Laurel, 1967.
A reasonably priced paperback series of six volumes, each containing full color
reproductions and thorough historical explanations. Vol. 1 - *Ancient and
Classical Art*; Vol. 2 - *Medieval Painting*; Vol. 3 - *Renaissance Painting*; Volume
4 - *17th and 18th Century Painting*; Volume 5 - *19th and 20th Century Painting*; Volume 6 - *Far Eastern Art*.

Canaday, John. *What Is Art?* Knopf, 1980.

Hess, Hans. *How Pictures Mean*. Pantheon, 1974. A comprehensive text that analyzes
pictures in context of each artist's background. Illustrated with 92 pictures.

Hibbard, Howard. *The Metropolitan Museum of Art.* New York: Harper & Row, 1980. Contains 1,050 illustrations, 608 in color.

Jacobs, Jay. *The Color Encyclopedia of World Art.* New York: Crown, 1975.

Jaffe, Hans, ed. *The History of World Painting.* New York: Alpine, 1967.

Janson, Cora, and Janson, H. W. *The Story of Painting: From Cave Painting to Modern Times.* Austin: Galahand, 1977.

Rothenstein, John, ed. *The Great Artists.* New York: Funk and Wagnalls, 1978. 25 large paperback volumes with very large full color prints especially appealing to children. Each volume is about a specific artist and contains an historical sketch of the artist and a brief description of each print.

Walker, John. *The National Gallery of Art, Washington.* Abrams, 1975. Contains 1,120 illustrations including 1,028 plates in color.

See also *The Search for Personal Freedom* under Historical and Pedagogical Reference Sources and *The Time-Life Record Series: The Story of Great Music* (which presents a general art history as well as a social and music history in its text) under Supplementary Literature.

MUSIC EDUCATION FOR THE HANDICAPPED

Alvin, Juliette. *Music for the Handicapped Child.* New York: Oxford, 1976.
　　　　　Music Therapy for the Autistic Child. New York: Oxford, 1979.

Bailey, Philip. *They Can Make Music.* New York: Oxford, 1973.

Furneaux, Barbara. *The Special Child: Education of Mentally Handicapped Children.* New York: Penguin, 1969.

Lawrence, Sidney. *Challenges in Piano Teaching: One-to-One Lessons for the Handicapped and Others.* West Hempstead, N.Y. Workshop Music Teaching, 1978.
　　　　　"Music for Every Child: Teaching Special Children." *Music Educators Journal,* April 1982, entire issue. Reston, Va.: M.E.N.C. Press.

Orem, R. C. *Montessori for the Disadvantaged.* Boulder, Co.: Capricornus, 1968.
　　　　　Montessori and the Special Child. Boulder, Co.: Capricornus, 1969.

Ward, David. *Hearts and Hands and Voices: Music in the Education of the Slow Learner.* New York: Oxford, 1976.
　　　　　Sing a Rainbow: Musical Activities with Mentally Handicapped Children. New York: Oxford, 1979.

HISTORICAL AND PEDAGOGICAL REFERENCE SOURCES

Apel, Willi, and Daniel, Ralph. *The Harvard Brief Dictionary of Music.* New York: Washington Square Press, 1961.

Baker, Theo. *Dictionary of Musical Terms.* New York: Schirmer, 1923.

Bastien, James. *How to Teach Piano Successfully.* Park Ridge, Ill.: Kjos, 1973. A must for piano teachers. Thorough in pedagogy, technique, repertoire, history, survey of various methods. Contains a comprehensive bibliography of reading materials and music.

Campbell, Margaret. *The Great Violinists: A Fascinating History of the Violin, Its Makers and Its Masters.* Includes a discography. New York: Doubleday, 1981.

Carl Orff's Music For Children and Related Supplementary Materials. Belwin-Mills Publishing Corporation, Melville, N.Y. 11746. A catalog of Orff Materials.

Chosky, Lois. *The Kodaly Method: Comprehensive Music Education from Infant to Adult.* Englewood Cliffs, N.J.: Prentice Hall, 1974.

Cross, Neal; Lamm, Robert; and Turk, Rudy. *The Search for Personal Freedom,* Volumes 1 and 2. Dubuque, Iowa: Wm. Brown, 1977. A text that presents a unified study of the humanities, beautifully illustrated, and comprehensive (often with complete plays, music examples, art work) analysis of the history of music, art, architecture, dance, poetry, literature, drama, and so on.

Dalcroze, Emile-Jaques. *Rhythm, Music and Education.* Salem, N.H.: Arno-Ayner Co., 1921. Dalcroze education has much in common with the Suzuki philosophy. Talent Education benefits from use of Dalcroze type rhythmic activities.

Findlay, Elsa. *Rhythm and Movement: Applications of Dalcroze Eurhythmics.* Evanston, Ill.: Summy-Birchard, 1971.

Gill, Dominic, ed. *The Book of the Piano.* Cornell, 1981. Examines all aspects of the piano's history, design and music. Written by fourteen musicologists and musicians. Beautifully illustrated.

Gillespie, John. *Five Centuries of Keyboard Music.* New York: Dover Publications, 1972.

Hinson, Maurice. *Guide to the Pianists Repertoire.* Bloomington, Ind.: Indiana University, 1973.

Hitchcock, H. Wiley, ed. *Prentice-Hall History of Music Series.* Englewood Cliffs, N.J.: Prentice Hall, 1965-69. Eleven books by various authors that are comprehensive but engagingly written; for teachers, parents, and high school age students. Covers music history of the East and West.

Kendall, Catherine Wolfe. *Stories of Composers for Young Musicians.* Tucson, Ariz.: Toadwood, 1982. Includes biographies of composers found in *Suzuki Violin Method.*

Kochevitsky, George. *The Art of Piano Playing: A Scientific Approach.* Princeton, N.J.: Summy-Birchard, 1967.

Landis, Beth and Carder, Polly. *The Eclectic Curriculum in American Education: Contributions of Dalcroze, Kodaly, and Orff.* Washington, D.C.: Music Educators National Conference, 1972.

Lloyd, Norman. *Golden Encyclopedia of Music.* New York: Golden, 1968.

Nash, Grace. *Creative Approaches to Child Development; with Music, Language, and Movement.* Sherman Oaks, Calif.: Alfred Music, 1974. Incorporates ideas of Orff, Kodaly, and Laban.

Raebeck, Lois and Wheeler, Lawrence. *Orff and Kodaly Adapted for the Elementary School.* Dubuque, Ia.: Wm. C. Brown, 1977.

Salter, Lionel. *The Illustrated Encyclopedia of Classical Music*: A Guide to Composers and Recommended Recordings. London: Salamander Books, 1978.

Schonberg, Harold. *The Great Conductors.* New York: Simon and Schuster, 1967.
　　　　The Great Pianists: From Mozart to the Present. New York: Simon and Schuster, 1966.
　　　　The Lives of The Great Composers. New York: Norton, 1970.

Starr, William. *The Suzuki Violinist: A Guide for Teachers and Parents.* Knoxville, Tenn.: Kingston Ellis Press, 1976.

Stevenson, Victor and Unger-Hamilton, Clive, ed. *The Music Makers.* New York: Harry Abrams, 1979. A beautifully illustrated collection of one thousand biographies of musicians of all eras of music.

Wax, Edith. *Dalcroze Dimensions*. Roslyn Heights, N.Y.: Mostly Movement, 1983. Provides information about the Swiss music educator and his approach; includes a list of Dalcroze teacher training programs.

Wilson, Charlene. *Teaching Suzuki Cello: A Manual for Teachers and Parents*. Berkeley: Diablo Press, 1980.

Young, Phyllis. *Playing the String Game*. Austin: University of Texas, 1977.

SUPPLEMENTARY MATERIALS

Especially for Children

Carr, Rachel. *Be a Frog, a Bird, a Tree: Creative Yoga Exercises for Children*. New York: Har-Row, 1977.

Fuhrberg, Carolyn. *Treble Treasures*. Chicago: Fuhrberg, 1981. A composer study card game designed to make learning about composers fun.

Halls, Yvonne, and Steiner, Patricia. *I Love to Practice*. Kaysville, Utah: I Love to Practice, Inc., 1981. Sixty-three games and activities designed to encourage enthusiasm for practice for both parent and child.

Heald, Linda. *Magical Music Mirage*. Music Mirage Motives, Cedar Rapids, Iowa, 1982. A visual learning kit for Book 1 Suzuki piano students; contains lyrics to songs, reward decals, musical components game, flashcards, and other activities.

Mills, Elizabeth, ed. *In the Suzuki Style: A Manual for Raising Musical Consciousness in Children*. Berkeley: Diablo Press, 1973. A source book of ways for the Suzuki parent and teacher to use games and activities to motivate children, especially in their early years of study.

Nurmi, Ruth. *Playing Cards*. Bryn Mawr, Pa.: Music Now, 1983. A set of 21 colorful flashcards presenting in capsule form the building blocks of piano technique. Each card presents one technical bit with an appropriate animal drawing epitomizing that skill.

Parkinson, Marie. Judy, Mary, artist. *Mommy, Can We Practice Now?* Rexburg, Ind.: Parkinson-M & M Publications, 1981. Games, activities, practice hints, and supplemental materials are included.

Suzuki Variations Game. Gretna, Nebraska: Still Music, 1983. Three dimensional toys and games designed to introduce infants and beginning students to the Twinkle Variations.

Yurko, Michiko. *Musopoly*. Rockville, Md.: Music 19 (Box 2431), 1979. A motivating board game that is designed for teaching and reviewing the fundamentals of music theory.

 Perfectly Silly Perfect Practicing Game. Rockville, Md.: Music 19, 1983. A game designed to make practicing more enjoyable. The student plays sections of his music in crazy ways ("play with your mouth open," "play softly and click your tongue," etc.) that help his concentration.

 Orchestral Odyssey. Rockville, Md.: Music 19, 1980. A game designed to stimulate a student's interest in orchestral instruments, concert etiquette, conducting, and the symphony orchestra.

 The World Traveler Practice and Listening Club. Rockville, Md.: Music 19, 1983. A unique subscription club for helping students and parents develop consistency in practicing and listening. Subscribers receive a guide booklet, a schedule calendar, and a small national flag monthly.

RECORDINGS

Children's Listening Library. Dallas: Listening Library, Inc., 1982. Selections that are especially recommended by Dr. Suzuki for listening - for all ages, infants and up. A two cassette collection accompanied by a booklet of background information.

The Composers' Library Series. Neptune City, N.J.: Paganiniana Publications, 1981. A series of albums about famous composers. Each album contains a book with a comprehensive text and photographs, and three cassettes - one a spoken biography, the other two recordings of the composer's music with narration by Martin Bookspan.

The Enjoyment of Music. New York: Norton - Columbia Special Products, 1972. Nine records of music of all periods. The selections are discussed in the corresponding book of the same name. (book by Joseph Machlis, published by Norton, 1970).

Essential Piano Library. Cincinnati: Baldwin, 1982. Eight recordings by famous artists begin at about volume VI Suzuki level and give examples of a broad range of literature through the most advanced levels. Features a book of performance suggestions by the artists. The corresponding musical score is an excellently edited volume, *The Student's Essential Classics*, New York, Peters, 1981.

Four Hundred Years of the Violin. Los Angeles: Baroque–Everest. An anthology of outstanding violin repertoire beautifully performed by Steven Staryk. Contains six records of music of all eras.

Introduction to the Great Composers and Their Music, Los Angeles: Everest. An eleven record set, narration by David Randolph. A comprehensive study of many composers found in the Suzuki method. Excellent examples are performed and good insights are given about periods of history. Good for all ages.

Philippe Entremont Plays Sonatinas: Kuhlau, Clementi, Haydn, Dussek, Mozart, Beethoven. New York: Columbia, 1974. A two record set that contains many of the sonatinas and sonatas found in the *Suzuki Piano School* as well as many additional sonatinas.

The Pianist's Guide to Bach: Baroque Performance Practice, A Guide for Pianists, Teachers, and Music Lovers. Laurette Goldberg, Artistic Director. Notes by Carol Hess. San Francisco, Ca.: Suzuki Music Association of California, 1983. A cassette recording of many Bach pieces (including some found in the *Suzuki Piano School*) with emphasis on style and correct embellishments. Includes an excellent book that summarizes baroque performance style.

The Seraphim Guide to the Classics. Hollywood: Seraphim-Capitol. Ten recordings in a survey of Western music from the Middle Ages to the present.

Stereo Review Guide to Understanding Music. New York: Ziff-Davis-Columbia Special Products, 1973. Four records, narrated by David Randolph. Discusses the elements of music, sense and sensation in music, form, and interpretation.

Time-Life Records. Excellent series of recordings. Many packaged with corresponding booklets. Especially recommended: *Mozart, Arthur Fiedler's Favorites, Great Men of Music, Beethoven Bicentennial Collection, Great Performers, Great Moments of Music, The Story of Great Music.* Each album contains several records. Catalog available from Time-Life Records, 541 N. Fairbanks Court, Chicago, Illinois 60611.

NOTE-READING AND THEORY MATERIALS

Ausharian, Evelyn. *Natural Way to Note Reading.* Ann Arbor: Shar, 1980. Makes use of games, flashcards, movable notes, duet parts that use Suzuki rhythms and keys.

Clark, Frances, and Goss, Louise. *The Music Tree.* Princeton, N.J.: Summy-Birchard, 1973. A comprehensive series with a novel beginning approach that starts with teaching simple concepts such as up and down. (Piano)

Comnick, Claire. *My Music.* Columbus, Ohio: J. Arthur, 1980. Five books designed especially for introducing reading to the preschool child. With corresponding recordings. Illustrated stories and creative games. (Piano)

Fink, Lorraine; Muller, Frederick; and Rusch, Harold. *Quick Steps to Note Reading.* San Diego: Kjos, 1979. Volumes especially designed for Suzuki violin students of all ages. (Violin)

Lawrence, Sidney. *A Guide to Remedial Sightreading for the Piano Student: A Study in Corrective Teaching Techniques and Procedures.* West Hempstead, N.Y.: Workshop Music Teaching Publications, 1964. (Piano)

Lethco, Amanda; Manus, Morton; and Palmer, Willard. *Alfred's Basic Piano Library - Theory Books.* San Diego: Alfred, 1981. Six books that include attractive repertoire selections that incorporate new concepts. (Piano)

Movement, Sound and Reading Readiness. River Forest, Illinois: Prince Publications, 1983. Auditory and rhythmic exercises for group sessions.

Schoening, Ruth. *From Sound to Symbol.* Racine, Wis.: Agei, 1976. Five music workbooks for students ages seven to twelve. Uses sound to reading to writing approach. (All instruments)

Schreck, Suzanne. *Sight Reading Skills* (For Suzuki Violin Students). Norfolk, Va.: Schreck, Inc., 1984. Contains 50 lessons that introduce one concept at a time.

Shannet, Howard. *Learn to Read Music.* New York: Simon and Schuster, 1956. Especially designed to teach adults the basic fundamentals so that they might help their children in note-reading.

Starr, Constance. *The Music Road.* Knoxville, Tenn.: Kingston Ellis Press, 1981. Three books, large print. Designed for teaching basic concepts to beginning piano students.

Van de Velde, Ernest. *Method Rose.* Tokyo, Japan: Ongaku No Tomo Sha Corp., 1947. Used by many Japanese teachers. (Piano)

Yurko, Michiko. *No H in Snake: Music Theory for Children.* Sherman Oaks, Calif.: Alfred, 1978. A step-by-step, child-oriented approach to teaching theory through games. (Piano)

REPERTOIRE BOOKS

Pianists should consult Beverly Tucker Graham's *Suzuki Pianist's List for Supplementary Material: An Annotated Bibliography* (Athens, Ohio: Ability Development Associates, 1981) for a graded, thorough list.

The Ability Development catalog has an excellent selection of piano, flute, and string repertoire. *How to Teach Piano Successfully* by James Bastien (Park Ridge, Ill.: Kjos, 1973) has a comprehensive listing for pianists.

For Piano

Anson, George, ed. *Anson Introduces Series*. Cincinnati: Willis Music Co., 1959. Includes *Scarlatti, Handel, Bach, Second Accompaniments for Bach,* and others. Level of difficulty - Suzuki Vols. 2–3 and up.

Clark, Frances, and Goss, Louise, ed. *Frances Clark Library*. Princeton: Summy-Birchard. Graded volumes in *Contemporary Piano Literature,* (1961) *Piano Literature of the 17th, 18th, and 19th Centuries* (1964), *Playtime: Supplementary Music,* 3 parts (1976), *Supplementary Solos: Levels 3 and 4* (1976)

Diller, Angela. *Duet Albums for Beginners: The Green Duet Book* and *The Brown Duet Book*. New York: G. Schirmer, 1950. Each book contains 30 folk duets about Suzuki Volume 2 level.

Glover, David, and Noona, Walter. *An Adventure in Jazz,* Books 1, 2, 3, 4. Melville, N.Y.: Belwin Mills, 1972. Music in various jazz styles, intermediate to difficult levels.

Hughes, Edwin, ed. *Master Series for the Young*. New York: G. Schirmer, 1967. Twelve books, one each for *Bach, Beethoven, Chopin, Grieg, Handel, Haydn, Mendelssohn, Mozart, Schubert, Schumann, Tchaikovsky, Weber*. Easier compositions for piano in their original versions.

Introduction Series. Sherman Oaks, Calif.: Alfred, 1970s. Each book summarizes the stylistic characteristics of a composer or period; includes ornamentation, phrasing, and articulation. Edited by Willard Palmer, Margery Halford, George Lucktenberg and others. The series contains books on *Bach, Baroque Era, Bartok, Beethoven, Chopin, Classical Era, Early English Music, Grieg, Handel, Haydn, Kabalevsky, Masterworks, Mendelssohn, Mozart, Romantic Era, Scarlatti, Schubert, Schumann, Theme and Variations*. Pieces range from easy to moderately difficult.

Landers, Ray. *Second Piano Accompaniments for Students and Teachers*. Chicago: Daniel Press - Suzuki Music Academy of Chicago. Volume 1, 1982. Volume 2, 1984. Accompaniment parts of moderate to difficult levels to be played along with the original selections. Features many folk and well-known classical selections. Music books and cassette recordings.

Mehegan, John. *Jazz Piano Series*. New York: Sam Fox, 1961. Three separate series that begin about Suzuki Vol. 3 - 4 level and progress in difficulty: *The Jazz Pianist,* 3 books, with corresponding record for Volume 1: *Styles for the Jazz Pianist,* 3 Books: and *Contemporary Styles for the Jazz Pianist,* 3 books.

Meili, Roger, and Volpe, George, ed. *100 Children's Classics*. Miami Beach, Fla.: Hansen House, 1983. Original compositions in the early grades in baroque, classical, romantic, and contemporary periods.

Novik, Ylda, ed. *Young Pianist's Guide to . . . Bach, Bartok, Beethoven, Chopin, Haydn, Kabalevsky, Mozart, Schumann*. Hileah, Fla: Studio P/R - Columbia, 1976. Eight separate books with corresponding recordings. Easy to intermediate levels of difficulty; biographies on composers and suggestions on ornamentation are included.

Palmer, Willard. *A Contemporary Album for the Young*. Sherman Oaks, Calif.: Alfred, 1981. Eighteen short pieces of intermediate difficulty, arranged in approximate order of difficulty.

Palmer, Willard, ed. *Seven Centuries of Keyboard Music*. Sherman Oaks, Calif.: Alfred, 1981. Easy to intermediate, medieval to modern pieces edited from the original sources, with editorial suggestions in lighter print.

Van Slyck, Nicholas. *With Twenty Fingers*. Hastings-on-Hudson, N.Y.: General Music, 1973. Well written duets (one piano, four hands) in a contemporary style. Book 1 has easy, Book 2 - moderately difficult, and Book 3 - difficult repertoire.

For Cello

Easy levels:
Grant, Francis, ed. *Easy Solos in the First Position*. Cleveland, Ohio: Ludwig, 1973.
Grant, Francis, ed. *Intermediate Solos in the Positions*. Cleveland, Ohio: Ludwig, 1973.
Krane, Charles. *Classic and Folk Melodies*. Bryn Mawr, Pa.: Theodore Presser.
Otis, Edith. *First Book of Study Pieces*. Boston: Schirmer

Moderate levels:
Herfurth, Paul. *Classical Album of Early Grade Pieces*. Boston, Boston Music Co.
Hindemeth, Paul. *Three Easy Pieces*. London: Schott.
Bartok, Bela. *18 Duos*. Oceanside, N.Y.: Boosey and Hawkes.

Note:
   Gilda Barston has compiled a comprehensive listing of recommended cello repertoire for 10 levels of study. For information, contact Ms. Barston at the Music Center of the North Shore, 300 Green Bay Road, Winnetka, Ill. 60093.

For Flute

Moise, Marcel. *Tonal Development Through Interpretation*. New York: McGinnis and Marx.
   A collection of arrangements of selections, primarily operatic arias, that Toshio Takahashi uses in training teacher trainees.
Takahashi, Toshio. *Repertoire to Supplement Suzuki Repertoire—Levels 1 through 13*.
   A graded list of supplementary repertoire written by the originator of the Suzuki flute method. Write Mr. Takahashi in care of the Talent Education Institute in Japan for information (address on page 181).

For Viola

Bay, Bill. *Fun with the Viola*. Pacific, Mo.: Mel Bay Publications, 1978. Easy Level Solos.
Doktor, Paul, ed. *Solos for the Viola Player*. New York: Schirmer, 1959.

For Violin

Doflein, Elma and Erich Doflein. *The Doflein Method: The Violinist's Progress*. Princeton, N.J.: Summy-Birchard, 1972. A course of violin instruction combined with musical theory and practice in duet playing. 3 volumes.
Gingold, Josef, ed. *Solos For the Violin Player*. New York: Schirmer, 1961. Moderate to advanced levels.
Isaac, Merle. *Violin Quartet Album*. Norwalk, Ca.: Highland-Etling, 1980. Arrangements for four violins and optional piano accompaniments of music by Mozart,

Bach, Moussorgsky, Weber, and McDowell.

Jardany, Pal; Sandor, Friges; and Szervanszky, Endre, eds. *Violin Tutor*. Ocean-side, N.Y.: Boosey & Hawkes, 1969. Duets interspersed with etudes of folk and classical selections. Moderate to difficult levels.

Perleman, George. *Violin's First Solo Album, Volumes 1-2*. New York: Fischer. Selections in First position, Easy levels.

Sjenicki, Edmund. *Violin Quartet Album*. Arrangements for four violins and optional piano accompaniments of music by Mozart, Handel, Bach, Albeniz, and Grieg.

Suzuki, Shinichi, ed. *Home Concert*. Princeton: Summy-Birchard, 1972. Twenty-four folk songs and classics arranged by Suzuki for solo violin, two or three part ensemble. Requires intermediate reading ability. 2 volumes. Piano accompaniment also available.

Thirty-Seven Violin Pieces You Like to Play. New York: G. Schirmer, 1943. A collection of moderate to difficult classical selections with piano accompaniments—baroque through contemporary.

All of the above books, plus numerous other collections and single selections—solo, chamber, and orchestra—are available through Ability Development Co. or most music stores.

PERIODICALS

American Music Teacher, 2113 Carew Tower, Cincinnati, OH 45202.

American String Teacher, University of Texas at Dallas, Box 688, Richardson, TX 75080.

American Suzuki Journal, P.O. Box 354, Muscatine, IA 52761.

Clavier, 1418 Lake St., Evanston, IL 60204.

Clavier's Piano Explorer Newsletter, 1418 Lake St., Evanston, IL 60204.

Instrumentalist, 1418 Lake St., Evanston, IL 60204.

Music Educator's Journal, 1902 Association Dr., Reston, VA 22091.

Parents, 685 Third Ave., New York, NY 10017

Piano Quarterly, Box 815, Wilmington, VT 05363.

Psychology Today, P.O. Box 2562, Boulder, CO 80327.

Suzuki World, P.O. Box 460, Athens, OH 45701.

Talent Education Journal, 236 Spring Ave., St. Louis, MO 63119.

Ordering Suzuki Materials

National Distributors (Representative Listing)

Many books, recordings, instruments, and other supplies may be purchased through local music stores.

BOOKS, RECORDINGS, INSTRUMENTS, AND OTHER SUPPLIES

Ability Development Co., Box 887, Athens, OH 45701.

Kentuckiana Music Supply, P.O. Box 14124, Louisville, KY 40214.

Keynote Music Inc., P.O. Box 124, Chelsea, MI 48118.
Old Town Music Co., 32 E. Colorado Blvd., Pasadena, CA 91105.
Shar Products, P.O. Box 1411, Ann Arbor, MI 48106.
Summy-Birchard Co., Box CN 27, Princeton, NJ 08540.

STRING INSTRUMENTS–RENTAL, SALE, REPAIR, AND ACCESSORIES

Bein and Fushi, Inc., 410 S. Michigan Ave., Chicago, IL 60605.
Family Melody Centers, 77 S. Ocean Ave., Patchogue, L.I., NY 11772.
Kagan and Gaines, 207 S. Wabash Ave., Chicago, IL 60604.
H. Kamimoto Co., 198 Jackson St., San Jose, CA 95112.
Keynote Music Co., P. O. Box 124, Chelsea, MI 48118.
Manna Music Co,. 7729 Ellington Dr., St. Louis, MO 63121.
Southwestern Stringed Instruments and Accessories, 1228 East Prince Road, Tucson, AZ 85719.
Super-Sensitive Musical String Co., 6121 Porter Rd., Sarasota, FL 33582.
Suzuki Violin Co., Ltd., Nagoya, Japan (distributed in America by William Lewis and Son. Phone - 800-645-8004).
University Music Service, P.O. Box 354, Hershey, PA 17033.
William Moening and Son, Ltd., 2039 Locust St., Philadelphia, PA 19103.

PIANO SUPPLIES

Pedal Boxes

Electro Enterprises, 323 S. Franklin St., Suite 804-E 30, Chicago, IL 60606.
Rantapa Enterprises, 1390 Grantham St., St. Paul, MN 55108.

Footstools

Old Town Music Co., 32 E. Colorado Blvd., Pasadena, CA 91105.

Note: The inclusion of a listing in this bibliography does not necessarily imply an endorsement by Ray Landers or any Suzuki organization. A few of the listings are no longer in print but are included to provide a representative sampling of available materials; many of these may be found in libraries.

Index

Ability Development Co., 5-6
Ages for education, 2-3, 7, 104-5, 125, 126, 128-29, 133-34, 139, 148
See also Cognitive psychologists
American Montessori Society, 100
American Suzuki Institute, University of Wisconsin, 4
American Suzuki Journal, 4, 5, 46
Arithmetic, in relation to Talent Education, 4, 25, 42, 43
Art, in relation to Talent Education, 4, 25, 42, 43
Association Montessori Society, 100

Bastien, James, 105
Bereiter, Carl, 94-97
Benét, Stephen Vincent, vii
Bigler, Carole, xii, 26, 40
Biophilous personalities, 114-15
Bloom, Benjamin, 85, 118-19
Bowing, 11, 17, 35, 124
Brain, hemispheral development, 115-18
Brooks, Nancy Greenwood, 41
Bruner, Jerome, 84, 89
Busch, Fritz, 2

Calligraphy, in relation to Talent Education, 4, 25, 43
Cello, 4, 25
Charles, Dorothy Mae, xii
Chicagoland Suzuki Music Festival, 23
Chomsky, Noam, 106
Clark, Frances, 68
Cognitive psychologists, 83-87, 89-98, 102-4
Communication problems between Japanese and English, 67, 130-31
See also Cultural differences
Competition, 19, 127, 141
Concerts, faculty, 57, 64-65, 141-42
Concerts, students, 6, 14, 15, 19-21, 23, 58, 73
Contests, 58
Contracts, faculty, 51
Contracts, parents, 55-57
Cook, Clifford, xii, 129-30
Cornell University, 128

Criticisms mentioned about Talent Education, 39-41, 121-32
Cultural differences between America, Europe, and Japan, 67, 78-79, 80, 101-12, 122, 125, 127, 129-32, 144

Dennis, Wayne, 103-4
Developmental stages of childhood, 85-89, 112-115
Diffusion, effects on intelligence, 102-3
Discipline vs. freedom, 82-83
Doman, Glenn, 97-98, 128, 129

Early Development Association, Japan, 4, 25, 84
Early Training Project, Tennessee, 102-3
Edwards, Betty, 115-16
Eastman School of Music, 4
Einstein, Albert, 2, 131
Elman, Mischa, 1
Engelmann, Siegfried, 94-97
English, in relation to Talent Education, 4, 25, 43
See also Language
Environment: *see* Heredity vs. environment
Eto, Toshiya, 3
Eurhythmics and rhythmic games, 16, 63, 70, 71, 74, 78
Expectations, in relation to standards, 58

Faculty concerts: *see* Concerts, faculty
Faculty requirements: *see* Teaching, requirements
Farb, Peter, 105-6
Fink, Lorraine, 23
Flute, 4, 25
Foundation for Mind Research, 117
Fromm, Erich, 87-88, 114-15

Gagné, Robert, 108-12
Games, 15-16, 76-78
Gardner, John, 81-82
George Peabody College, 102
Goldberg, Laurette, 76
Gordon, John, 43
Graduation system, 11, 22-23, 39, 127, 139
Graham, Beverly, 40

183

Note: The above index is for the text and appendixes only. Refer also to the bibliography.

About the Author

Ray Landers has a bachelor of music degree in piano from the Sherwood Conservatory of Music, a master's of music degree in piano from Northwestern University, and a doctor of music degree in piano pedagogy from Indiana University. As a pianist, Dr. Landers has performed often as an accompanist and in solo, chamber music, and concerto programs in the United States, Canada, Europe, and Australia, and has made numerous television and radio appearances. Orchestras with which he has appeared as soloist include the Chicago Chamber Orchestra, the Gold Coast Chamber Orchestra, the Indiana University Philharmonic, and the Sherwood Symphony. Other instruments he has played include the clarinet, harpsichord, and organ. He specializes in modern music and improvisation and often performs solo recitals featuring his own compositions as well as those of other contemporary composers. In 1970 Dr. Landers represented Indiana University at the Tchaikovsky Competition in Moscow. At that time the Indiana *Herald-Telephone* critic said, "Landers is an absolutely fantastic pianist—worthy of any kind of international award. He is subtle, concerned with what he is saying. He understands each work down to its most infinitesimal feeling and makes possibly obscure music perfectly clear . . . with enviable gifts of comprehension and communication." Other national festivals in which he has participated include the Vianna da Motta International Concourse in Lisbon, Portugal, in 1971 and the Rockefeller Foundation International Piano Competition in 1978. Dr. Landers is well known for the many duets he has written to accompany piano repertoire. He often performs these at Suzuki institutes. His publications include *The Talent Education School of Shinichi Suzuki—an Analysis, Is Suzuki Education Working in America?, Second Piano Accompaniments for Piano Students and Teachers* (Music and Recordings) *Volumes 1 and 2*, and numerous articles (see bibliography).

Through study in major areas of piano performance and pedagogy and minor areas of education, theory, psychology, and music history, Dr. Landers became interested in new approaches to music education. He has studied piano and piano pedagogy with Madeline Webster, Roberta Savler, Herbert Renison, Guy Duckworth, Pauline Lindsey, Ivan Davis, Evelyn Starkey, and Walter Robert. He has attended piano workshops presented by Frances Clark, Sidney Foster, Jorge Bolet, Alfonso Monticeno, Joseph Banowitz, Robert Pace, and James Bastien and has studied various aspects of the Dalcroze and Kolady methods. He has had intensive Suzuki training at more than ten Talent Education institutes in Japan and America including seminars under Dr. Suzuki and numerous other Suzuki experts. His doctoral dissertation at Indiana University was on the application of Talent Education to piano instruction. He has taught at many Suzuki programs throughout America, Canada, and Australia, including the American Suzuki Institute at the University of Wisconsin, Stevens Point.

Dr. Landers has taught at Indiana University and Chicago State University. Since 1975 he has been director and piano instructor at the Suzuki Music Academy of Chicago, a preparatory program in piano, violin, cello, and flute which he founded. He is also founder-director of the Annual Chicagoland Suzuki Music Festival and the Summer Chicago Suzuki Institute. Dr. Landers is a certified Parent Effectiveness instructor, having taken the Thomas Gordon P.E.T. Instruction Course in 1979.

Dr. Landers is listed in 1980-84 editions of *Who's Who in the Midwest*, the 1980 *International Who's Who in Education*, and the 1983-84 *International Edition of Men and Women of Distinction*. He served on the National Board of the Suzuki Association of the Americas for the term 1981-84 and is a sanctioned teacher trainer for the SAA.

The following is a statement by Ray Landers:

Underlying all of my ambitions is the desire to help myself and others seek happiness through music. Through my studies, I have learned many approaches to education—experimental as well as traditional. I seek to find the best individual approach for each learning-teaching situation.

I am interested in the growth of personality and its relation to musical talent. Often, educational institutes and teachers are not concerned enough with the individual student's personal needs, and many students suffer as a result. I have been greatly influenced by Shinichi Suzuki; through his Talent Education philosophy I have gained insights that have helped in my own development as a performer, teacher, and human being. I have in common with Dr. Suzuki a late start in the study of music (Dr. Suzuki began violin at age 17, I began clarinet at 12 and piano at 14) and a great interest in helping children start in the earliest years.

I am interested in the new—the future—and am especially excited about performing contemporary music. But, I'm also passionate about the study of all types of music: I strive to be open-minded about experimental, rock, soul, country-western, popular, and jazz music as well as all types of classical music—music of all ages and cultures. I believe that this kind of openness makes for a fuller life. By showing interest in whatever music a student appreciates, I feel that a teacher helps the student gain more respect for other types of music that the teacher might introduce.

I believe strongly that discipline leads to freedom and creativity. A disciplined and joyous system of education such as the Suzuki Method can provide seriousness and fun, knowledge, the ability to use that knowledge, self-assuredness, and cooperation. . . . it can provide the best of the East and the West. Music education is a continual search into the past, present, and future. To me, Talent Education is an ever-changing method; it is based on basic principles that remain the same, but as man learns more and incorporates the new, Talent Education continues to evolve. Dr. Suzuki is constantly expressing interest in "new ideas" as should all educators.

I hope to always work in an environment that encourages open attitudes toward change. Besides teaching and performing I am interested in composing, theater, opera, ballet and modern dance, cinema, art, and literature, but, most of all, I want to express my uniqueness; I want to grow and help others grow—especially through the media of the arts.

Ray Landers may be contacted at the following address:

c/o The Suzuki Music Academy of Chicago
Fine Arts Building - Suite 401
410 S. Michigan Avenue
Chicago, IL 60605
(312) 663-0038

About the Photographer

Arthur Montzka has an associate of arts degree from George Washington University, a bachelor of music education from Oberlin Conservatory, and a master of music degree from the Eastman School of Music. He serves as orchestra director in the Dekalb, Illinois, schools and is conductor of the Kishwaukee Symphony Orchestra. He is contributing author to the book *Free to Choose—Career Choices for Young Men.*

In 1971, Mr. Montzka, while teaching a Suzuki pedagogy course at Oberlin College, was asked to take photographs at the first American Suzuki Institute, Stevens Point, Wisconsin. He has combined his knowledge of photography and young children (the Montzkas have four children—all Suzuki students; the eldest two are in college studying to be Suzuki teachers) and taken numerous photographs at various national and international Suzuki conferences since then. He has a file of more than ten thousand pictures of Suzuki violinists, violists, cellists, pianists, flutists, and harpists.

Arthur Montzka